Glenstal Abbey

THROUGH THE SEASONS

Glenstal Abbey

THROUGH THE SEASONS

With photographs by Valerie O'Sullivan

First published in 2019 by

columba BOOKS

23 Merrion Square North, Dublin 2

www.columbabooks.com

ISBN: 978-1-78218-363-1

Cover and book design by Alba Esteban | Columba Books

Project editor Colmán Ó Clabaigh OSB

Photographs by Valerie O'Sullivan

Printed by L&C, Poland

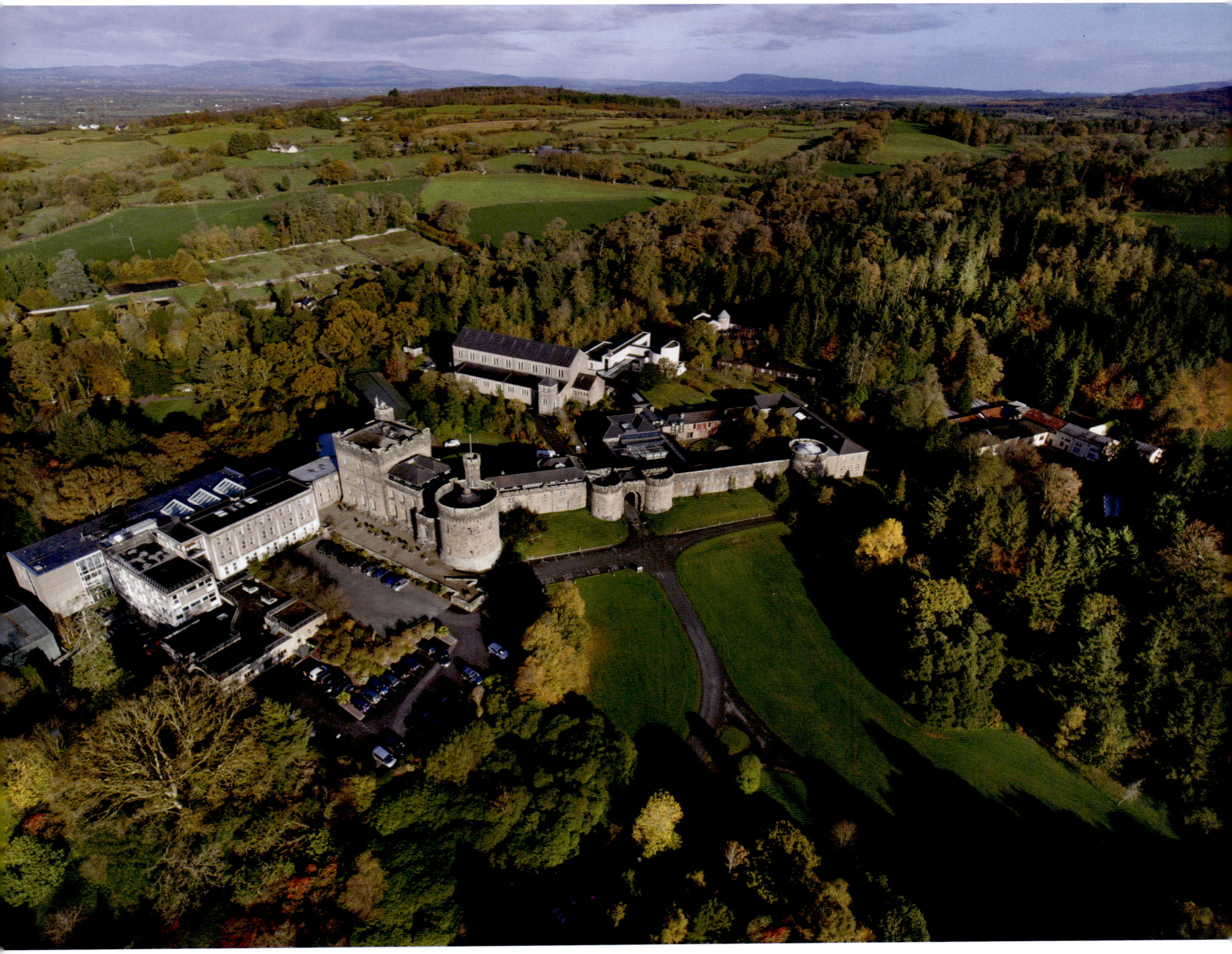

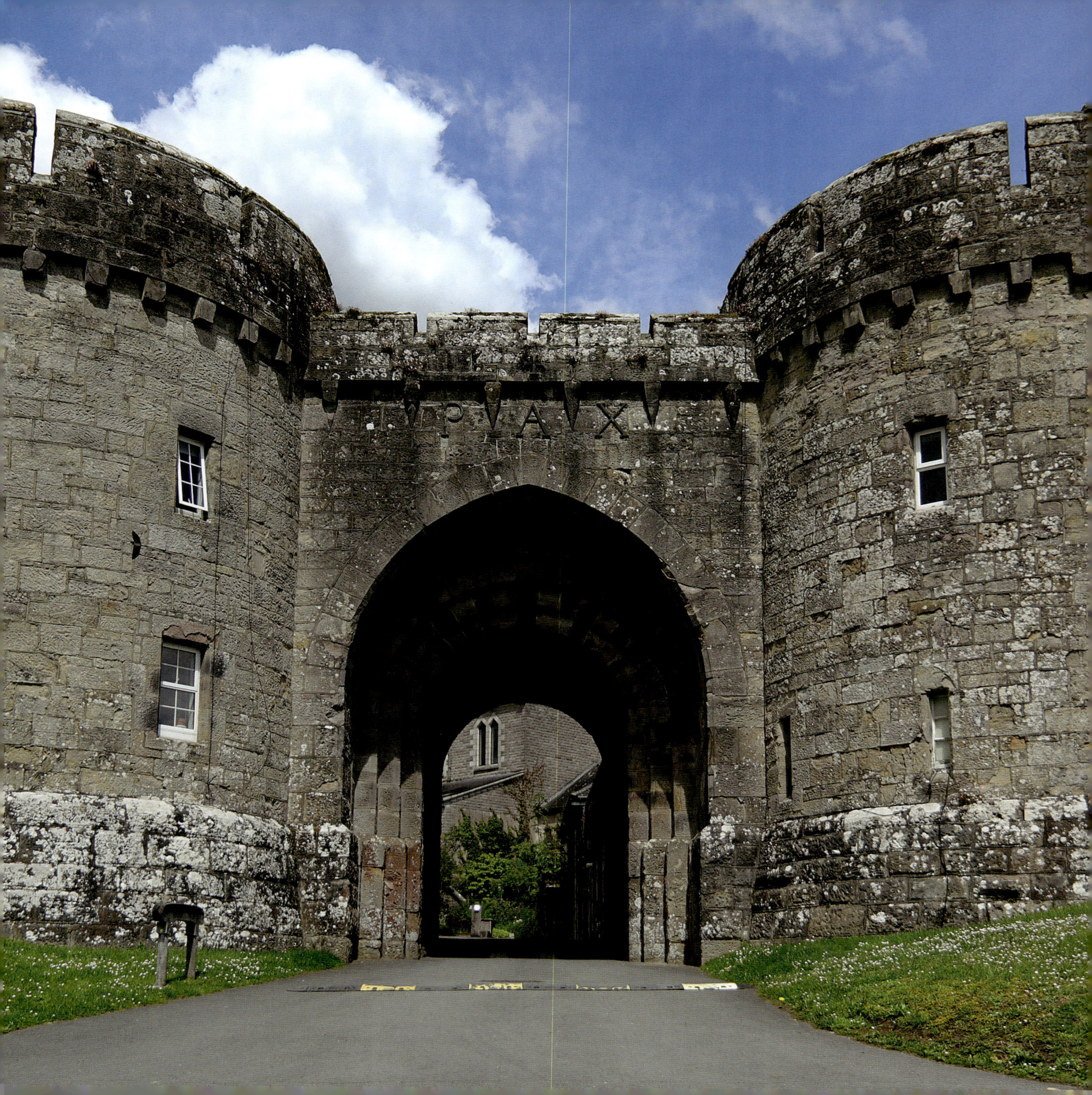
PAX

Foreword

Glenstal Abbey is situated on the slopes of the Slieve Felim mountains in the rural heartland of East County Limerick. Evidence for human settlement here dates back to the Bronze Age and the remains of a ringfort, Cistercian grange, tower house, fortified house, Mass rock and terraced gardens indicate the impact successive occupants have had on the landscape. Throughout the 19th and into the early 20th centuries, Glenstal was the seat of the Anglo-Irish Barrington family whose imposing Norman revival style castle is the most prominent feature of the grounds. Their influence can also be seen in the parkland and forests that comprise the estate. The careful husbandry and farsighted planning of previous generations means that we enjoy an environment of outstanding natural beauty.

Since 1927 Glenstal has been home to a community of Benedictine monks. Established from Maredsous Abbey in Belgium, it was the realisation of the dream of that community's Irish abbot, Blessed Columba Marmion, to re-establish male Benedictine life in his homeland for the first time since the dissolution of the monasteries in the 16th century. Although he died before this could happen, his memory is preserved in the inclusion of his baptismal and monastic namesakes in the monastery's dedication: the Abbey of Saints Joseph and Columba at Glenstal.

The primary purpose of a monastery is the praise and worship of God and the sanctification of its members. Consequently, the daily celebration of the Eucharist and the Liturgy of the Hours lies at the heart of our life here, our very raison d'être. Everything else that we do flows from this. Whether it is the work of education in the school, the reception of guests, or the myriad of ways in which monks put down a day, all find their focus when we gather as a praying community around the altar.

Through the words and images that follow, we invite you to watch a year unfold in the life of the Glenstal community, to see for yourself the beauty of the changing seasons in nature and the unfolding of the Christian mystery in the annual cycle of the liturgy. Witness also the different stages of the monastic journey from the first steps as a novice, through the lifelong commitment of solemn profession to the final conclusion in death. Human life in all its phases is to be found here and a wide variety of occupations. Here you will see the various activities in which the community engages as it seeks to earn its daily bread.

Above the entrance gate to Glenstal the word PAX is inscribed in large bronze lettering underneath a bronze cross. Meaning 'peace', it is what we seek for and strive after here. It is our wish that those who come here will also experience something of this Peace of Christ. It is also our hope that, through the pages of this book, you too will experience it in whatever circumstances these words and images reach you.

Abbot Brendan

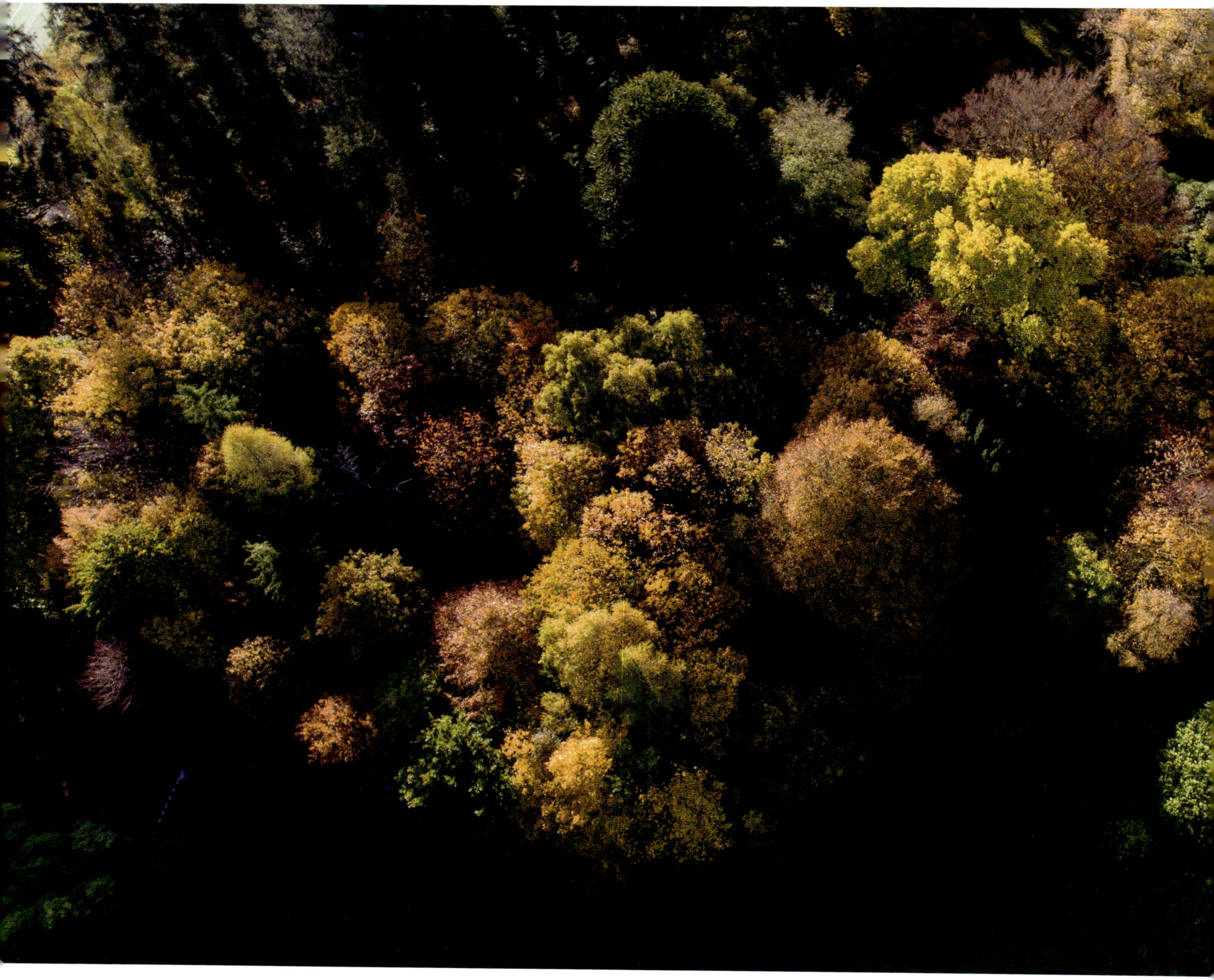

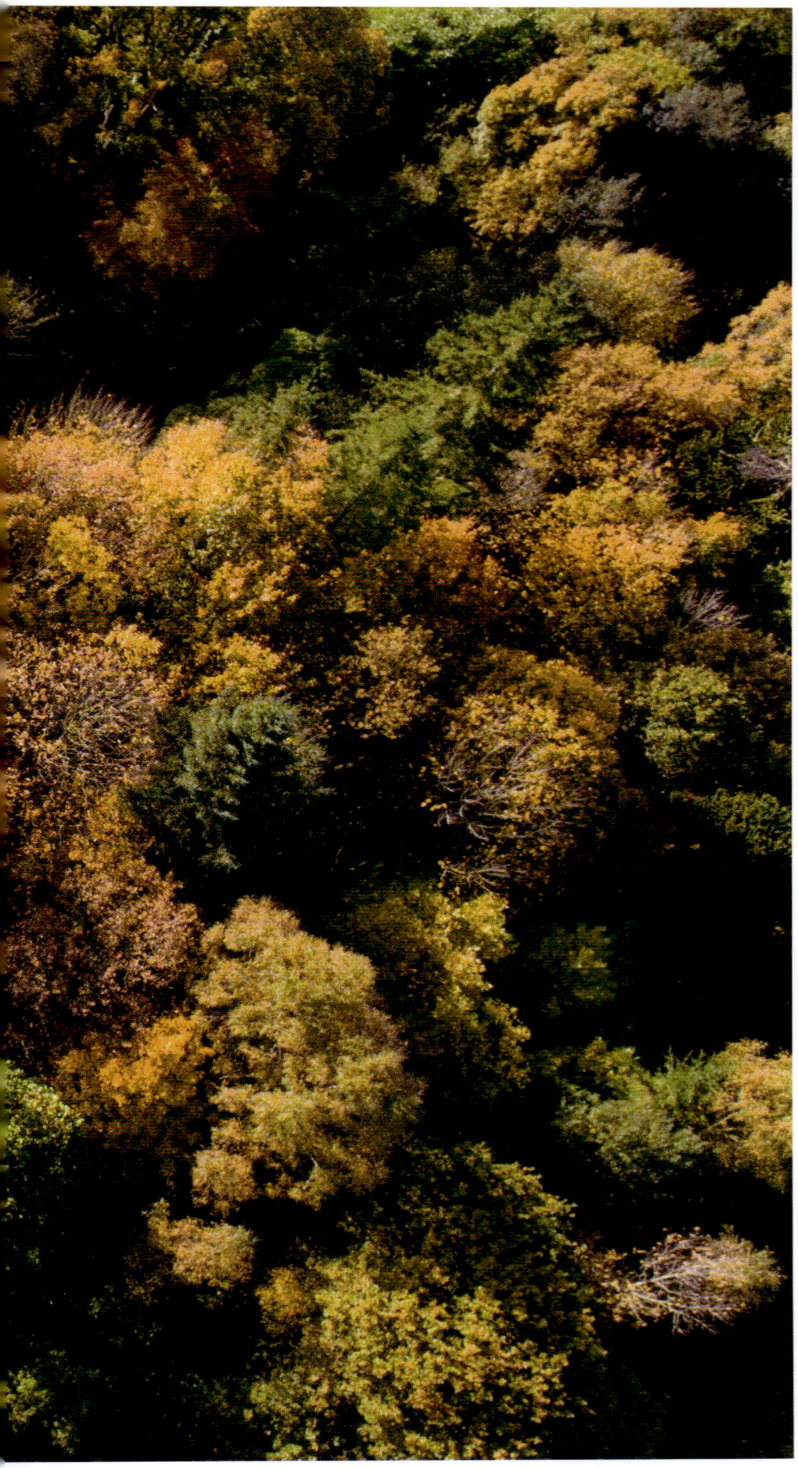

Acknowledgements

The inspiration for the book came from Valerie O'Sullivan and the team at Columba Books. Following the success of her photo-essays on the female monastic communities at Kylemore Abbey, Co. Galway and Glencairn Abbey, Co. Waterford, it was decided to broaden the approach and to examine the life of a contemporary male monastic community. We are grateful to Valerie for chronicling a year in the life of Glenstal Abbey and to Garry O'Sullivan, Lorna Siggins, Alba Estaban and the team at Columba Books for making this vision a reality.

Our greatest debt however, is to the people who make Glenstal what it is. The benefactors, casual visitors, colleagues, friends, guests, neighbours, parents, retreatants, staff and students who share this place with us and whose support and generosity have enabled the monastic community to exist here since 1927. We are mindful of the previous generations that have bequeathed this place of outstanding beauty to us and of the duties that this gift brings. Through these combined efforts may Glenstal continue to be, in the words of St Benedict, a 'household of God'.

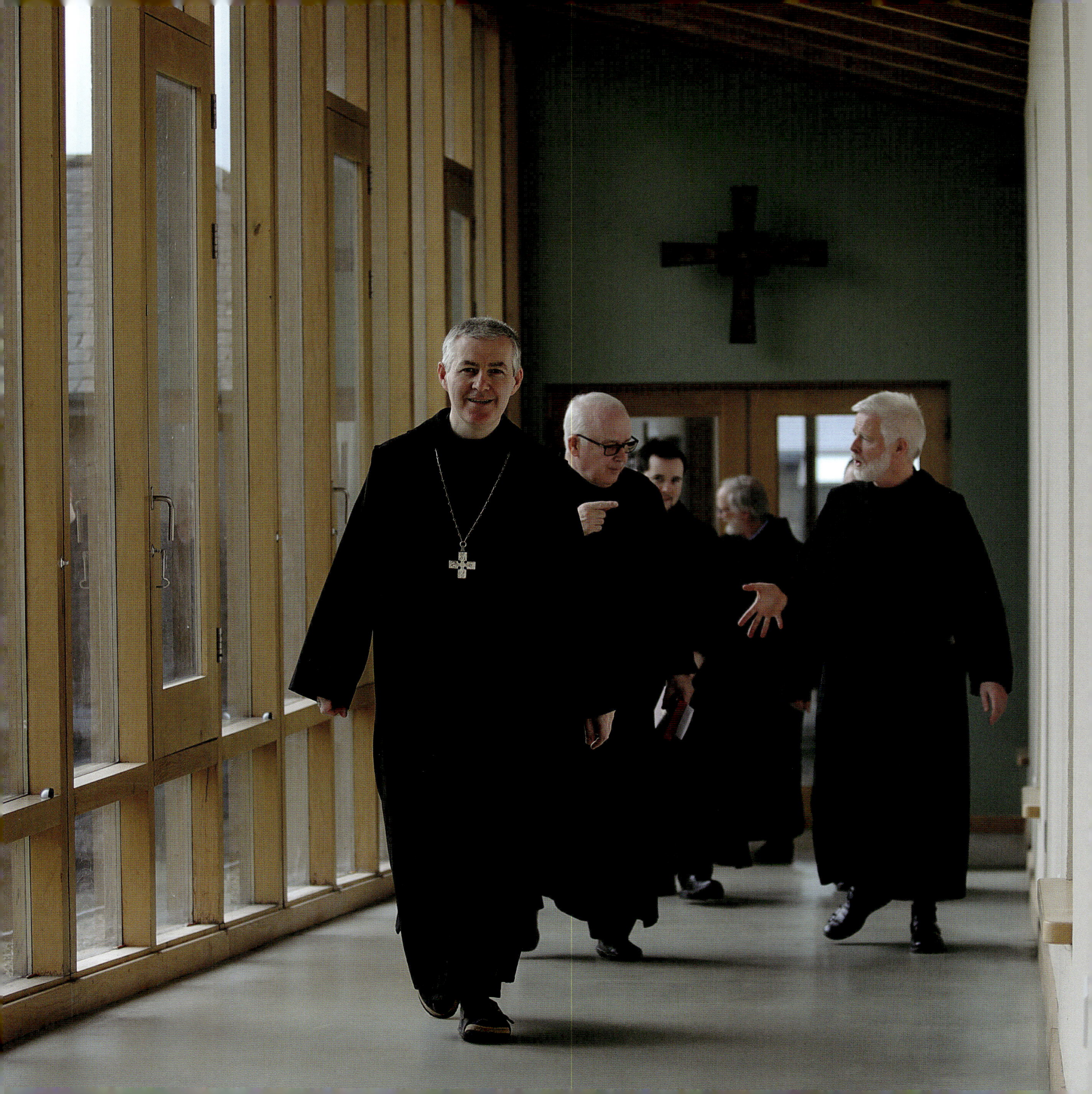

Contents

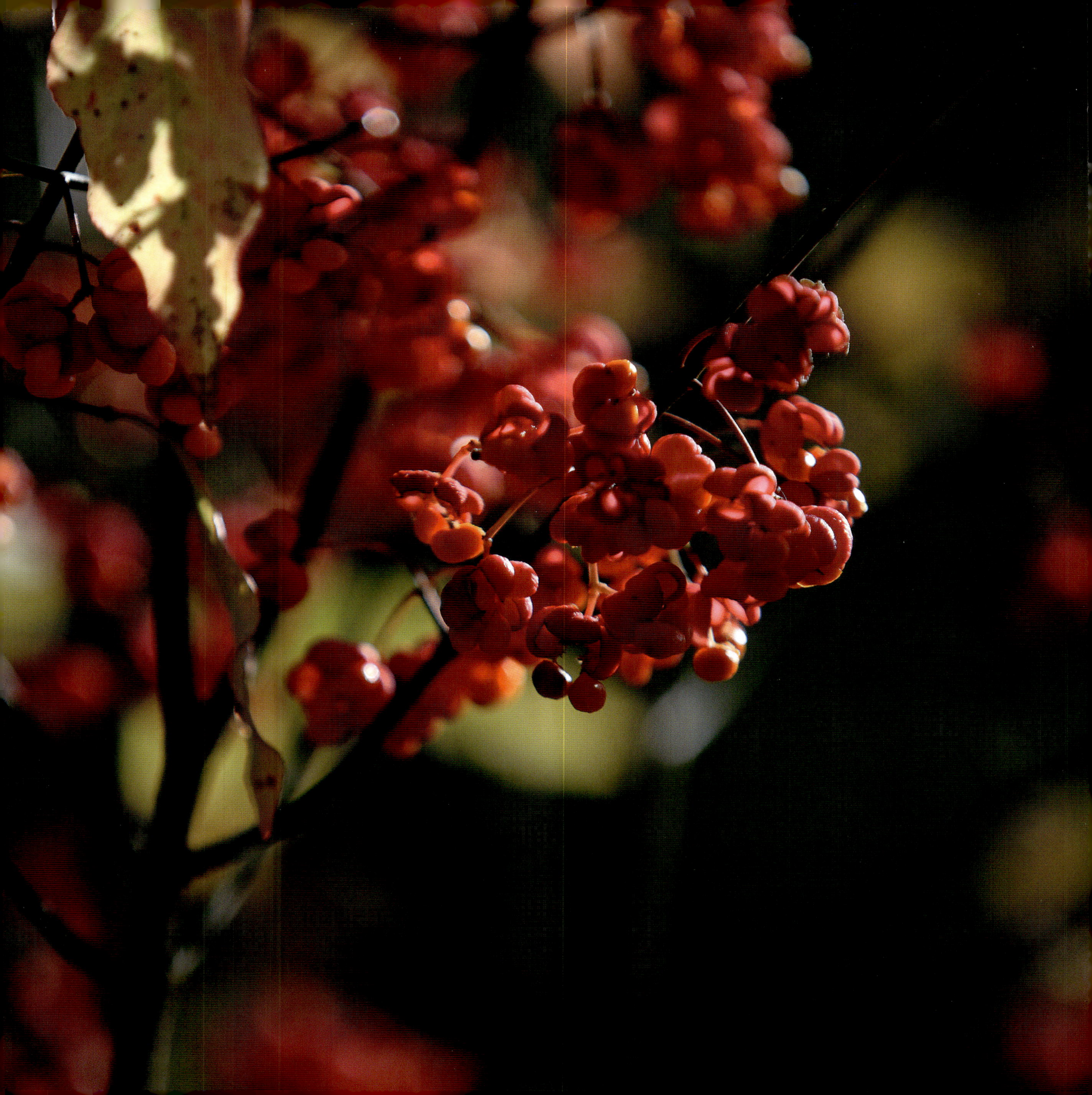

Autumn

The year has a number of beginnings in Glenstal, each with its own distinctive aspect. Of these new starts, the opening of the academic year at the end of August generates the most energy as we prepare for the influx of new and returning students. The community has been involved in secondary education almost since its origin in 1927 and remains committed to the ministry of providing a Catholic education in a monastic setting for those students who chose to attend it.

As an institution it has witnessed many changes, most recently the introduction of day boarding and the construction of a fine new academic block. The small size of the student body encourages close relationships in which everyone knows everyone else. In addition to their academic and sporting endeavours, the boys are encouraged to develop their skills as musicians, public speakers, swimmers, rowers or whatever other talent they've received. Even with the recent expansion of numbers, the ethos has remained constant as both students and staff strive to create an environment where learning may flourish, characters develop and in which God may be glorified in all things.

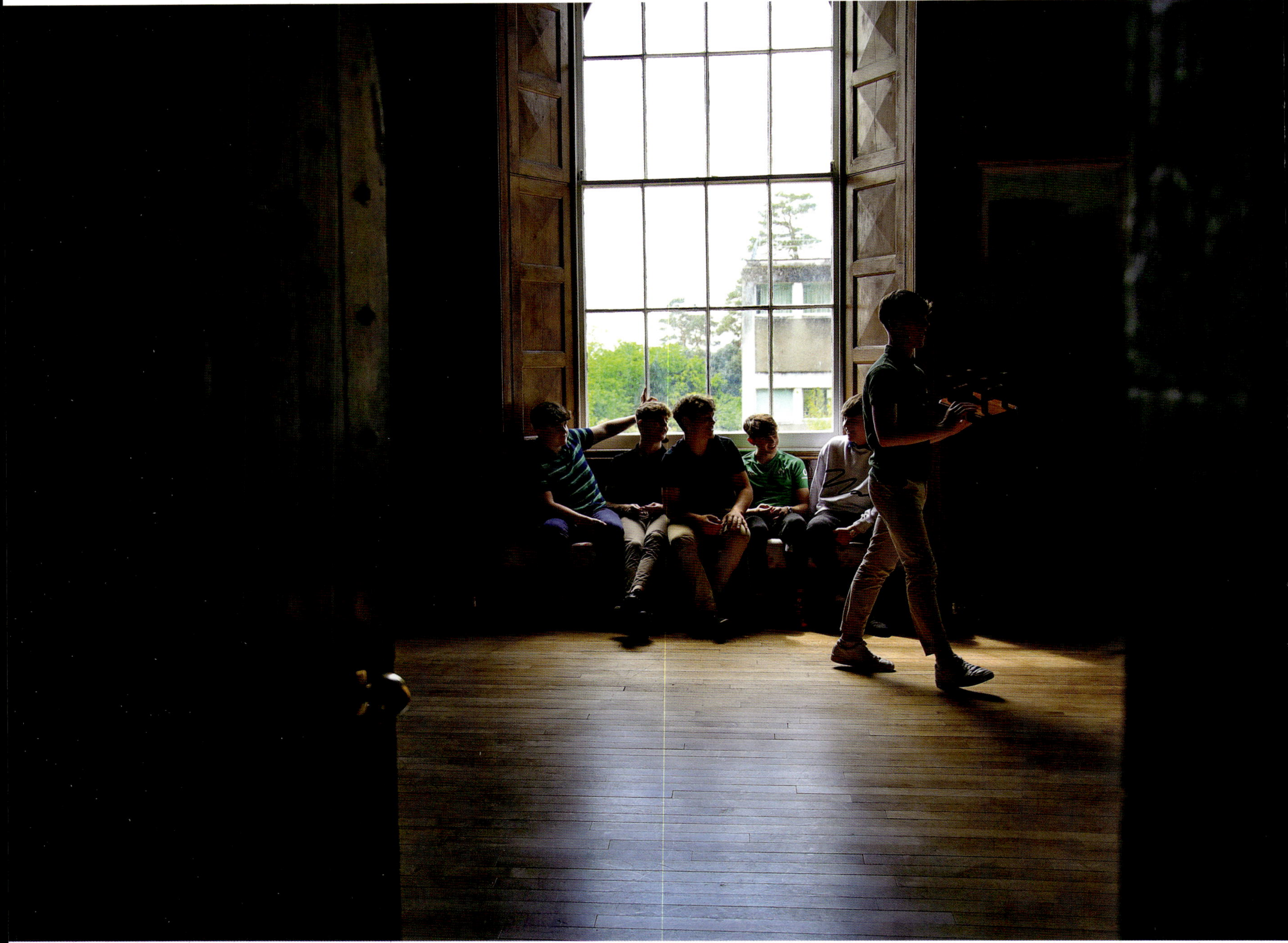

Dermot Hughes, William Cahir-Whelan, Stefan Caufield-Dreier, Andrey Casey, Lughaidh Shortt and Michael Buckley, students at Glenstal Abbey School.

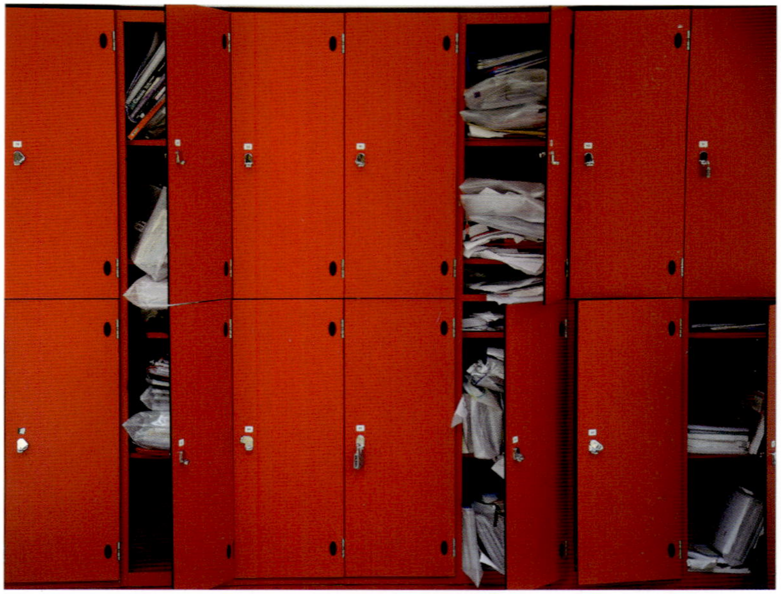

Before the school returns, long hours go into the planning of timetables and schedules that govern the various academic, sporting and recreational activities. The fine September weather means that the boys are largely oblivious to all this as they catch up with old friends and make new ones.

Below: Students Michael Buckley and Dermot Hughes at the water fountain.

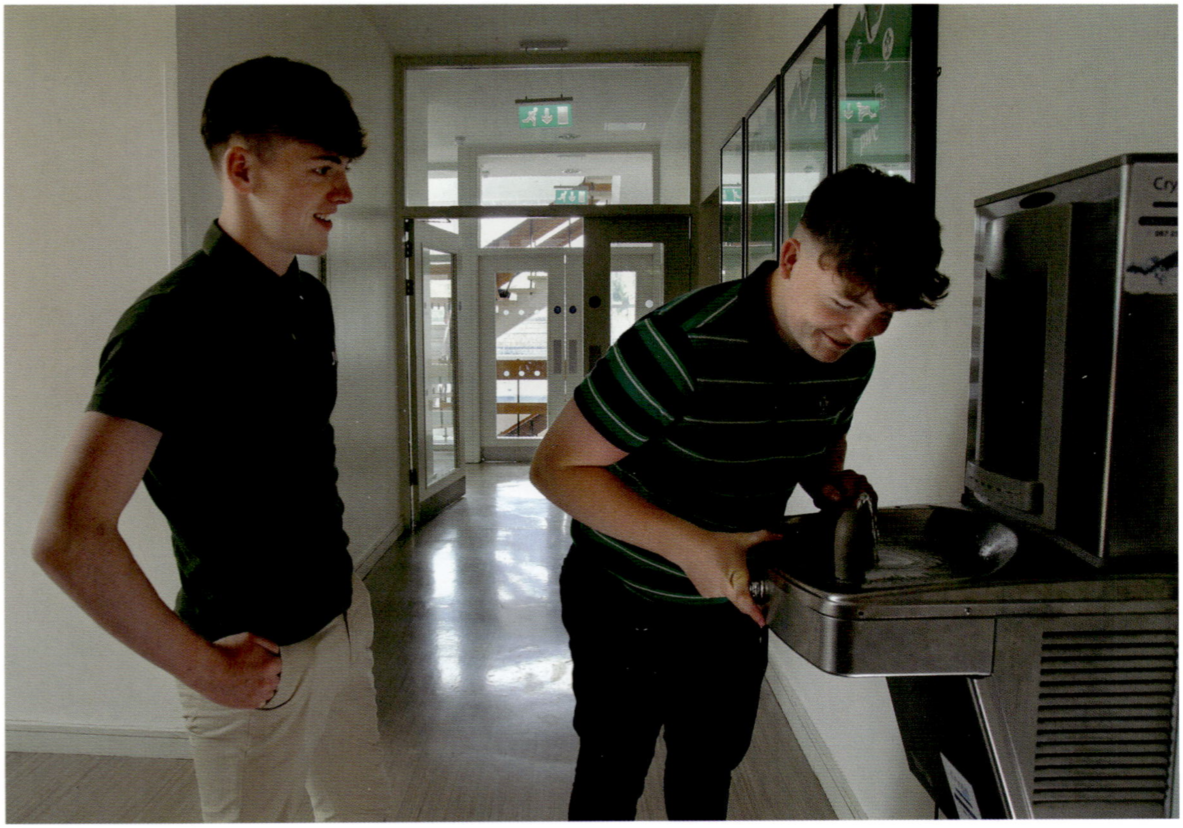

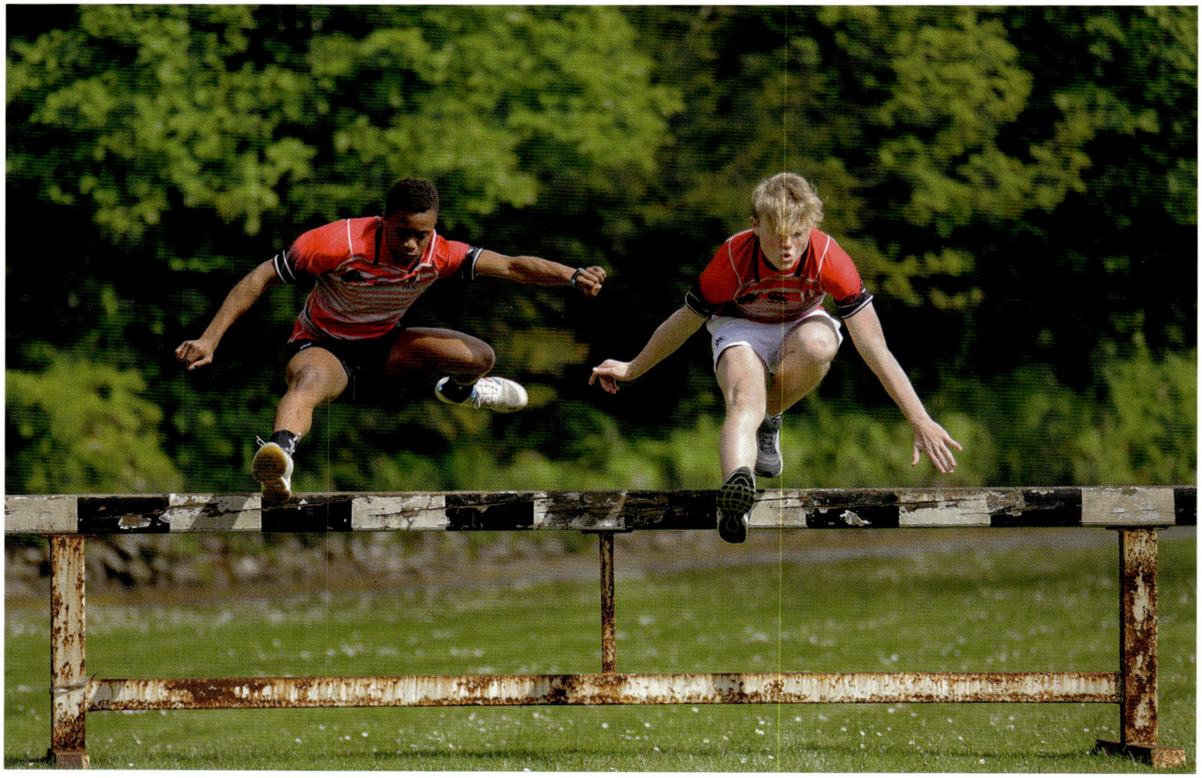

Above: Nyoleme Agbanobi and Thomas McAllister, training at Glenstal Abbey, Co Limerick.
Right: The art of fencing taught at Glenstal Abbey School
Opposite: Caolan Dooley, left and Daniel O'Mahony going for the ball.

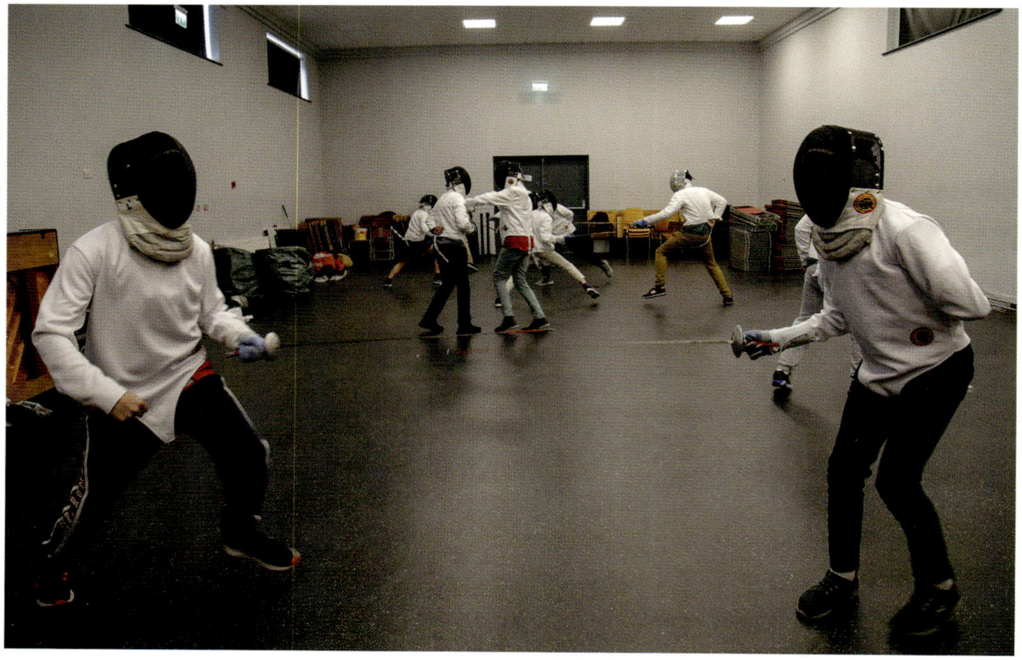

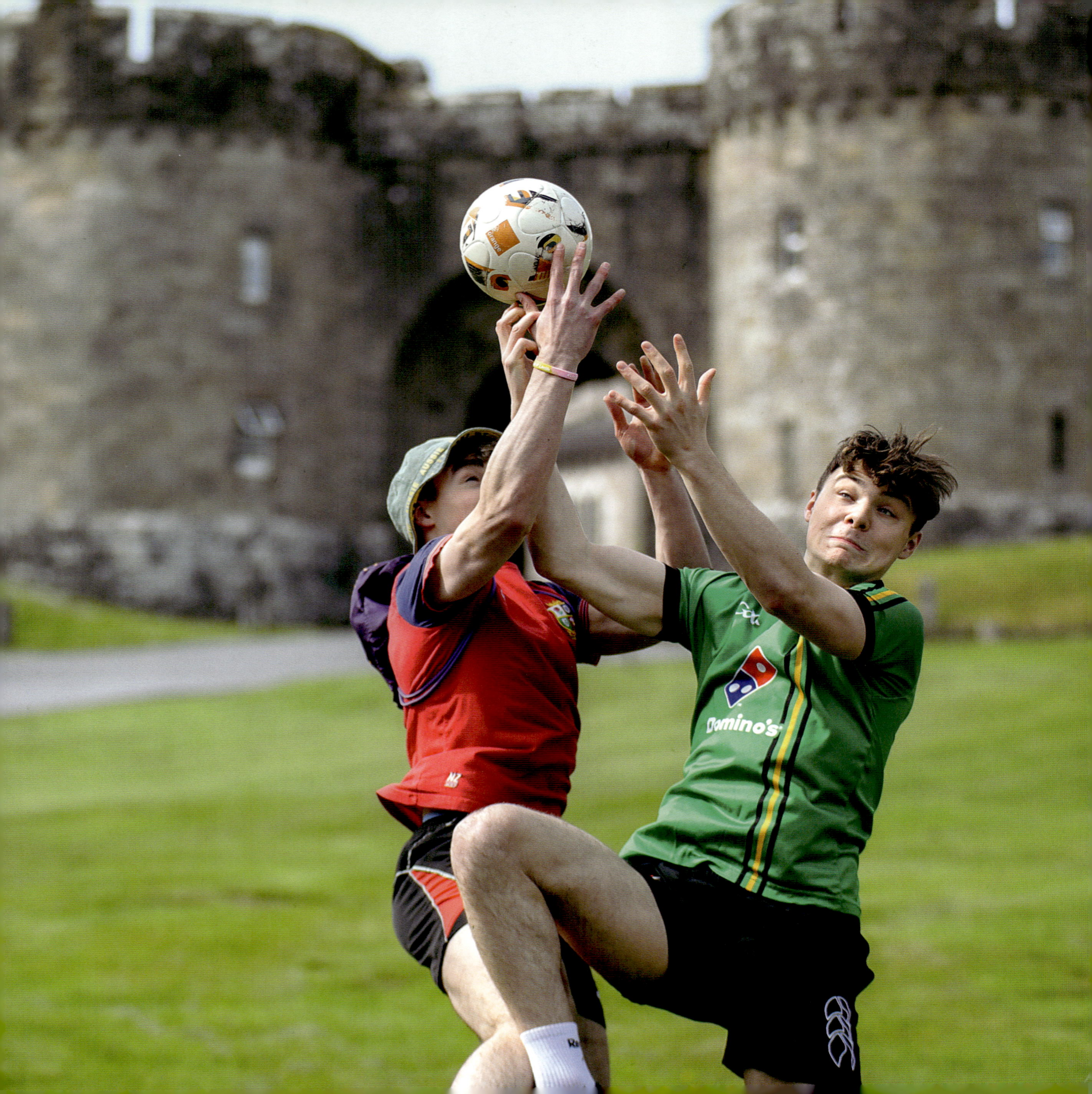
Domino's

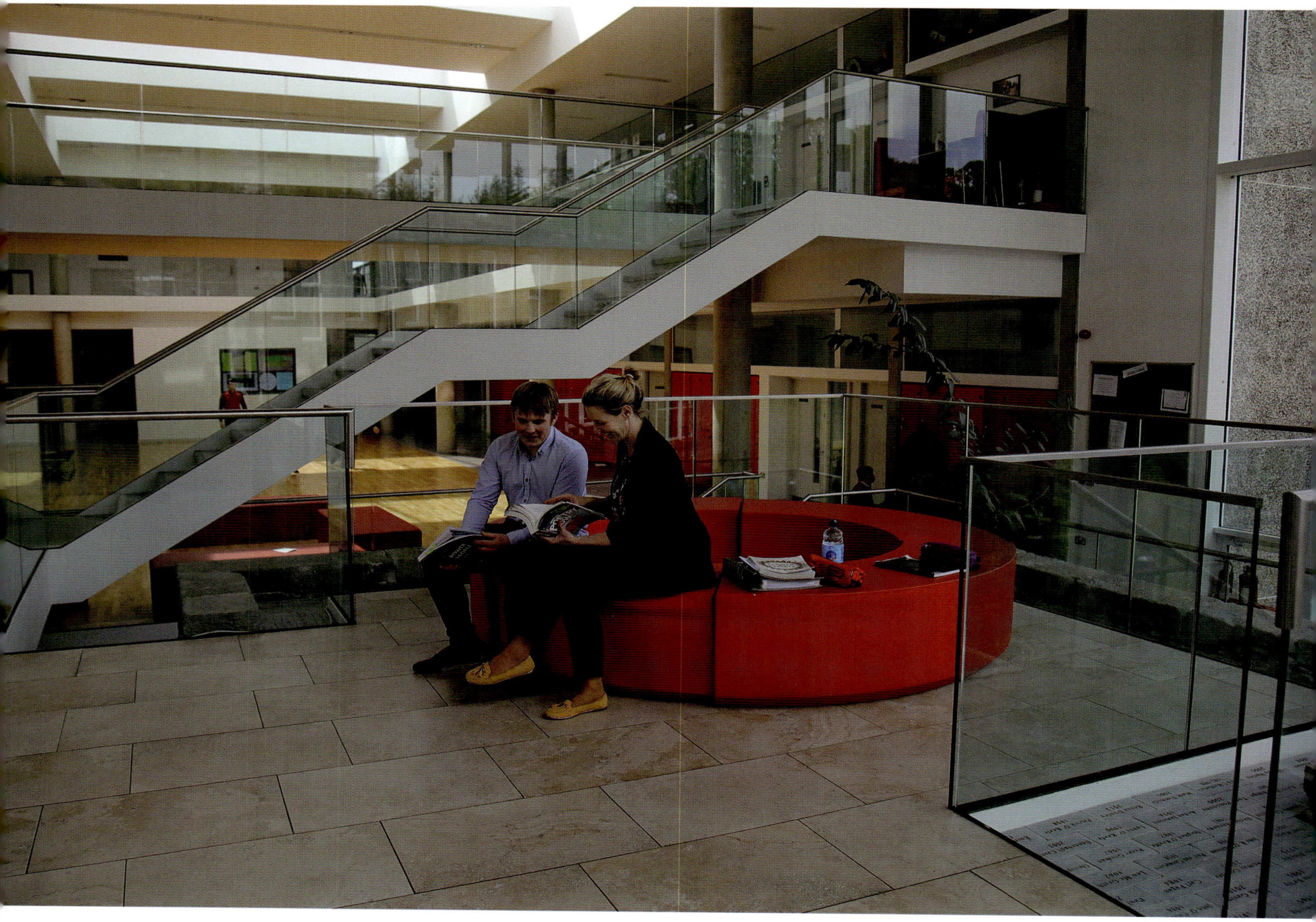

Matthew Lynch with Music Teacher Hazel O'Herlihy.

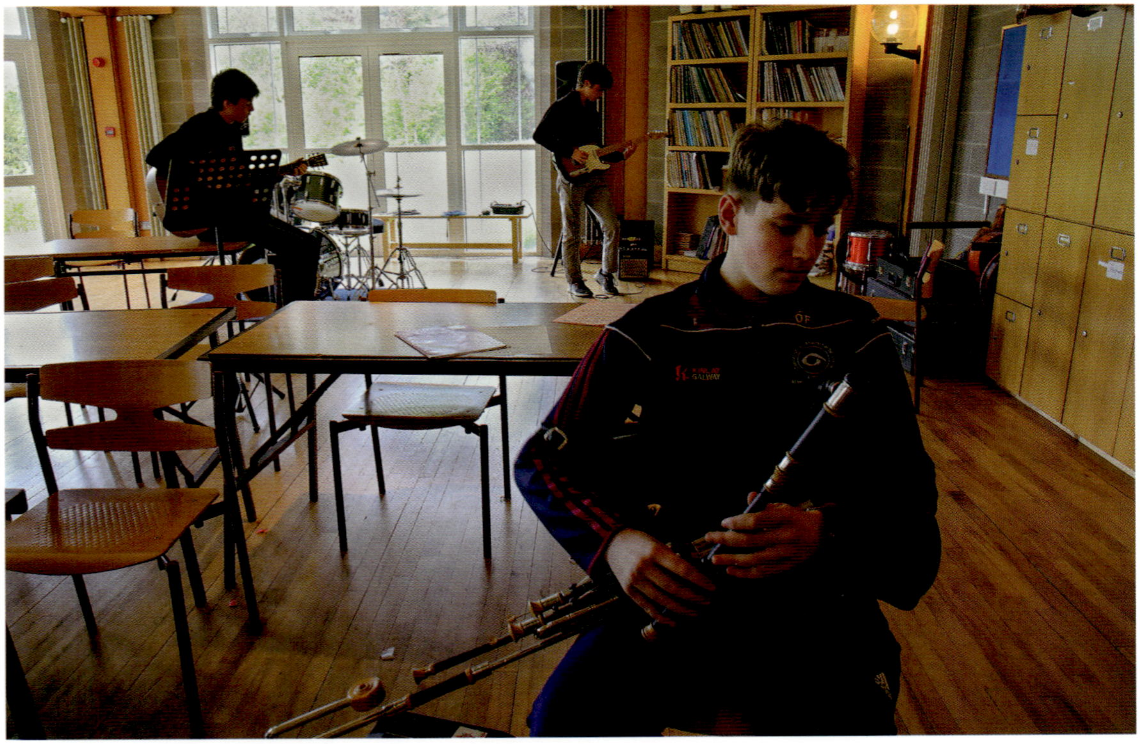

Ódran Furlong on the Uilleann Pipes, Tim Hyde and Richard Enright on guitar.

Receiving a novice

September is often a time of new beginnings in the monastery also as the feast of the Triumph of the Cross on September 14th is the traditional date for receiving novices and clothing them in the monastic habit. The novitiate is a year of probation in which candidates experience the monastic life at first hand, seeking to discern if this way of life is the one to which God has called them.

During this time the novice is trained in the various disciplines that sustain him in his calling. These include classes in scripture, liturgy, monastic history, Latin and chant, but the most formative process is the (mostly) gentle attrition of living with 30 other people and facing up to what this reveals about human nature and about oneself. To assist this process of formation the community runs a Studium programme offering intensive courses on various monastic topics that has been well attended by junior monks and nuns from other communities as well.

In the past year we rejoiced in the reception of a novice and the solemn profession of another monk. Grateful for this, we pray that Lord will continue to call men to seek him in this place so that we may share with others the great mercy that we ourselves have received here.

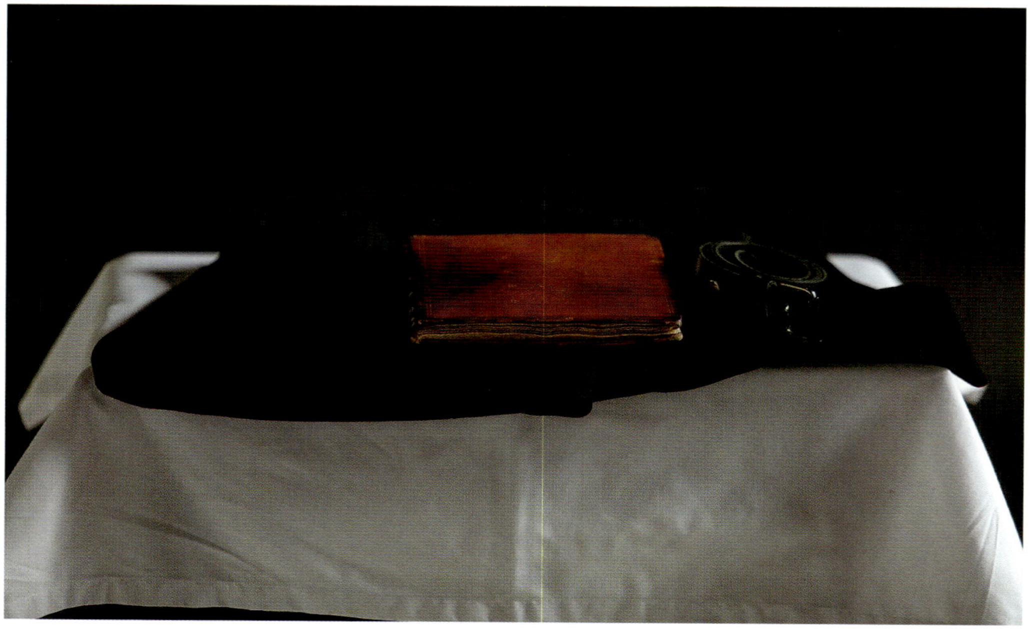

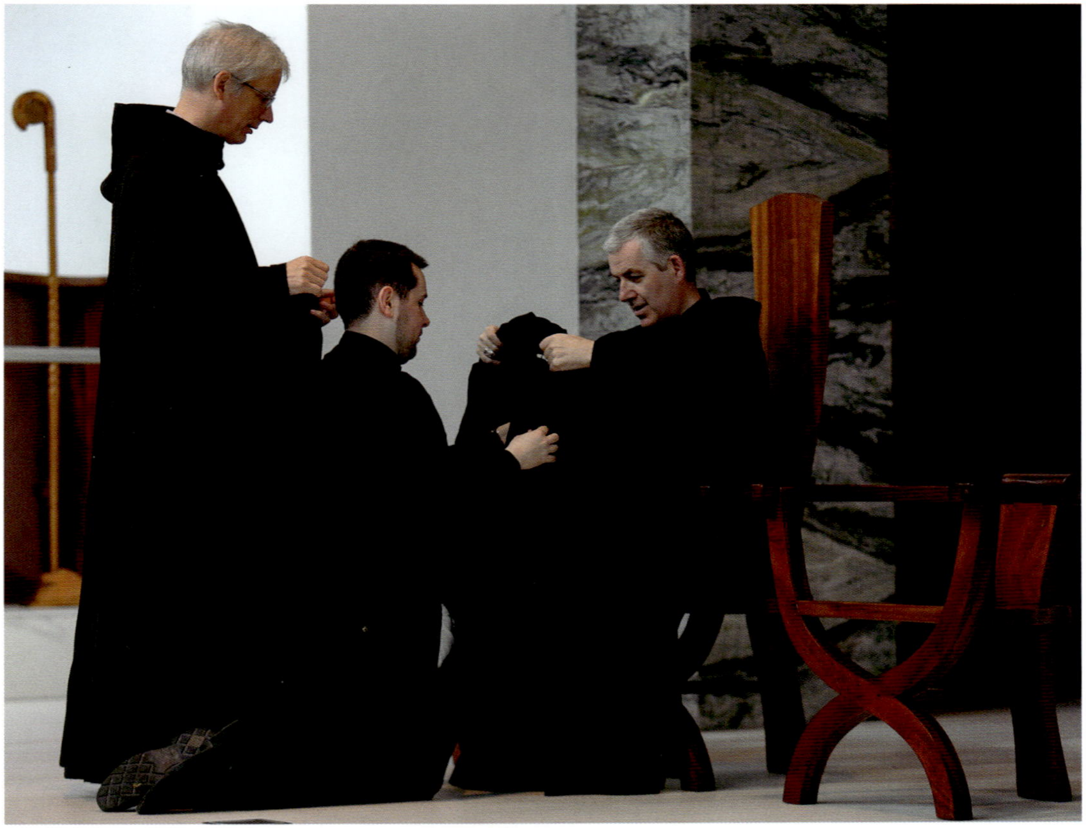

Under the watchful eye of Fr Columba, the novicemaster, Br Justin receives the monastic habit from Abbot Brendan. The habit consists of a long black tunic bound at the waist with a leather belt. Over this is placed the hooded scapular, which originated as a work apron. At solemn or final profession each monk receives the voluminous, long-sleeved garment known as a cowl that is the traditional garb of a monk or nun.

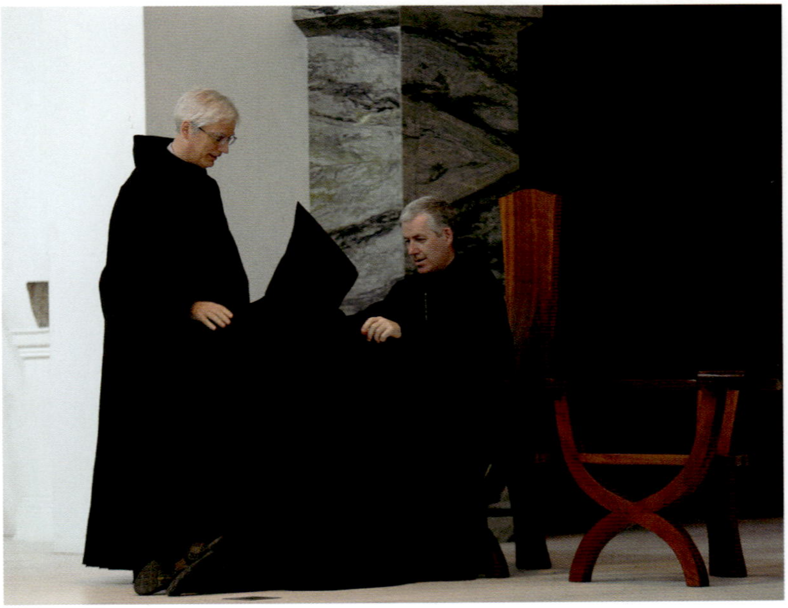

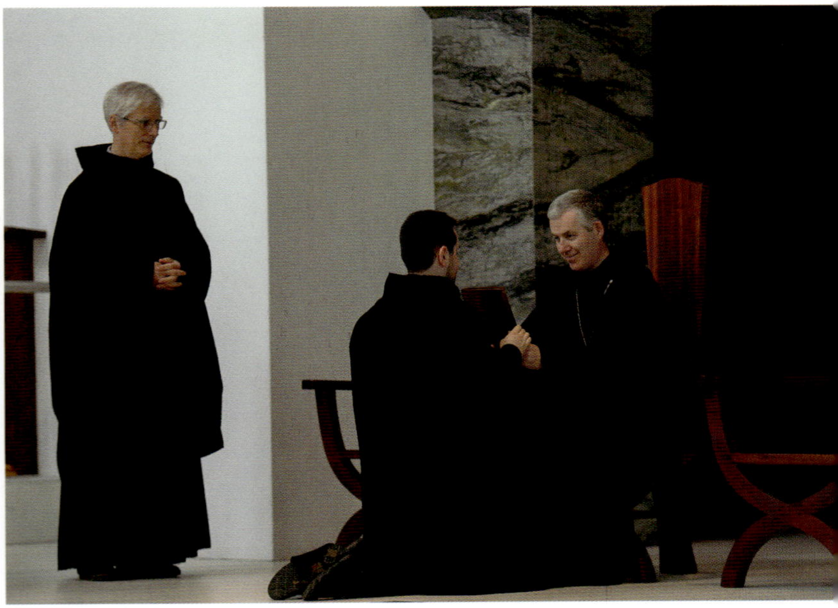

The woods in autumn

As autumn progresses, the grounds become more spectacular as varying hues of red and russet, gold and brown, bedeck the trees with only the pines standing green and steadfast against the declining year. The grounds at Glenstal have been carefully planted and tended since the early 1800s, and we are now the beneficiaries of two centuries of landscaping and forest management.

Numerous specimens of broad-leafed native trees can be found in the grounds along with one of the largest collections of pine trees in the country. There are some exotic specimens as well: Monkey Puzzles and Redwoods along with several stands of ancient oaks .

In the orchard, vast quantities of apples have ripened and are ready for harvesting. In the past, this seasonal glut and what to do with it had always been a challenge as there's only so much apple tart one can eat. The solution last year was to press the surplus and to produce apple juice that has been as refreshing as it is popular.

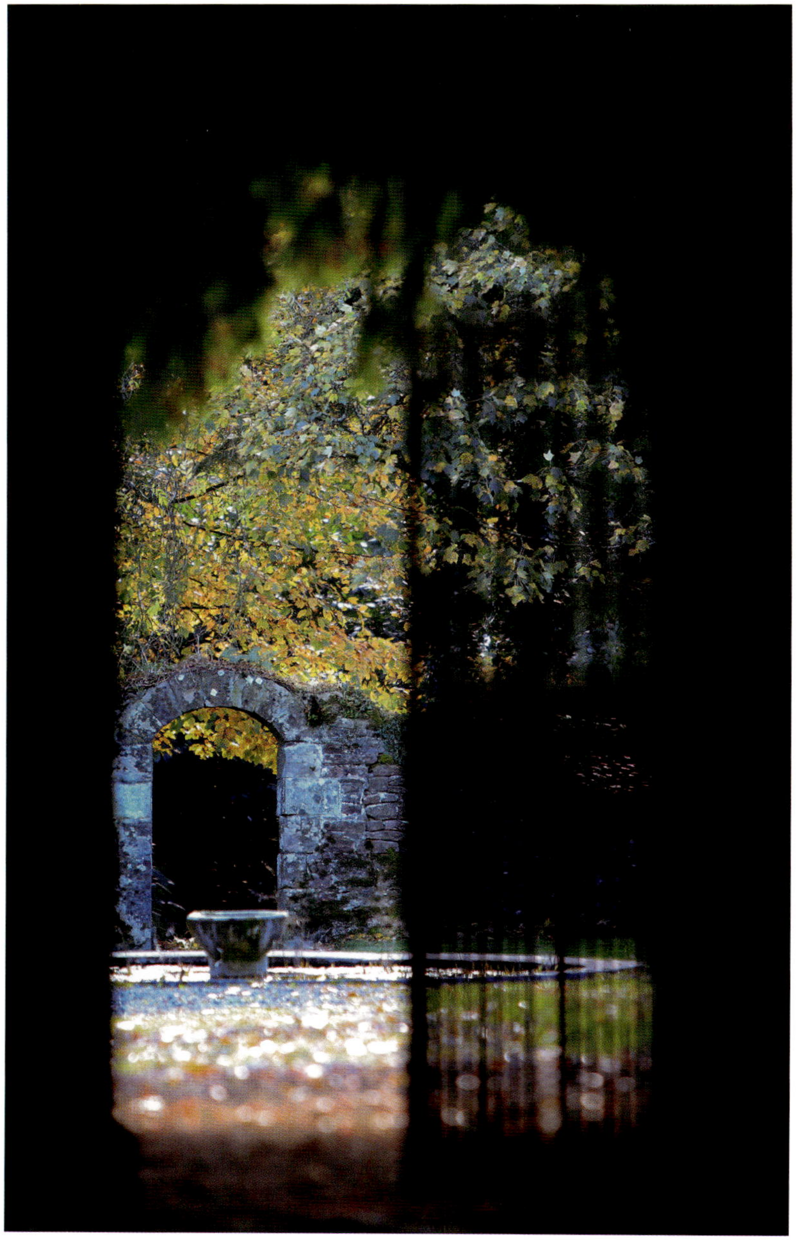

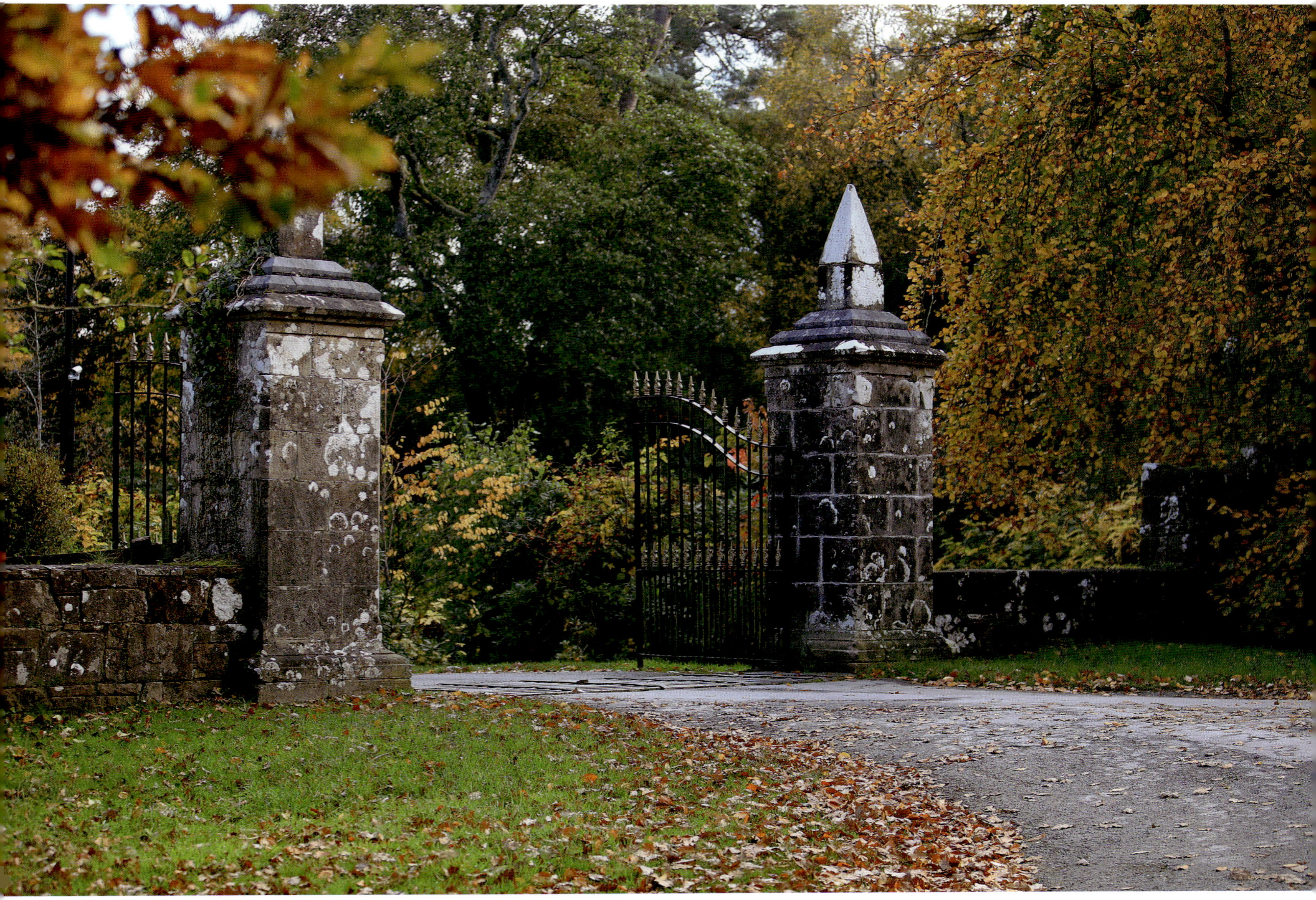

“

The trees are in their autumn beauty
The woodland paths are dry,
Under the October twilight the water
Mirrors a still sky…

– W.B. Yeats

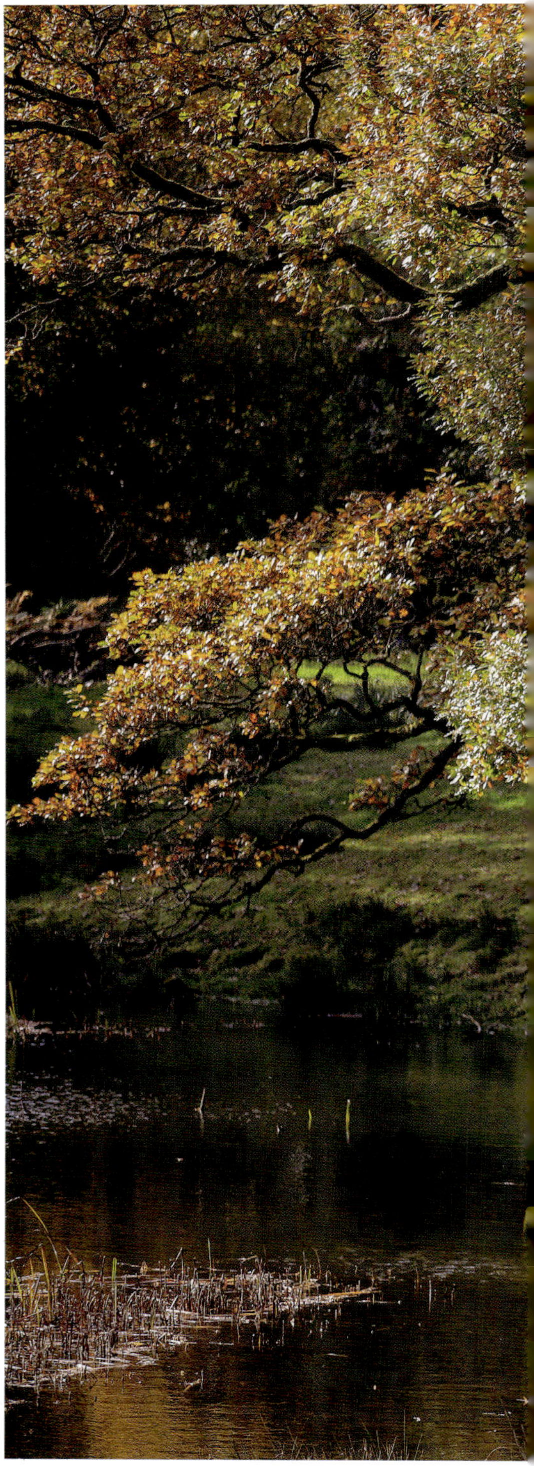

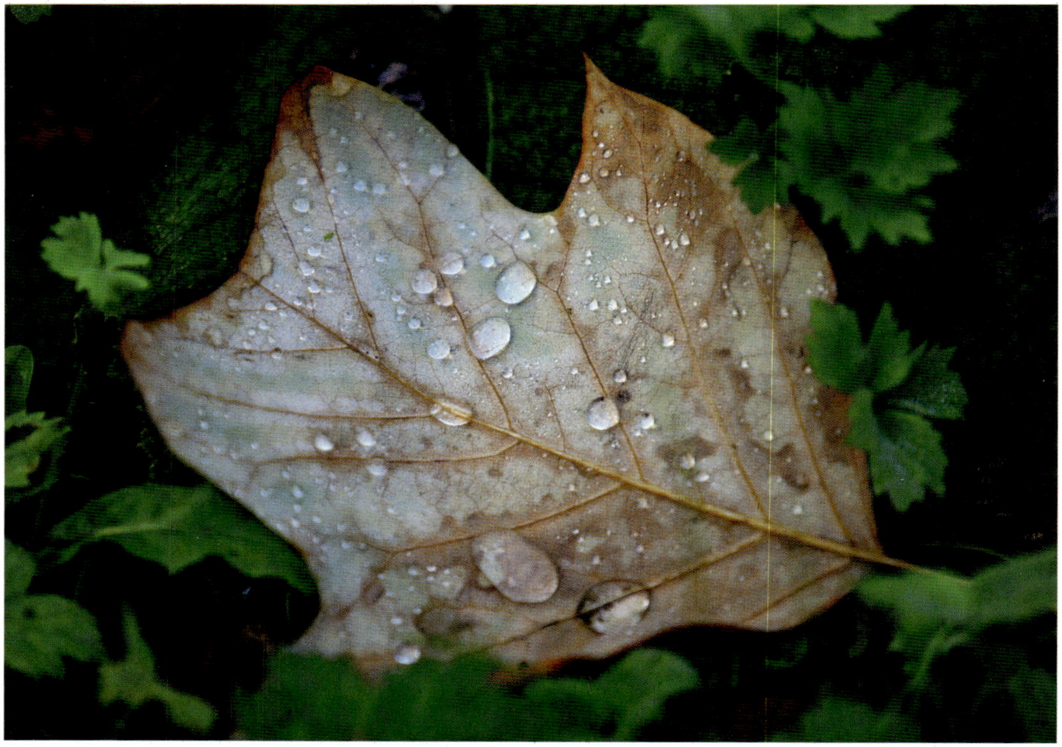

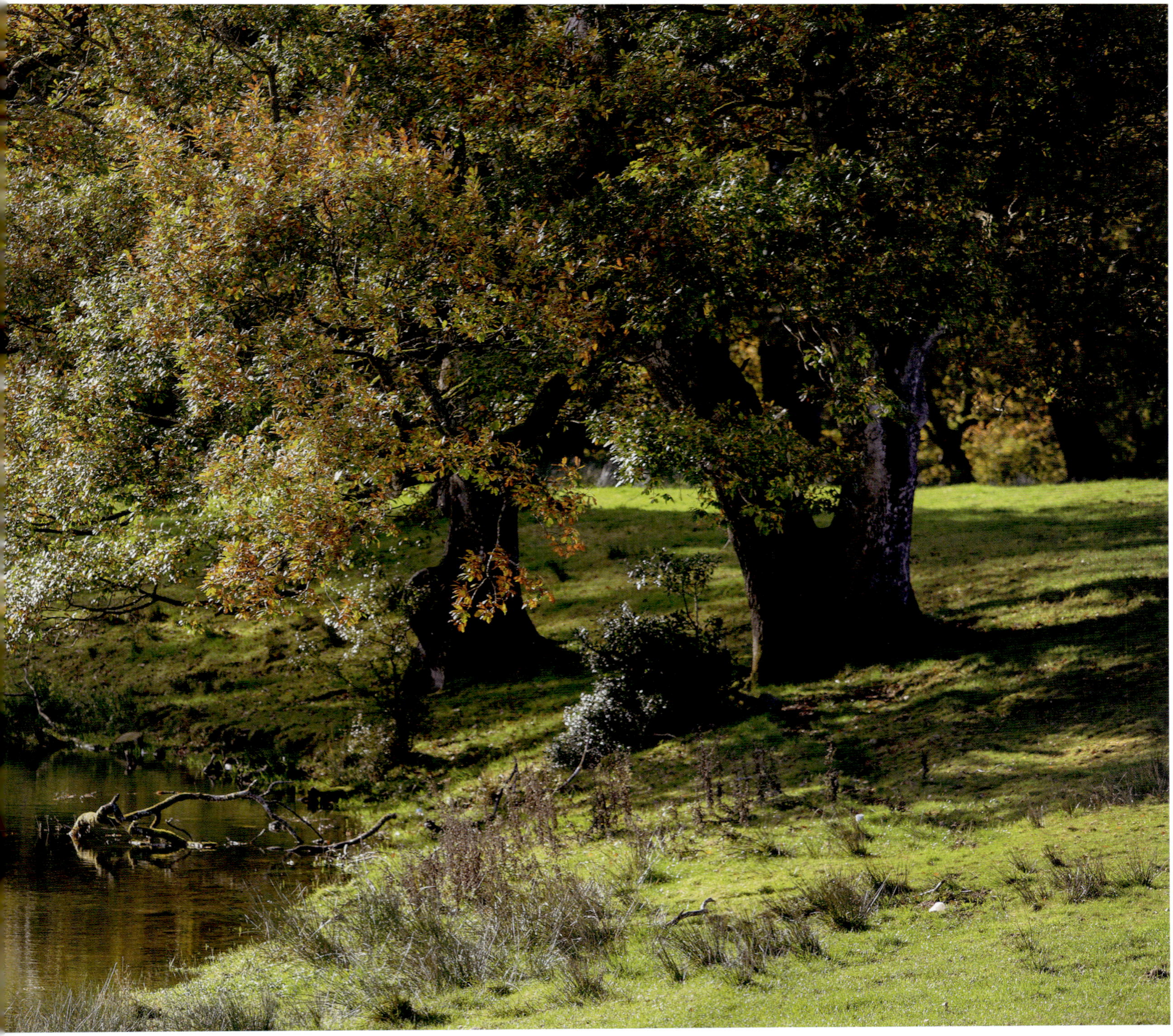

The Gardens

There are two walled gardens in Glenstal, each with its distinctive character and history. The 19th-century Barrington garden, known as the Lady Garden, is closest to the castle and is typical of a 'Big House' walled garden although the walls were much reduced later in its history. The original paths have been restored, as has the fountain and the painstaking work of restoration is an ongoing labour of love. In addition to an attractive flower garden, the garden also holds a stand of white birch trees, each one commemorating one of those executed in the wake of the 1916 Rising. Set slightly apart, another tree commemorates Winifred Barrington, the daughter of the house, who died in an IRA ambush in May 1921.

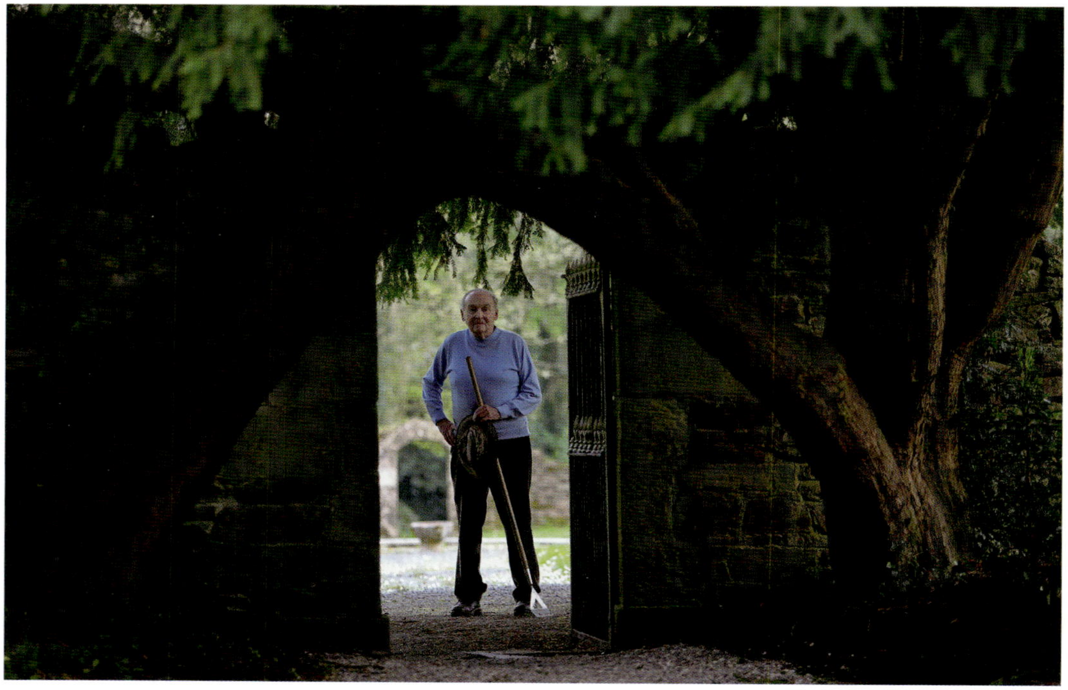

Fr Brian, gardener, in the Glenstal Lady Garden

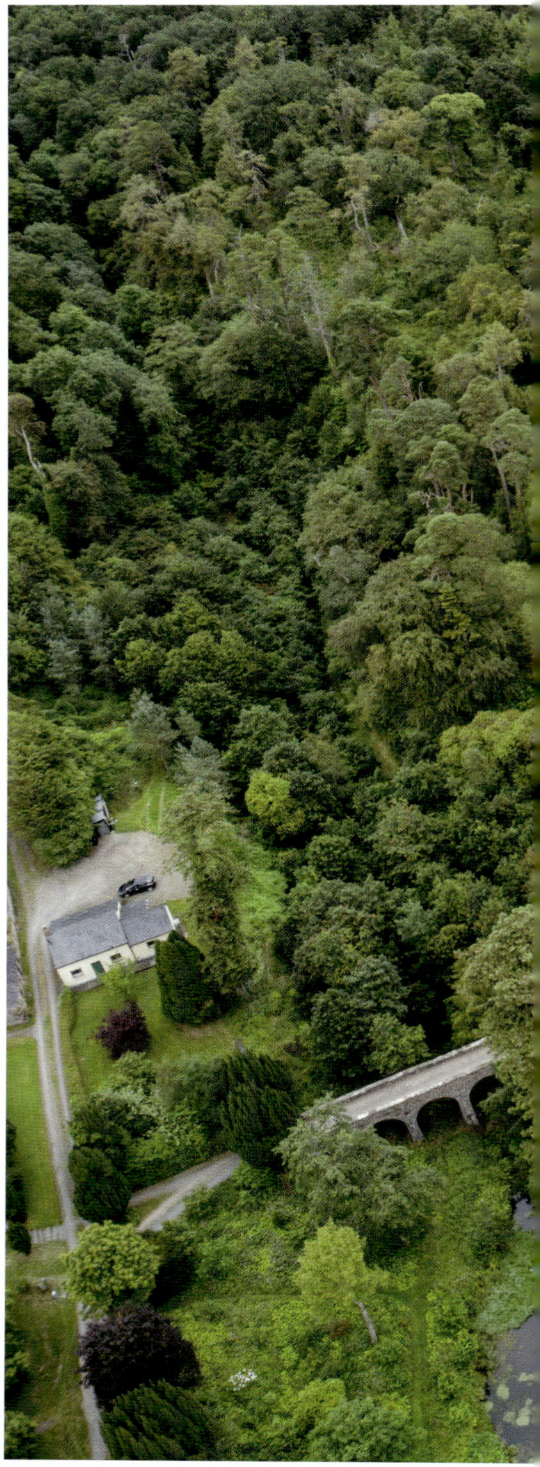

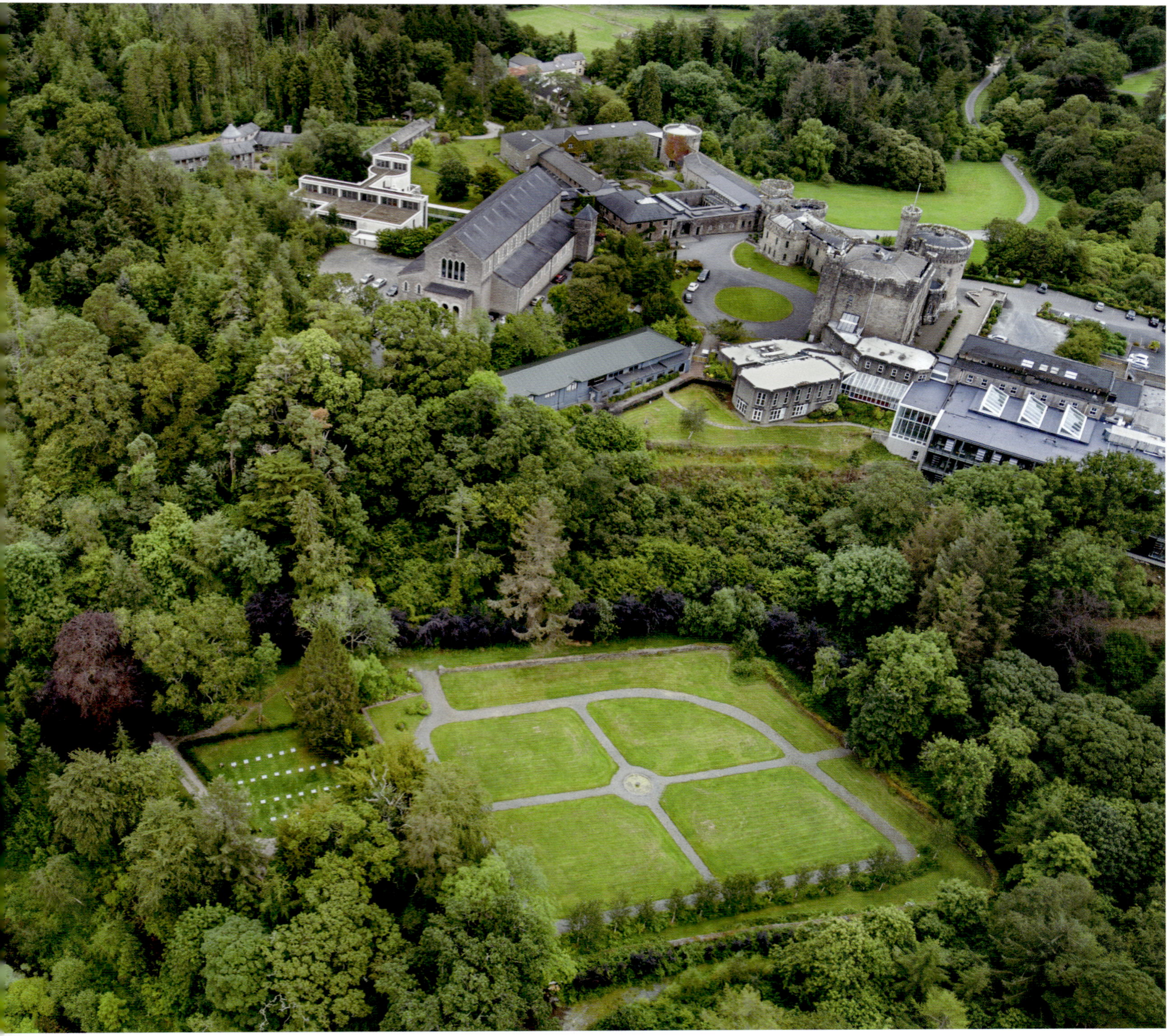

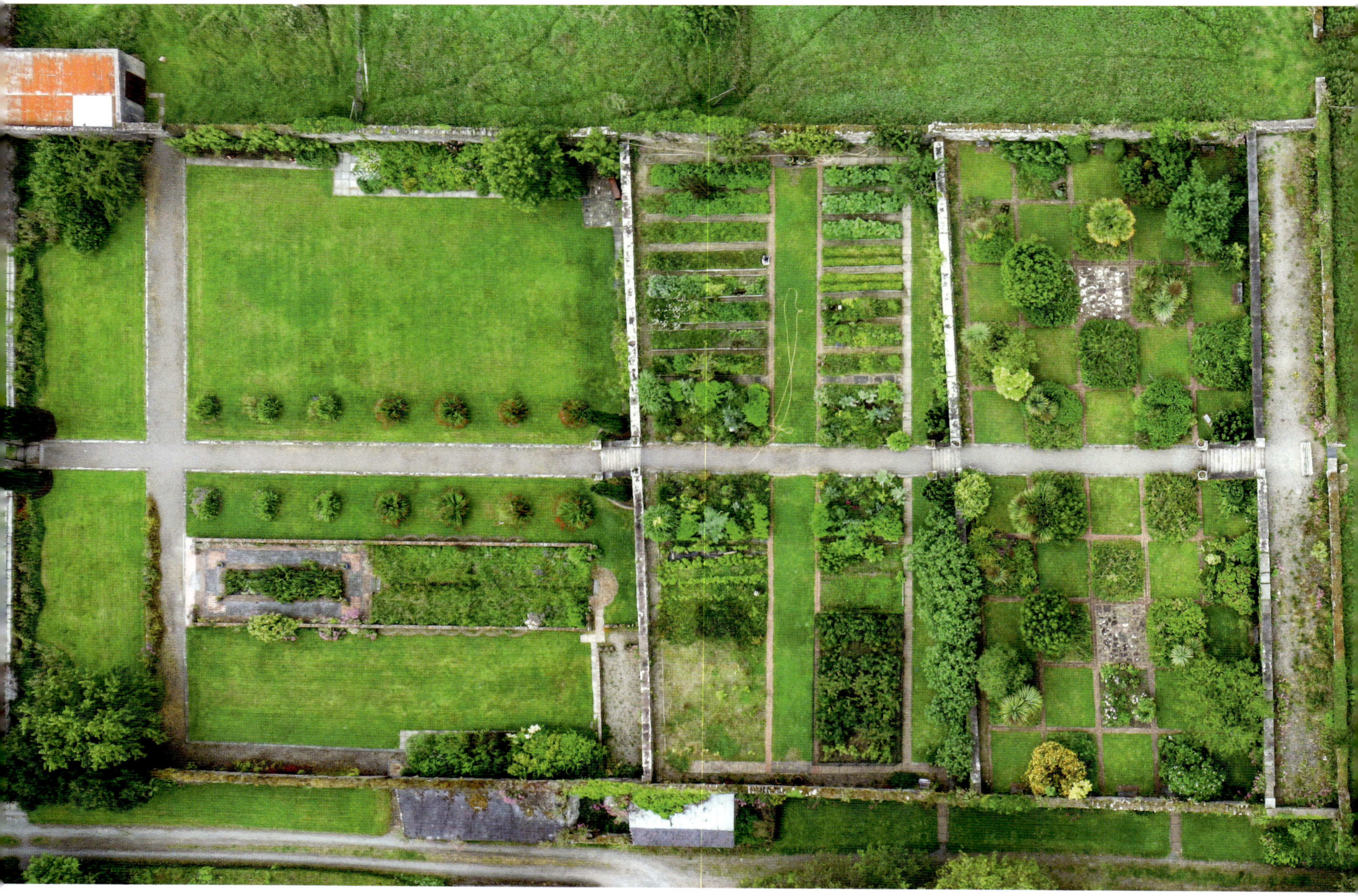

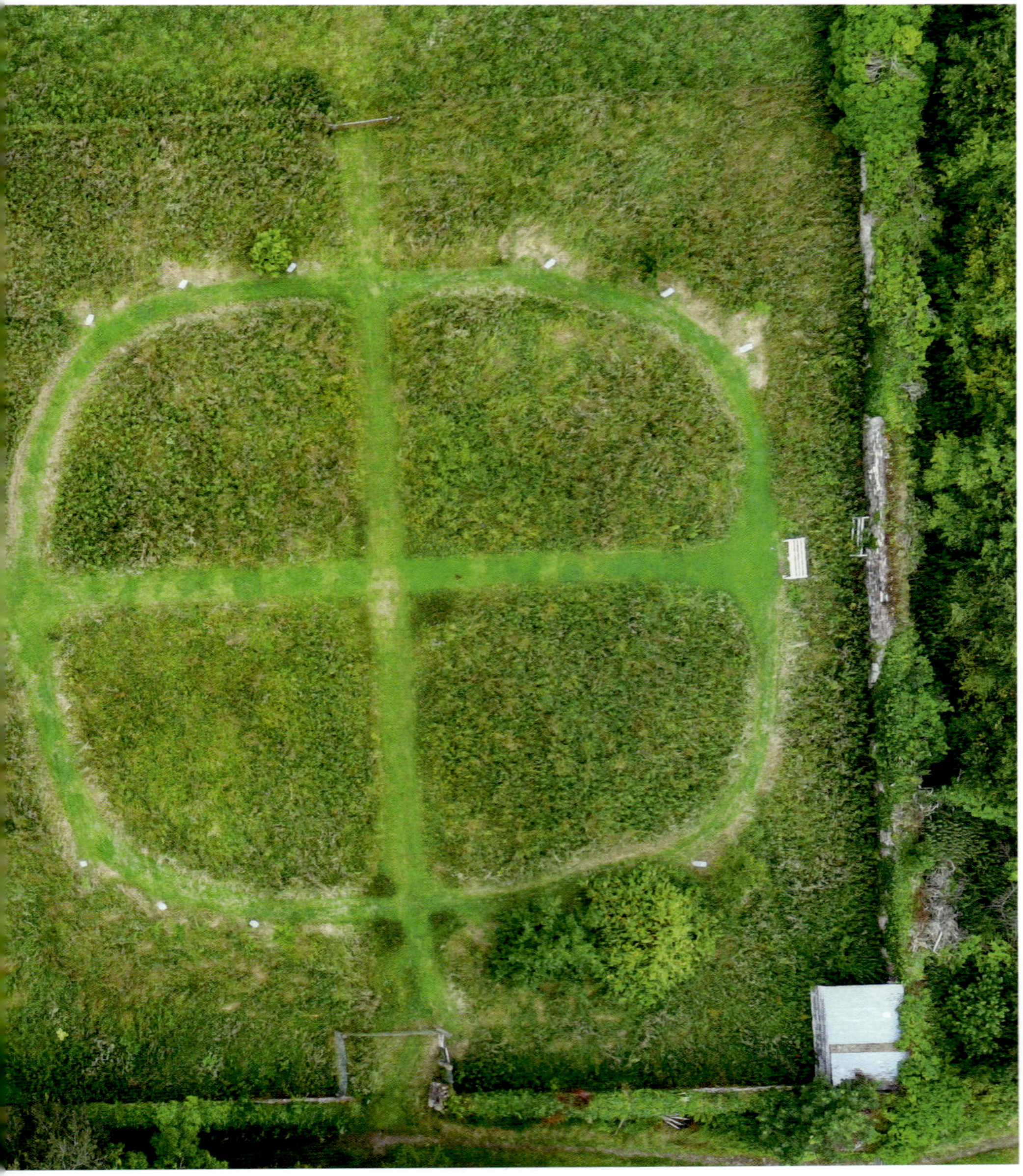

The Terraced Garden dates to the late 17th century and formed part of the domestic complex of the now vanished Capercullen House. It consists of three walled areas each containing approximately an acre of ground. For many years this magnificent amenity was neglected but following a concerted effort by monks, guests, students and men-of-the-road, it is now restored to something approaching its former elegance.

One section consists of a working orchard complete with ecologically sensitive lawnmowers in the form of a small flock of Jacob's sheep. Another area has recently been restored in memory of Fr Seán Ó Duinn, a member of the monastic community and a renowned Celtic scholar. Here, a stand of trees has been planted in the shape of a Celtic cross with each tree representing a letter of the Ogham alphabet used by the ancient Celts.

The final part consists of three terraces, each with its own distinctive character and planting scheme. The bottom section contains examples of flowers and plants that were typically found in such gardens in the 17th century. The middle section contains a vegetable garden and soft fruit bushes including raspberries, blackcurrants, gooseberries and figs. The upper section is a bible garden, containing the various plants, shrubs and flowers mentioned in scripture that can flourish in the Irish climate.

The Icon Chapel

The Icon Chapel is situated in the crypt of the abbey church and contains a collection of Greek and Russian Orthodox icons ranging in date from the 15th to the 20th centuries. Established as the result of the generosity of two benefactors, the chapel was opened at Pentecost 1988 to commemorate the millennium of the baptism of Prince Vladimir of Kiev and the beginnings of Russian Christianity. Designed in the form of a Byzantine chapel and decorated with artwork by James Scanlan, the chapel is a spiritual oasis at the heart of the monastery and has been an important place of healing and comfort for many. It also provides an ecumenical link with the Orthodox churches as well as with our 'forgotten brothers and sisters': the Christian communities of the Middle East.

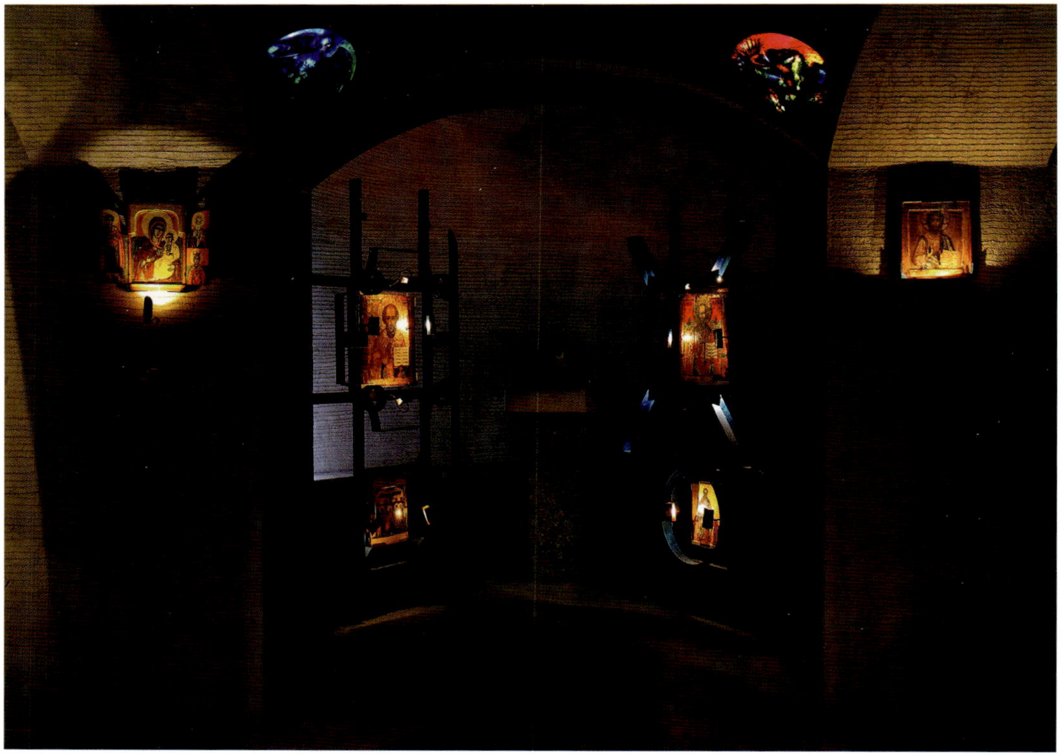

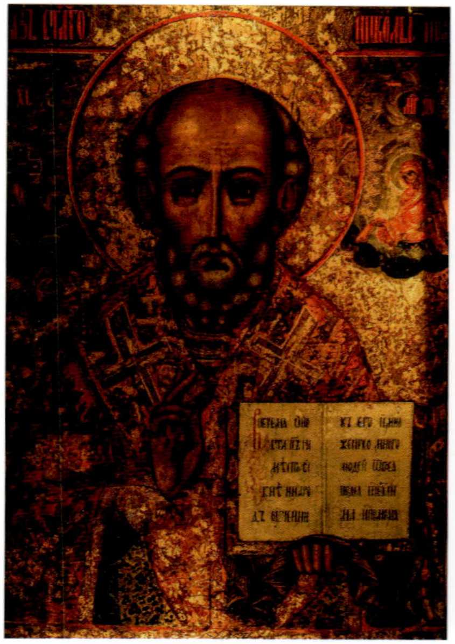

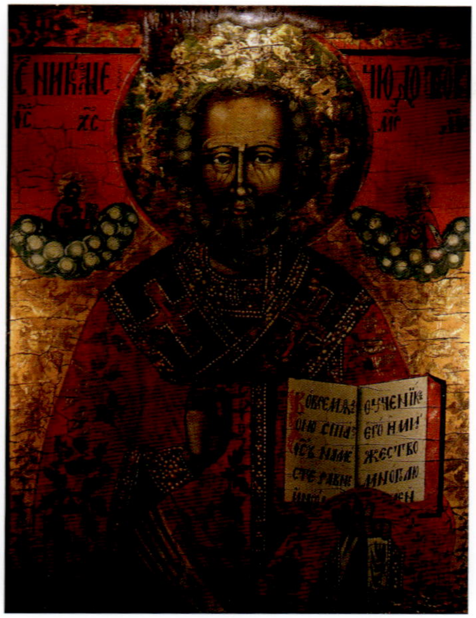

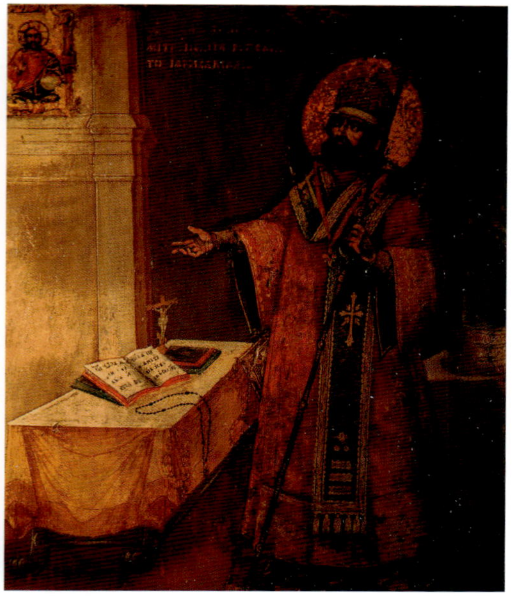

“

Drive away the darkness which surrounds us;
Spread around us the mantle of your light
Help us to know your will
And give us the courage to do it.

. . .

Cuir chun siúil gach dorchadas atá timpeall orainn.
Spré timpeall orainn do bhrat sholais.
Cuid linn do thoil a aimsiú agus
tabhair dúinn an mhisneach chun í a leanúint.

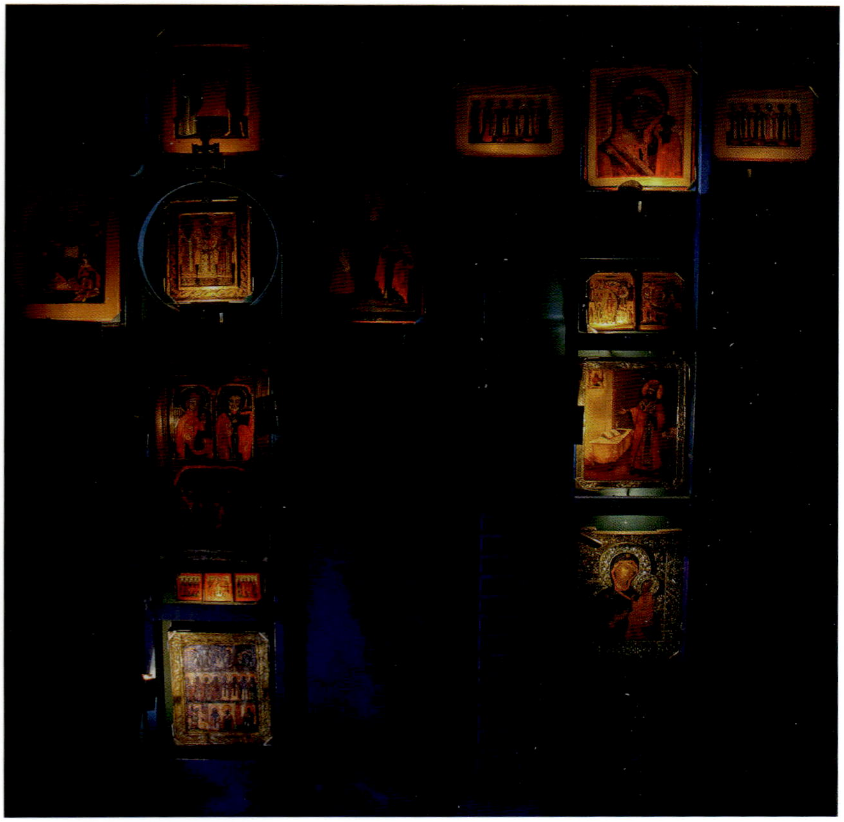

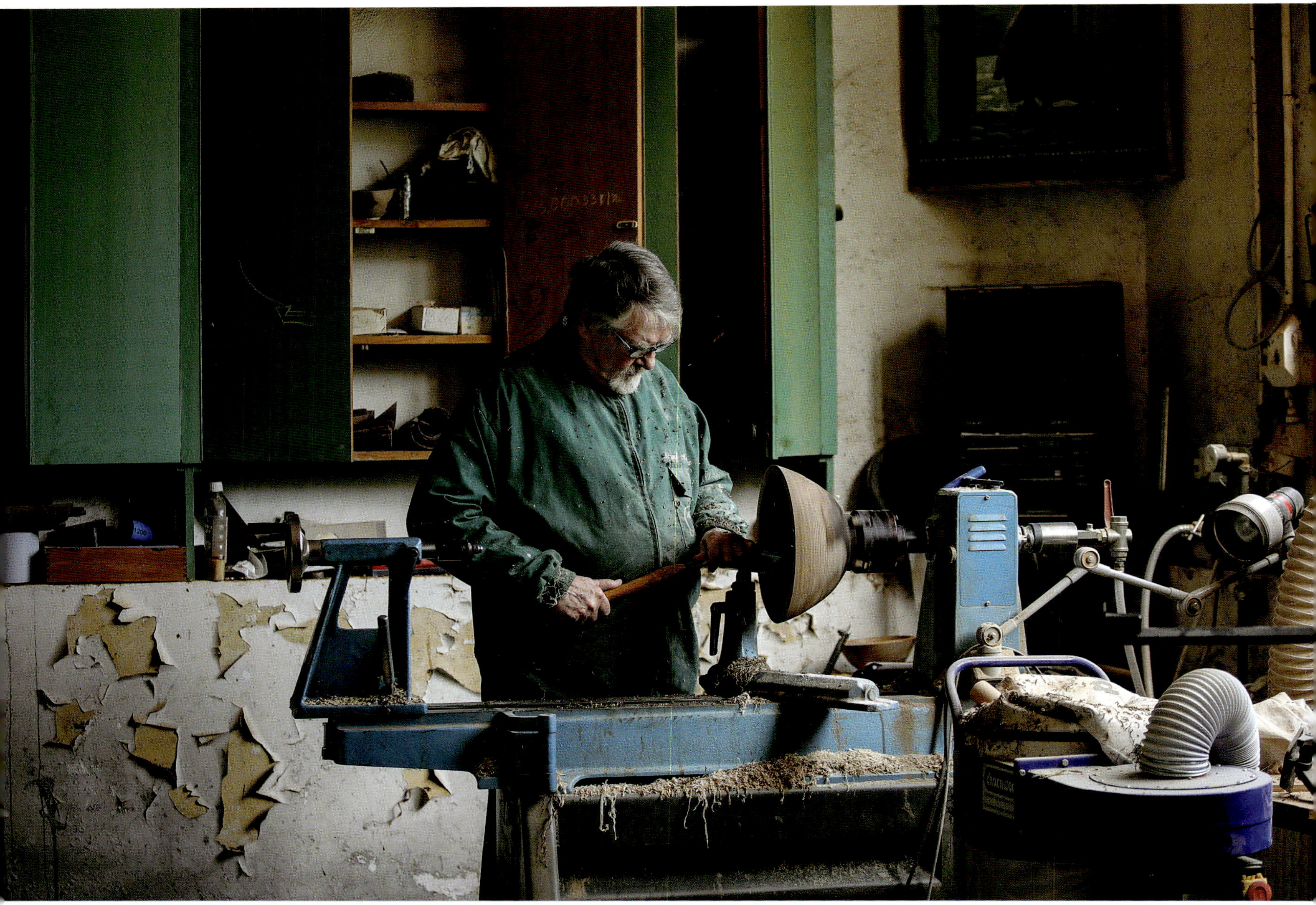

Br Ciarán has been a monk of Glenstal since 1961 and is one of Ireland's best-known woodturners. His interest began when two boys in the Abbey school brought a lathe to the carpentry workshop. The Glenstal woods provide abundant raw material for his craft.

The craftsmen of the monastery

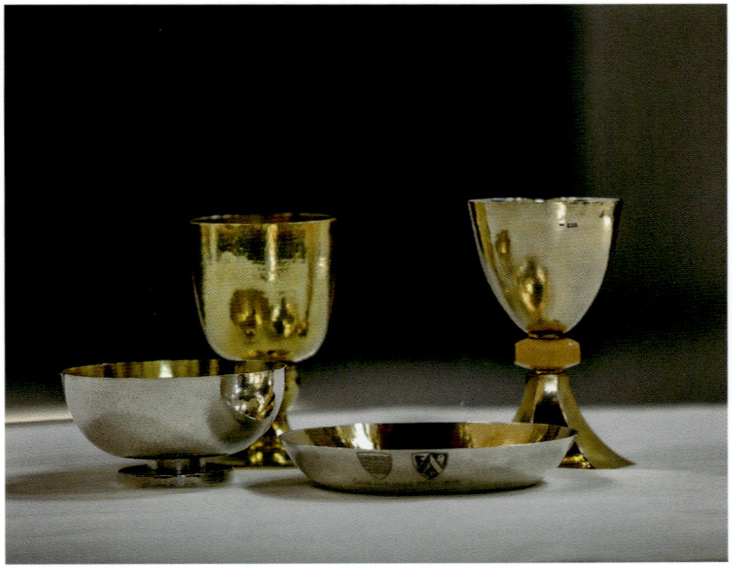

Chalices and patens made by Fr James and Fr Henry in the Glenstal silversmith's workshop

Monasteries have traditionally provided a place in which the arts can flourish, and Glenstal is no exception. The promotion of arts and crafts characterised the monasteries of Maredsous and Beuron, to which we owe our origins and traditions. The first educational project undertaken in Glenstal was the establishment of a school to train boys and young men from the locality as woodcarvers, sculptors, metal workers, joiners and painters. The expansion of Catholic institutions in the early to mid-20th century provided a ready market for their work and products of the Glenstal workshop may be found in monasteries, religious houses and churches across the country. The community's continental contacts provided a conduit for new ideas and influences that in turn influenced developments in Irish liturgical art, chiefly mediated through the annual Liturgical Conference that took place throughout the 1950s and 1960s and which has recently been revived.

The work of Br Benedict Tutty was of seminal importance, particularly in the period of liturgical renewal following the Second Vatican Council. Trained in Belgium and Germany and proficient in several artistic media, his work is found in churches throughout Ireland, England and even further afield. The abbey church in Glenstal contains fine examples of his skill in enamel, terracotta, metalwork and stained glass. It also houses specimens of the work of other monk-craftsmen and alumni of the Glenstal Arts School. The crafts practised in the community at present include bookbinding, carpentry, metalwork, painting and woodturning.

"

Should there be craftsmen in the Monastery, let them work at their crafts in all humility, ... that God may be glorified in all things.

– Rule of St. Benedict, Chapter 57

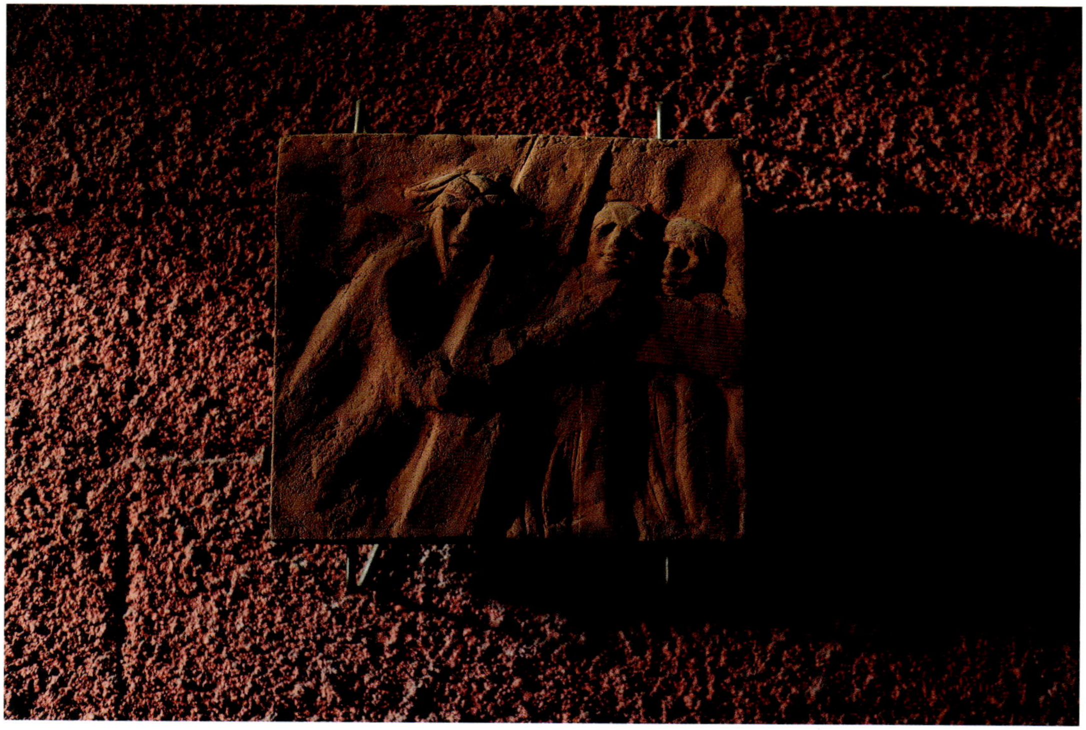

Jesus meets the Women of Jerusalem: Stations of the Cross in terracotta by Br Benedict.

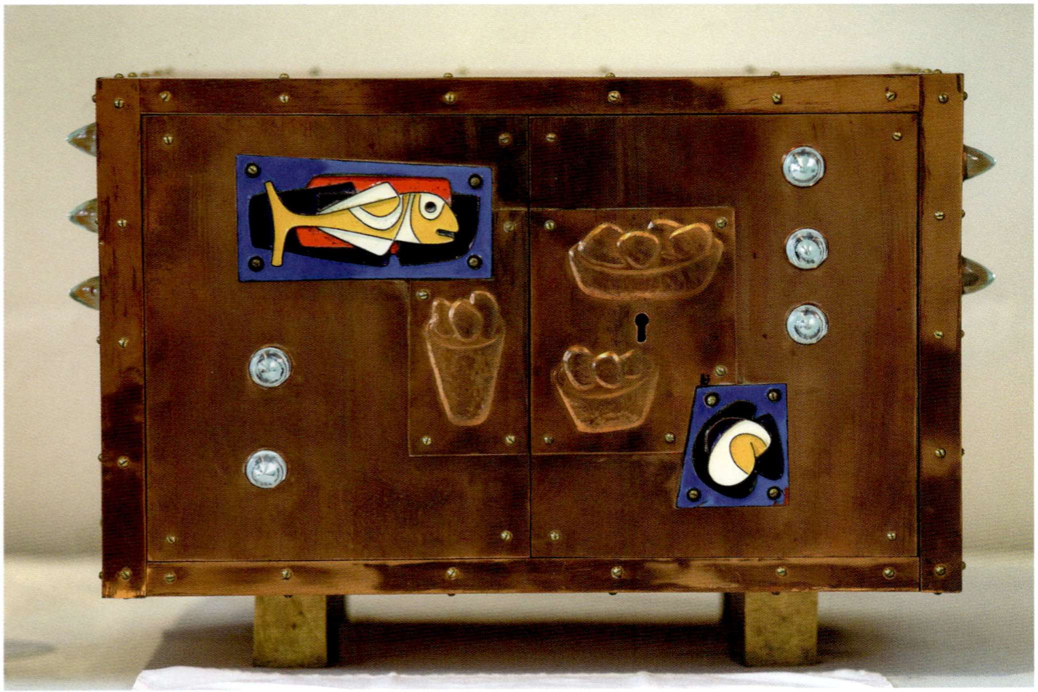

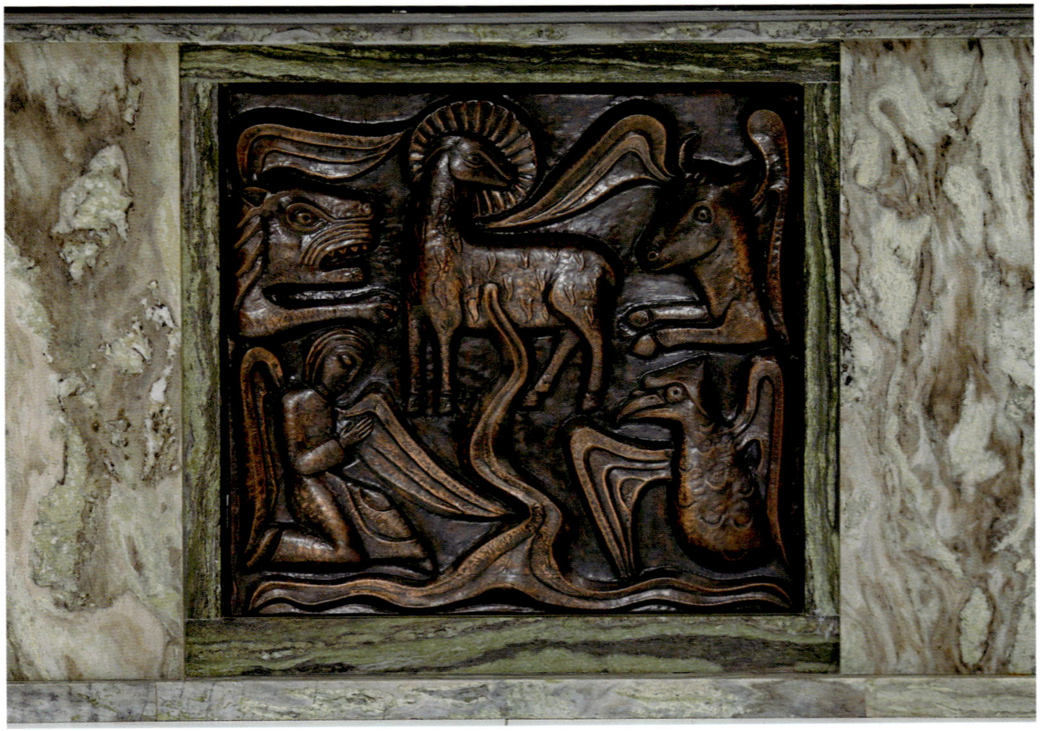

Top: Tabernacle depicting the miracle of the loaves and fishes by Br Benedict. Copper, enamel and rock crystal.

Left: The Lamb of the Apocalypse surrounded by the symbols of the four Evangelists by Brother Benedict. Beaten Copper.

Bookbinding has been practiced in monasteries from the earliest times and many of its painstaking traditional techniques are still employed today– stacking, folding, gluing, cutting, binding and stitching the spine. Here Fr Senan, the monastery prior, rebinds some liturgical books.

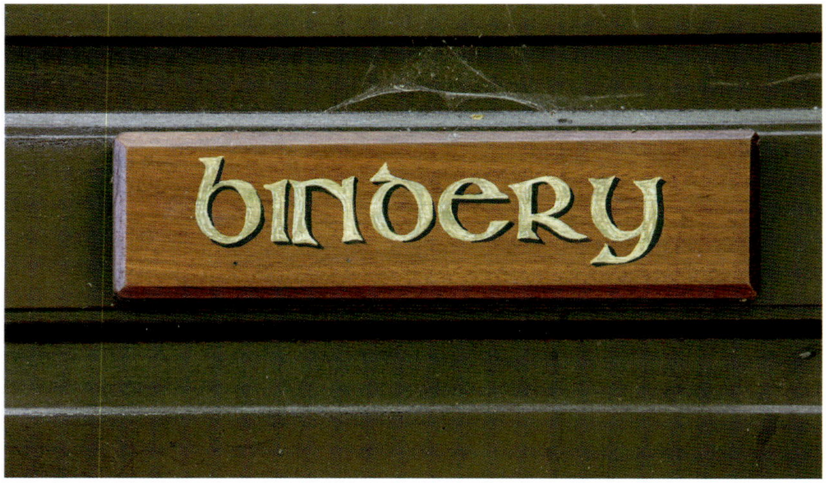

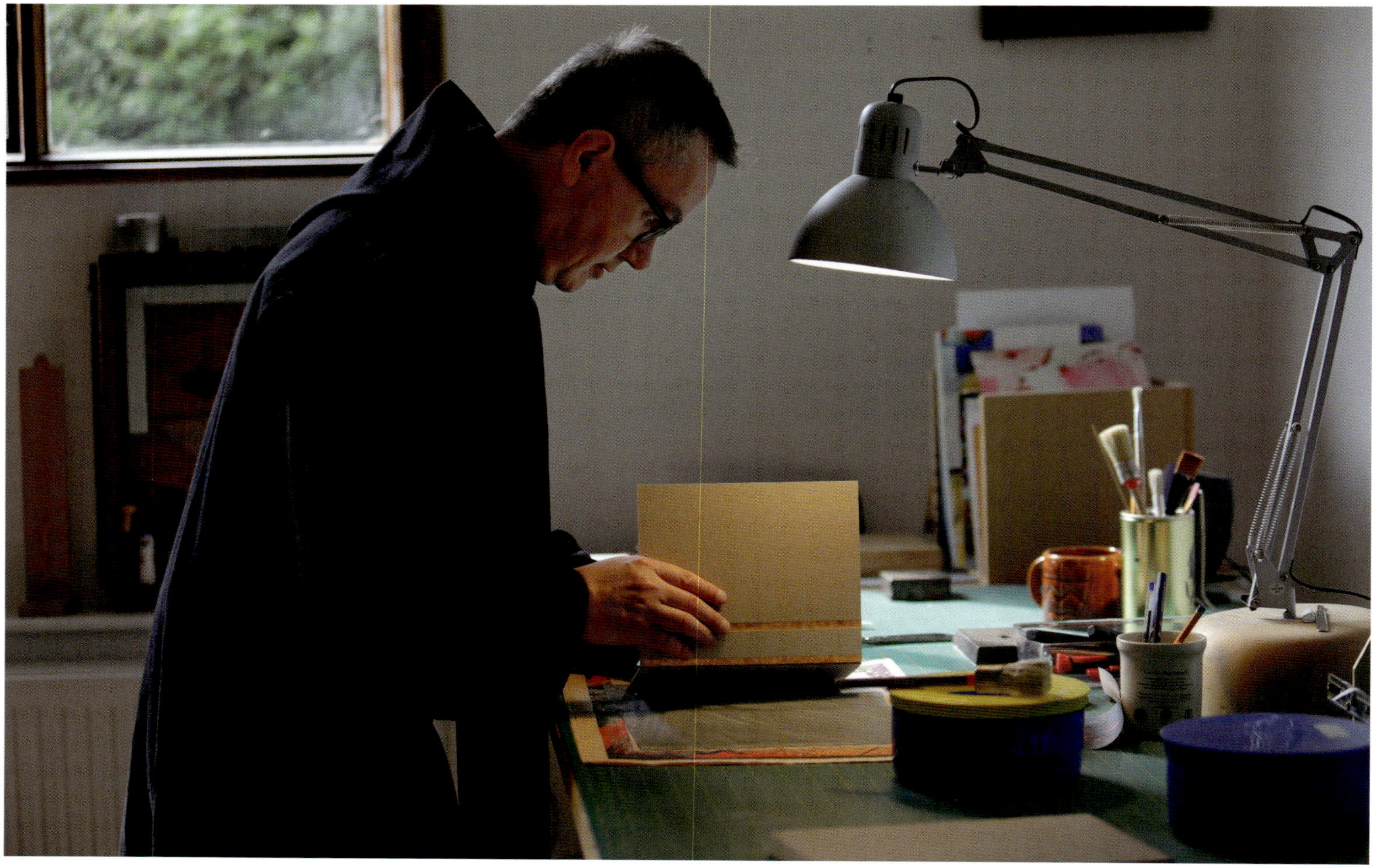

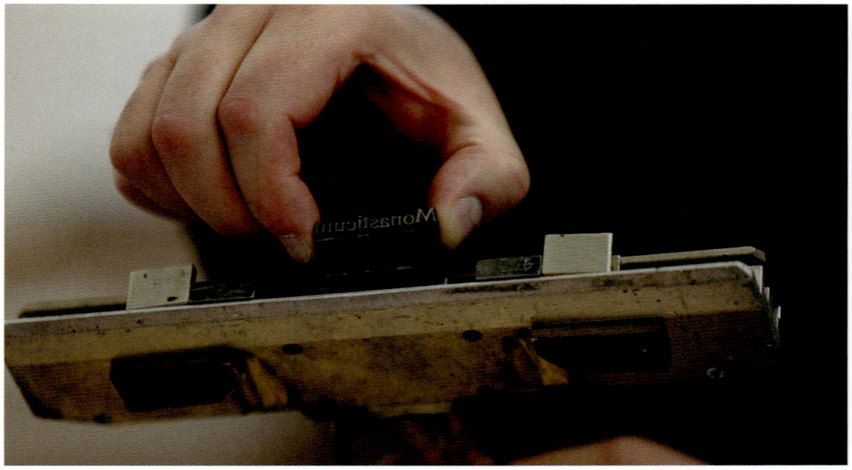

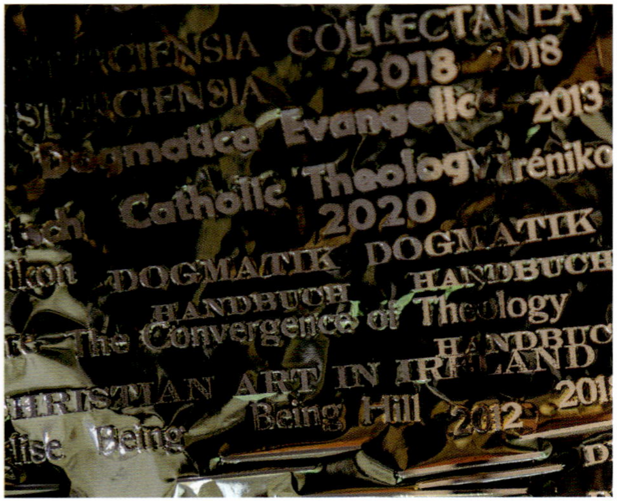
COLLECTANEA
2018
2013
Catholic Theology
2020
DOGMATIK DOGMATIK
HANDBUCH
The Convergence of Theology
CHRISTIAN ART IN IRELAND
Being Hill 2012

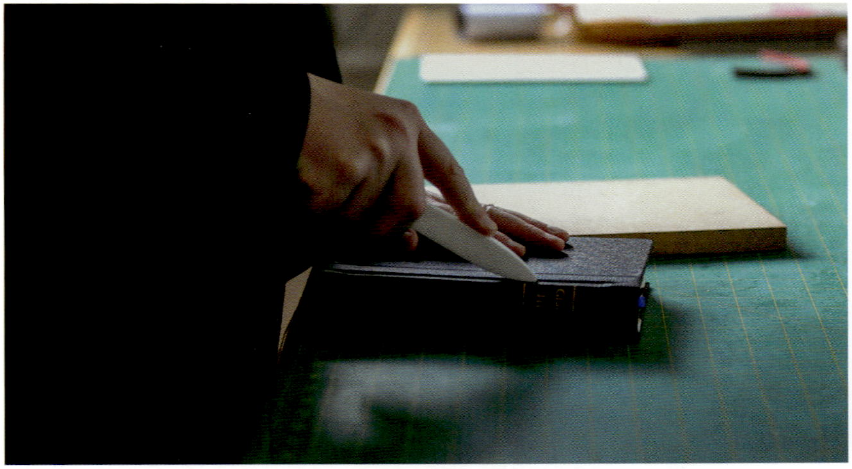

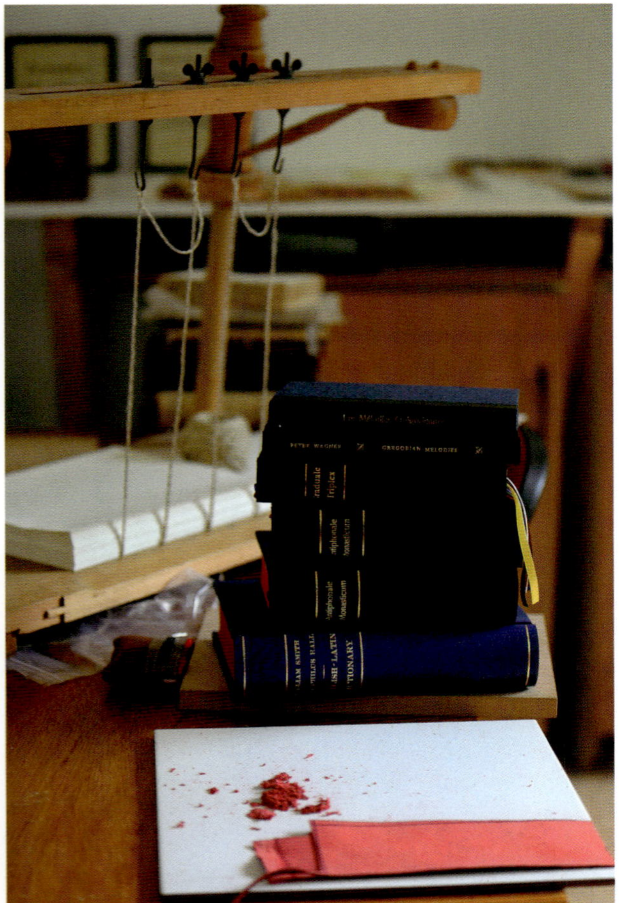
Graduale
Triplex

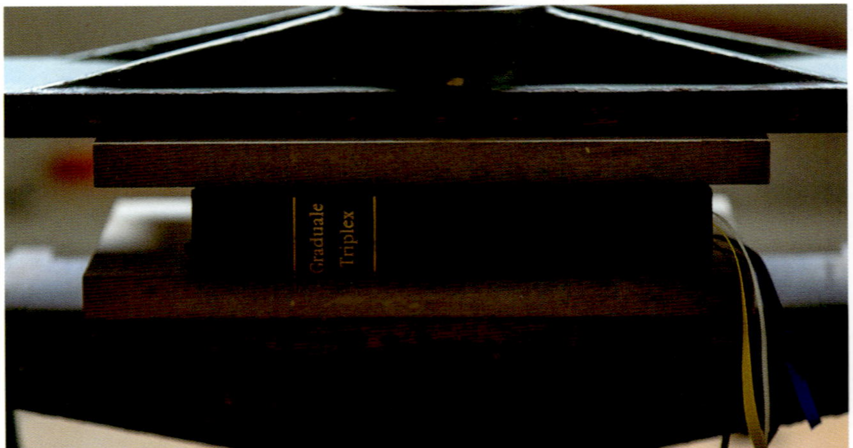
Graduale
Triplex

A Monk's Tale:

The Artist

Prior to my solemn profession at Glenstal Abbey in 2014, I worked as a graphic designer in Los Angeles, USA, for ten years after receiving my B.Des from the National College of Art and Design in Dublin. Currently a student at the University of St. Michael's College in the University of Toronto, Canada, I am about to enter my third year of doctoral studies. My area of research considers questions involving the need for contemporary liturgical art to adapt Christian iconography in terms of postmodern recontextualization.

Since entering Benedictine monastic life, painting has become a vital means of exploring the relevance of what the Incarnation suggests. The programme of studies in which I'm currently involved allows me to examine how art can be understood in terms of visual theology. For me, this begs the question of what change the Incarnation makes to our understanding of human flesh and blood. Like musicians in their chanting and the monks in their daily ritual, painting offers both a creative and disciplined means of responding to this mystery.

Art as theology builds upon the invitation that scripture extends to reflect on how encounter with Christ challenges preconceptions about the human body, especially in terms of identity and social relations. It suggests the need to adapt familiar Christian iconography in order to engage a viewer in a visual literacy appropriate to present-day concerns involving attitudes toward the human body.

The Woman at the Well, for instance, displayed at the entrance to our church, seeks to engage a viewer in more than a record of historical encounter with Christ. In much the same way as the paintings of the two disciples on the road to Emmaus (in the sacristy) or Saint Paul's being struck blind on the road to Damascus (in our library) suggest possibilities of what is involved in encounter with Christ, they also reflects the significance of the monk's *Opus Dei* in making that connection. In rendering the human figure naked 'to follow the naked Christ,' these paintings, like the Benedictine commitment to a life of daily conversion, echo the challenge to emulate the *paupertas, nuditas et humilitas Christi* and become, in ourselves, transparent images of the God who made us.

Br Emmaus

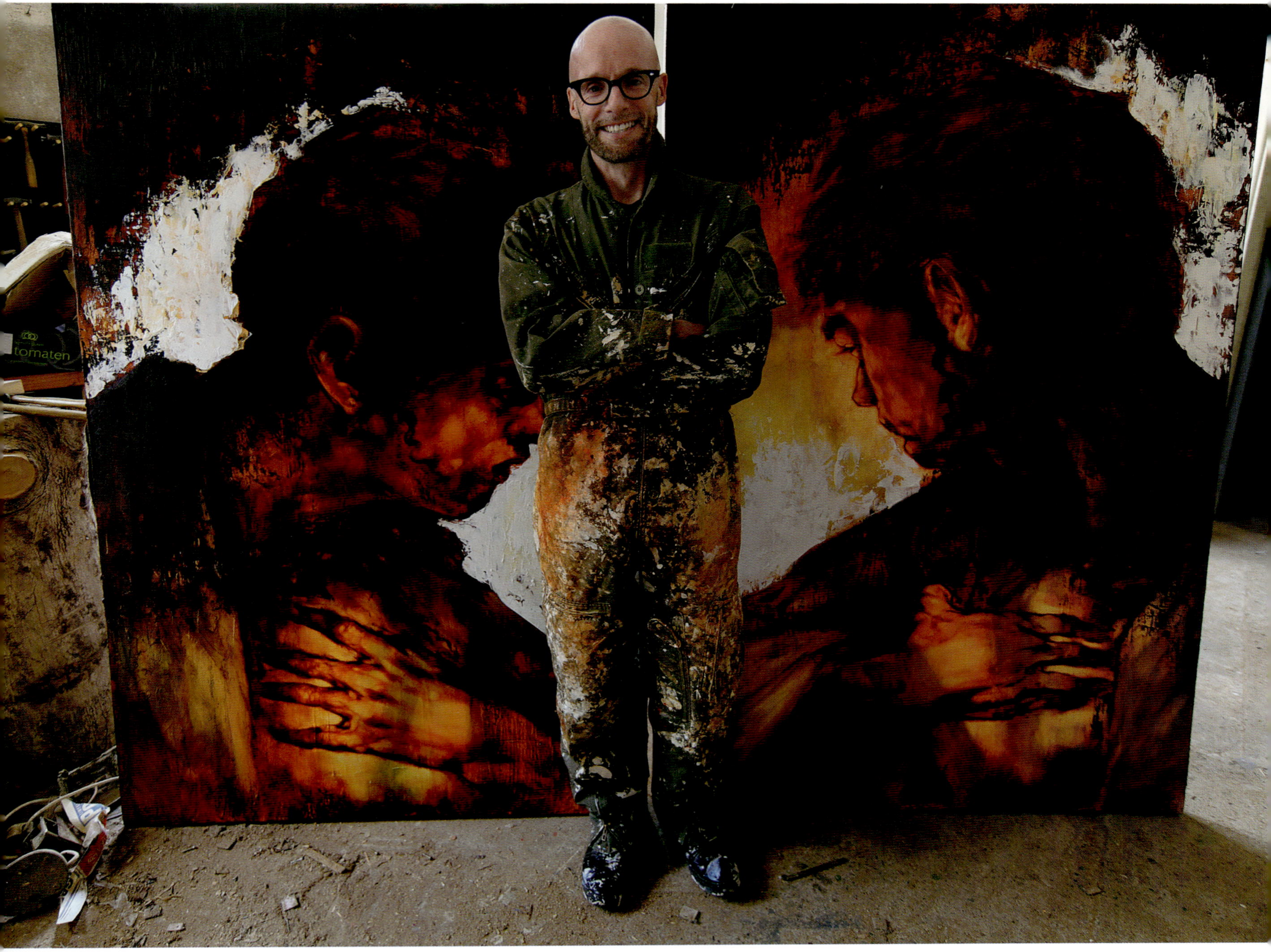
tomaten

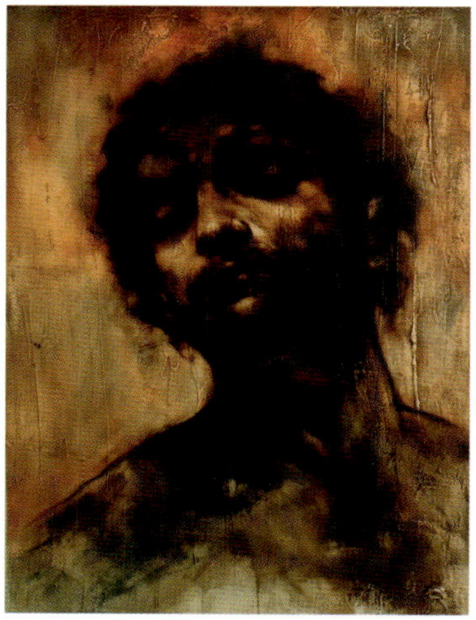

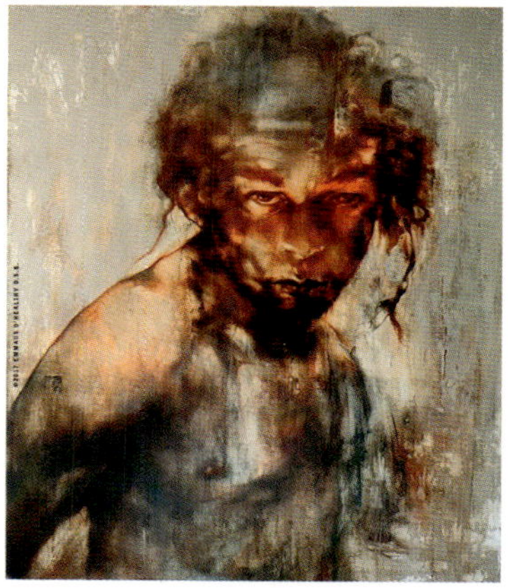

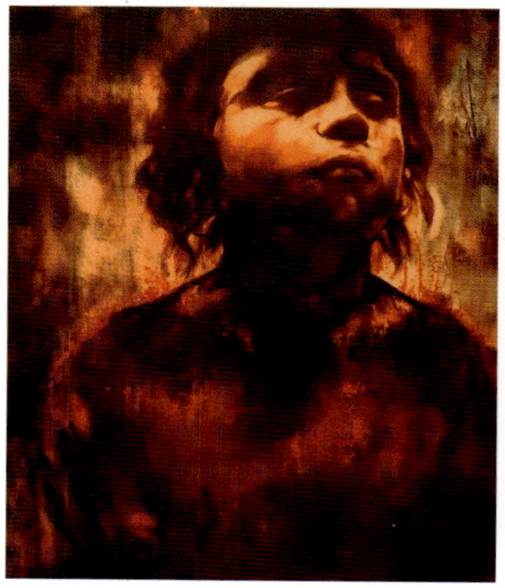

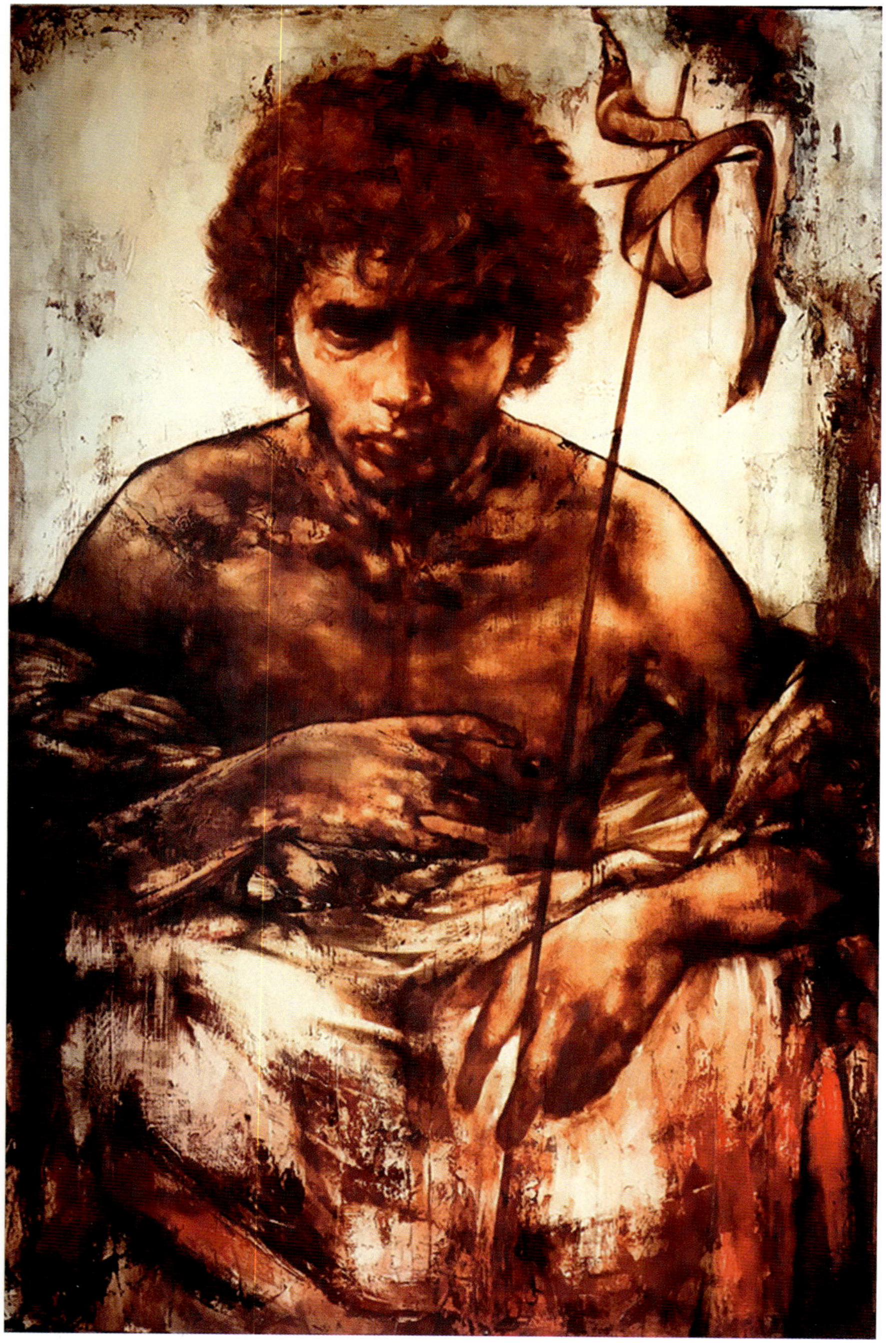

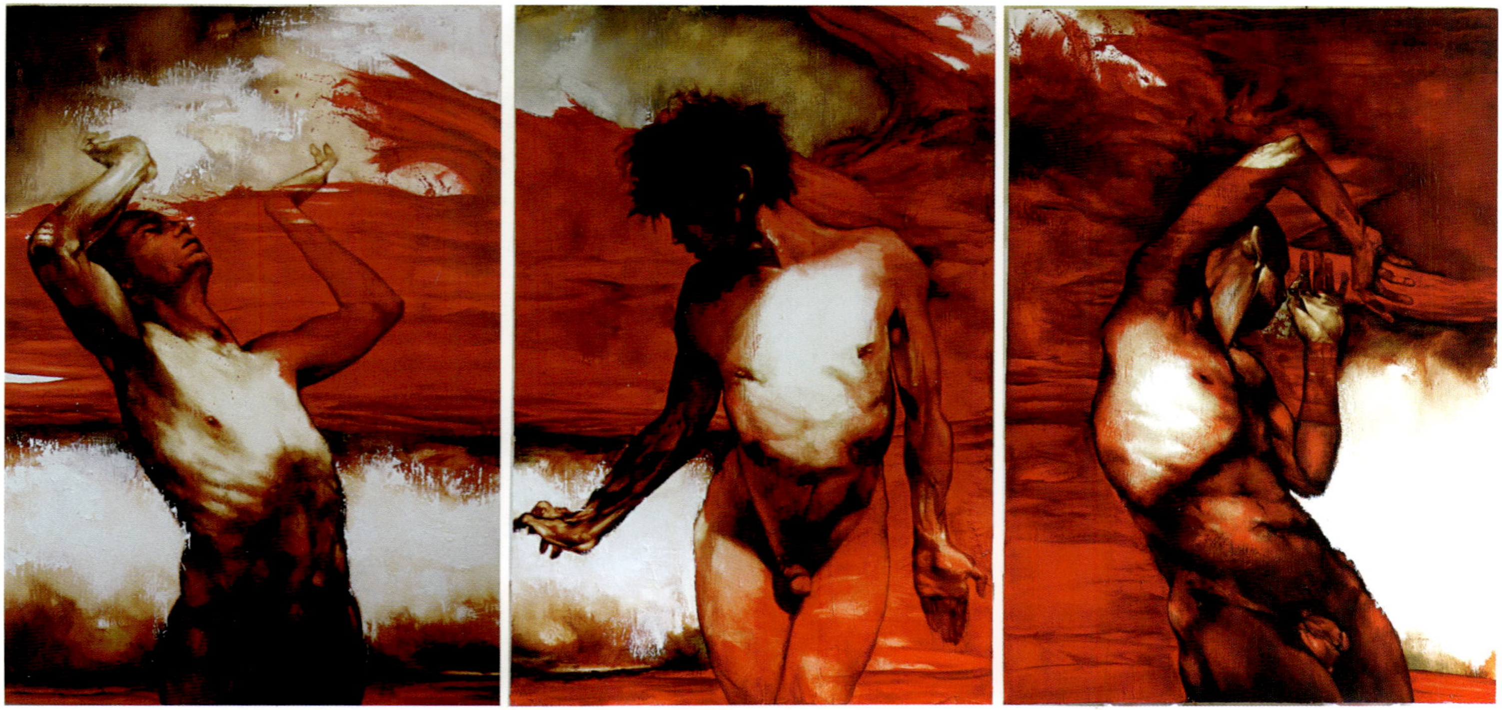

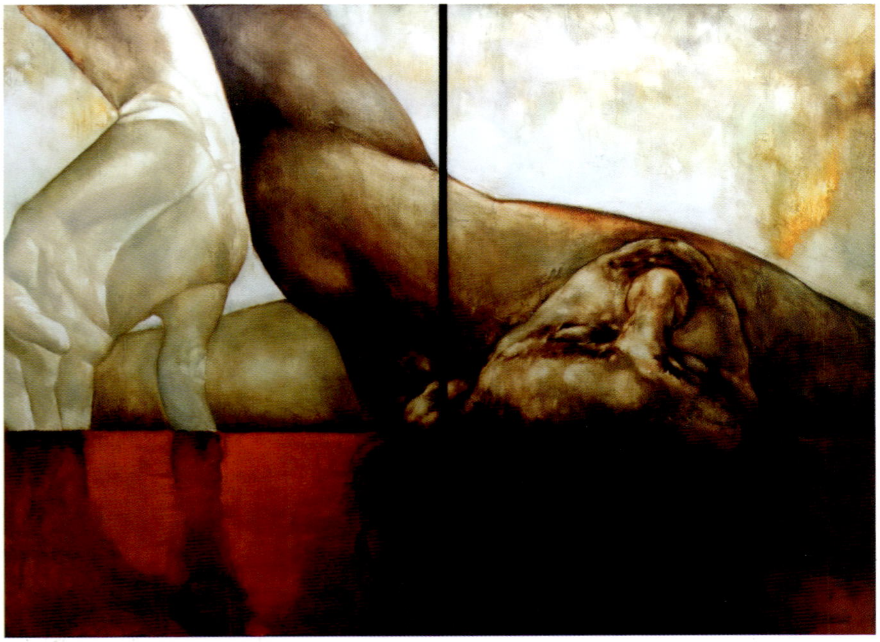

Above: The Good Thief

Right: The Conversion of Saul

Opposite: 'Vidi et Testimonium Perhibui Quia' – 'I have seen it and borne witness'

A Monk's Tale:

The Guestmaster

I came to the monastery, 49 years ago, with at least half a hope that I would work it out of my system and that I could get on with the rest of my life. In the meantime, I have spent the years and decades in an absorbing variety of occupations, teaching and housemastering in the school, accompanying and teaching the novices, helping to develop a monastic community in Nigeria, serving the community here, as prior and abbot, and now, as guest master and teacher in the school again, with some involvement in the garden and orchard.

Hospitality has developed enormously, since the construction of a purpose-built guesthouse 20 years ago. With 12 bedrooms, the dining-room, a meeting-room and a fine sitting-room, there is comfortable accommodation for a manageable group of individuals who enjoy quietness in beautiful surroundings. The monastic liturgies are a major attraction, while the extensive grounds allow for more or less challenging walks on the avenues and in the gardens. For many, a quiet stay provides a precious opportunity for reading or for accompaniment by one of the brethren. Then, the Icon Chapel can open a door onto another world of spirituality. For some, the evening supper with the community is an experience to treasure.

Many guests speak of seeking quiet space, to recover a sense of self and balance; sometimes, even, of healing. While the environment is obviously monastic, there is no hint of obligation to join in the monastic programme. If some like to speak with the guestmaster or another monk, others find what they need from encounters with other guests, or just with themselves.

There is general appreciation of the table-fare and of the gathering around the breakfast table, where the staple porridge plays a part for some. There is much exaggeration about its virtues, which are reducible to the following recipe (for 6):

- 1 cup porridge oats
- ¾ cup pinhead oats
- ¼ cup muesli
- 1 tsp salt
- 1 cup mixed seeds and walnuts
- 2 tablespoons sultanas (soaked in something alcoholic)
- 3 cups milk
- 4 cups water

Soak over-night and cook either at medium heat, stirring all the time; or in a slow cooker, for two hours at low heat.

Fr Christopher

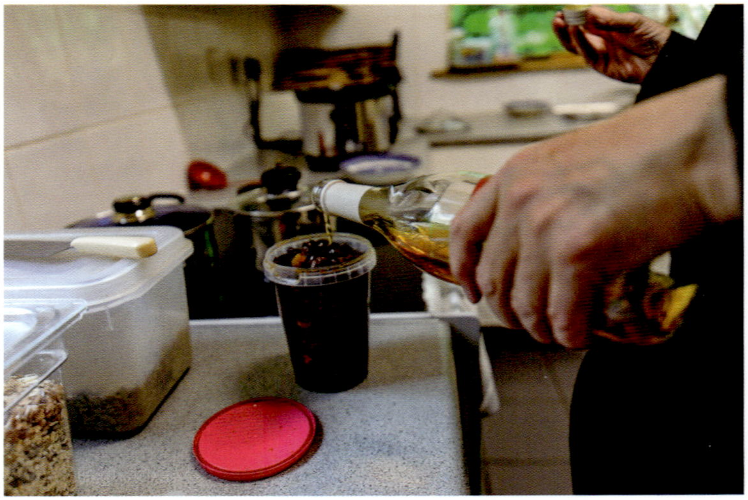

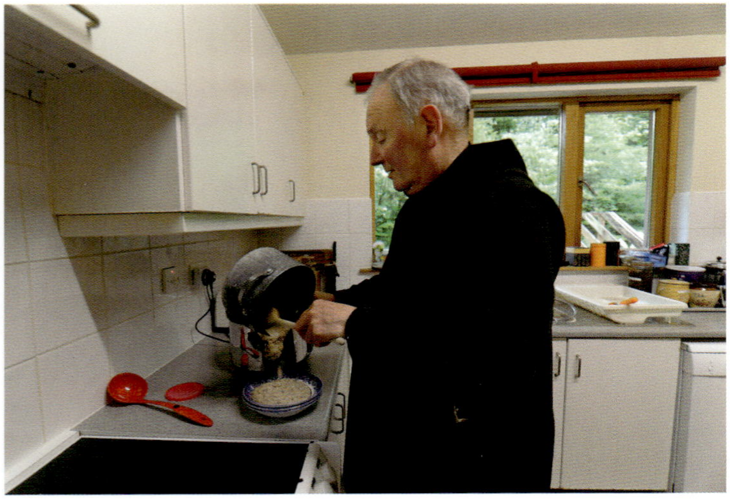

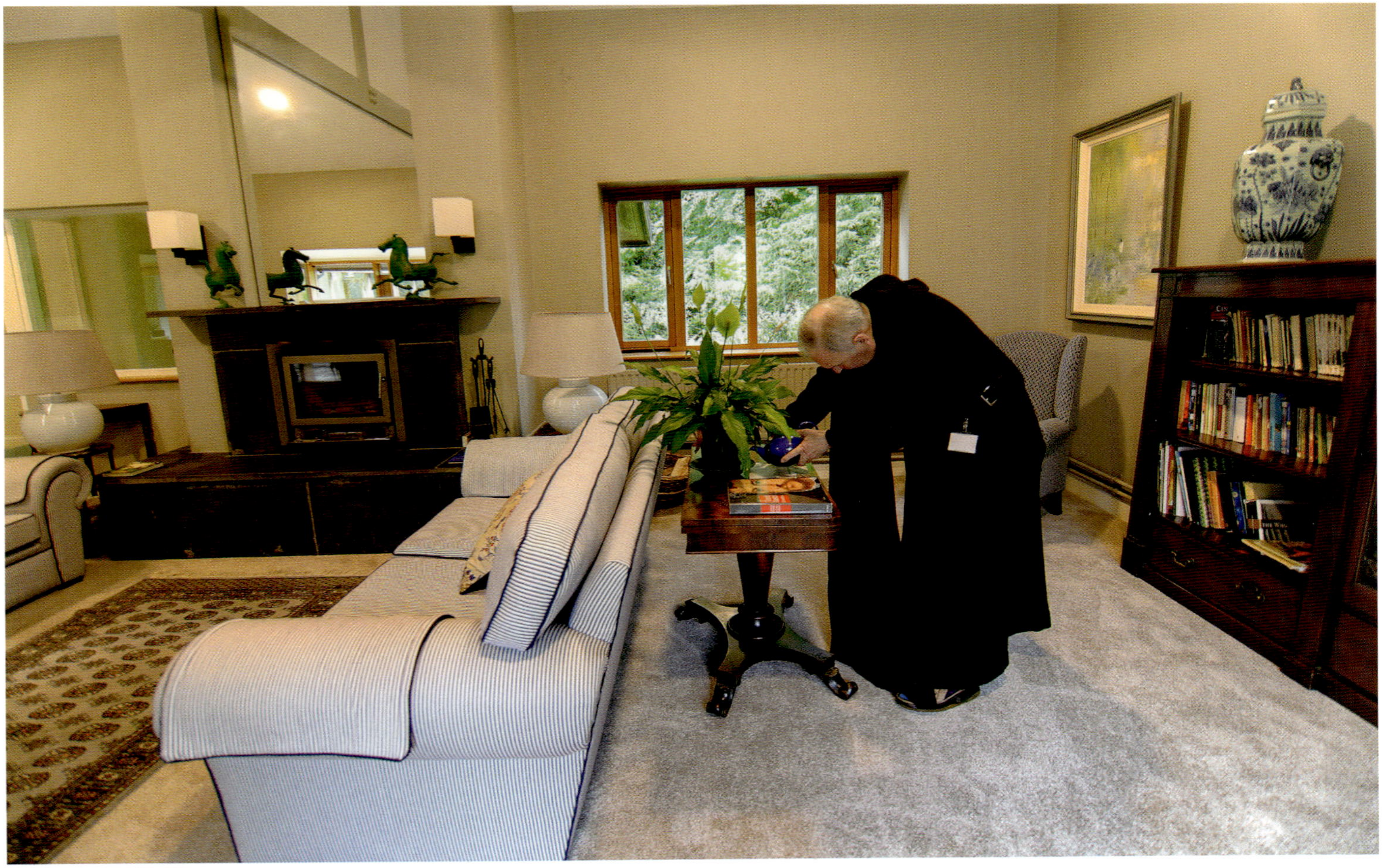

A Monk's Tale:

The Woodsman

That there should be a representative stand of the World Forest at the abbey comes perhaps as no surprise. The Temple of the Tooth at Kandy, which still protects the remnants of the great rain forest which once clothed Sri Lanka, the holy drunemetons of India and Saint Columba's beloved oak grove at Derry - where the only sound he feared was the ring of the steel axe - are but some instances of the connection between the sylvan and the saintly.

Of all the animals, we humans are perhaps the most vertically erect, upright and elegant. Within the kingdom of the plants, the same can be said for the trees. Therefore, when we stand in exultation and gratitude for our existence, and when we lift our limbs in prayer, we may often feel an affinity with our brothers and sisters of the forest. When Jesus cured a man blind from birth, the cured man's first observation was: I see men like trees walking.

To join a monastery where there is a forest that is known and loved is to join a community of praise, a place where the Divine Liturgy is already in progress. From its foundation in 1927, the monks of Glenstal have been happily appreciative of the arboreal inheritance of the place. Fathers Ghisbert, Gerard Francois, Daniel, Augustine and Oliver, are some of those monk-foresters whose names come to mind, ably and generously aided by Thomas Ryan Head, Christy Fitzgibbon, Martin Grant and many others.

Monks of old often felt their psalmody was joined by the chorus of the birds and that their good works found a resonance in the creation around them. The symphony of the forest offers a powerful amplification and extension through the cosmos of our song in choir. This symphony is so powerful that it can sometimes be almost heard by the ear of the senses. It is celebrated by the poet Venantius Fortunatus (d. 609). He encouraged the trees saying: 'Produce fronds, flower and germinate - *Frondete, flore, germine.*'

And to show how the trees can personally and exquisitely reveal the mysteries of salvation, he refers to red and purple flushed Lammas growth and to the Cross when he wrote: 'Decorous and splendid tree, adorned with the blood of the King – *Arbor decor et fulgida, ornata Regis purpura.*'

Fr Anthony

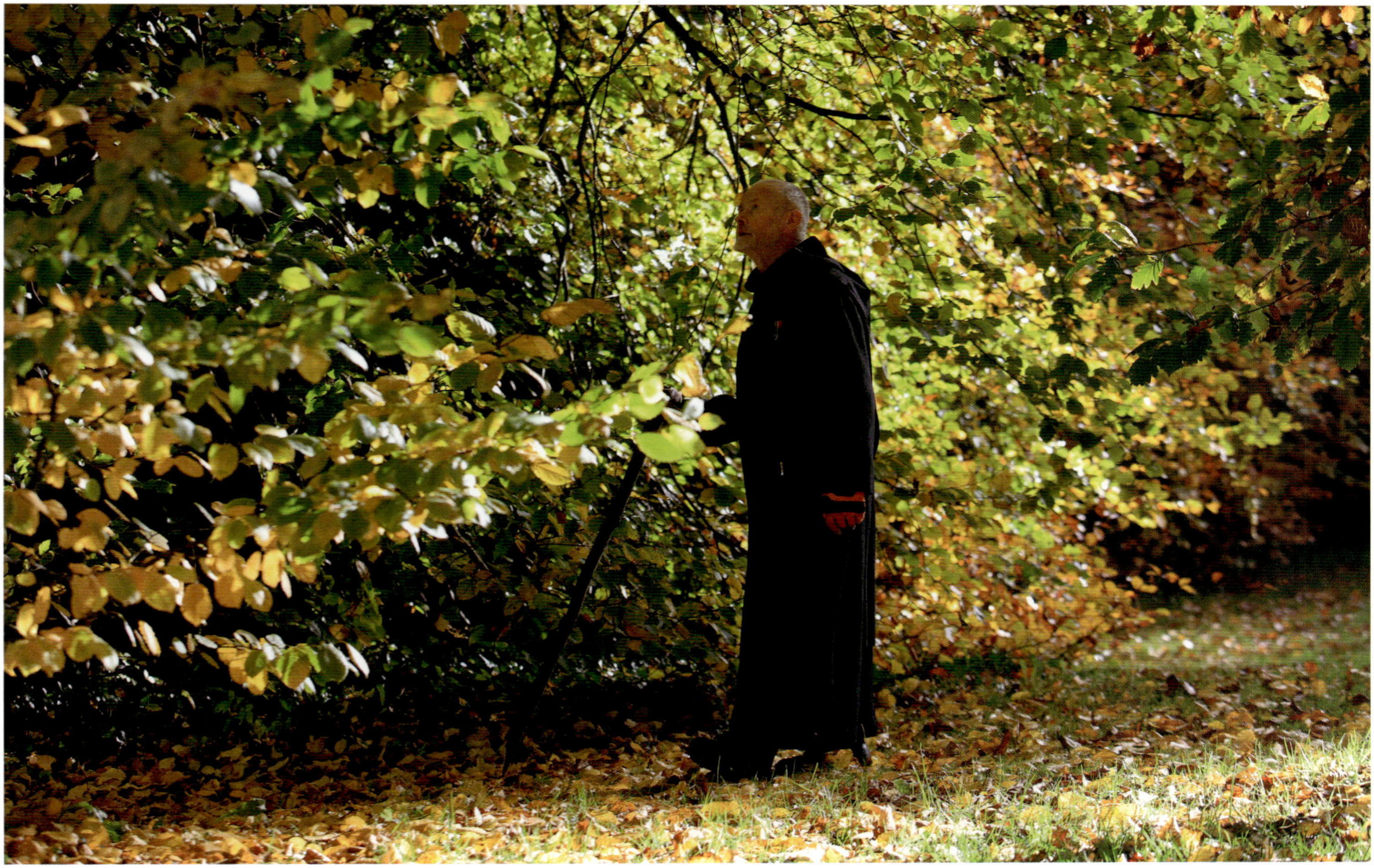

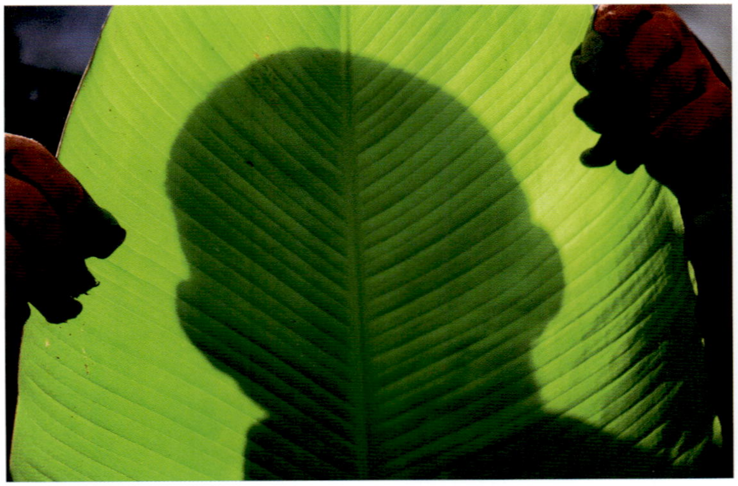

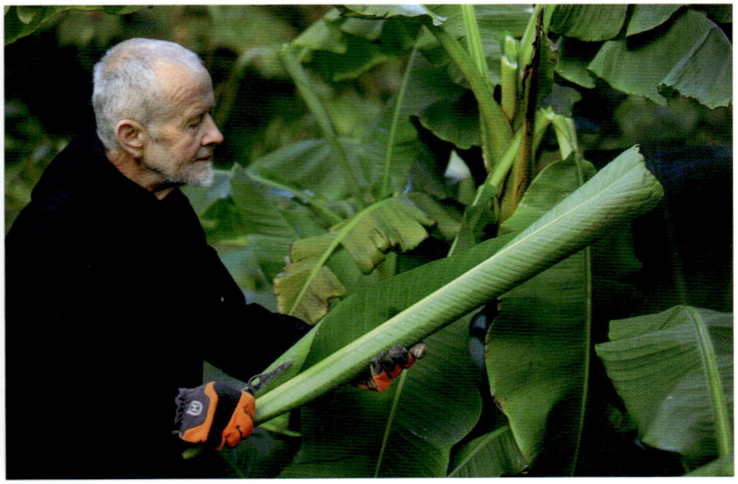

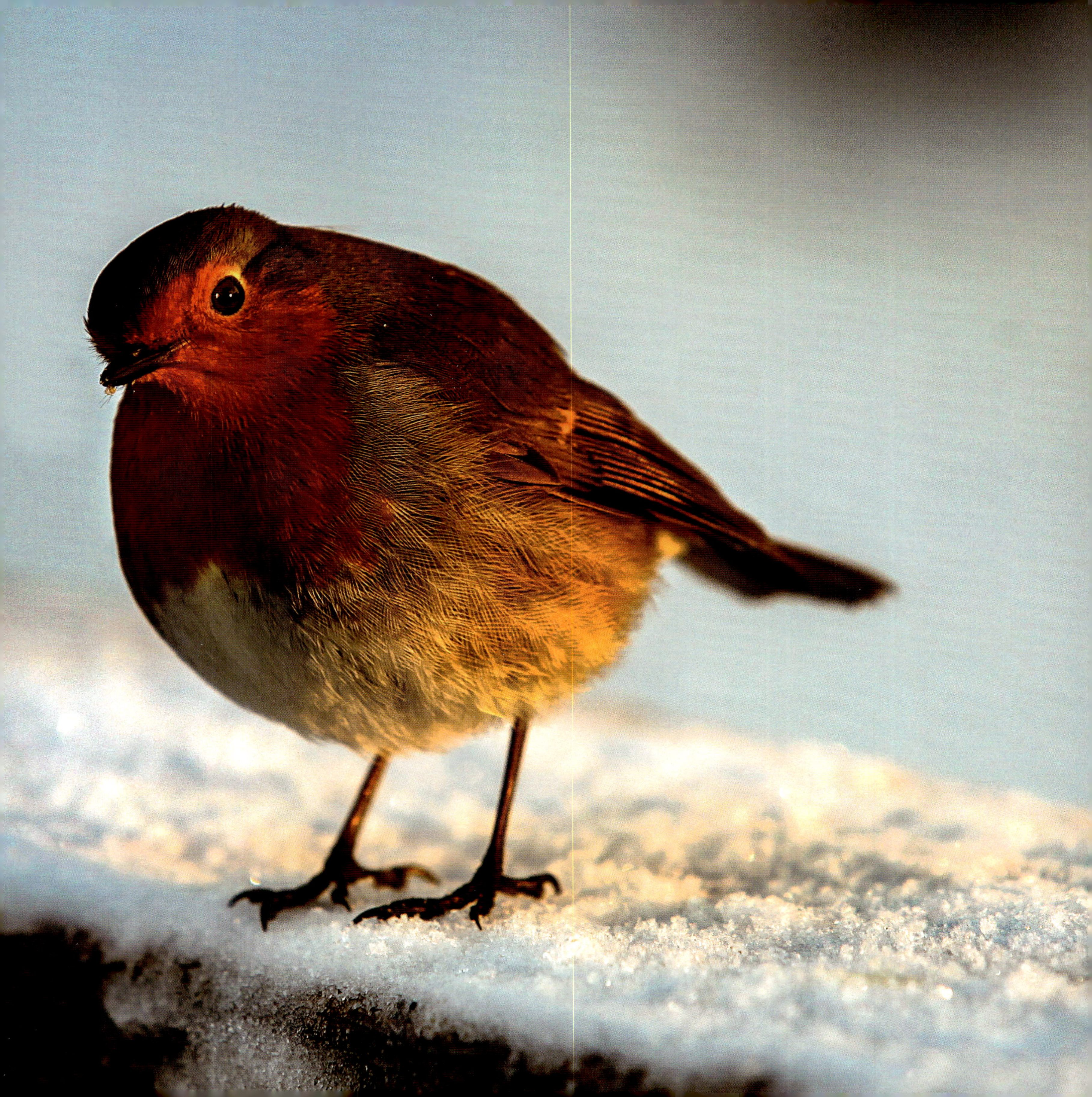

Winter

Winter marks both an end and a beginning. After the glorious colours of autumn have been swept away by the first storms, the grounds become stark, bereft and silent. The days shorten, the nights lengthen and grow cold, and the world turns in on itself.

Death seems to the fore in both life, and in liturgy. The celebration of the Solemnity of All Saints and the Commemoration of All Souls bring the departed to the forefront. Brethren visit the graveyard, remembering those 'who have gone before us marked with the sign of faith', and who now see more fully that for which all hope. Thirty-six lie buried there, more than half the community.

In the school, the inevitable colds and coughs do the rounds and eventually wend their way across the arch to the monastery. Despite the precautionary 'flu jabs, brethren start to cough and sniffle, there's a run on cough medicine, even rumours of the occasional hot whiskey... and the choir becomes croakier.

The North American poet Thomas Hood captures it well:

No sun - no moon!
No morn - no noon -
No dawn - no dusk - no proper time of day.
No warmth, no cheerfulness, no healthful ease,
No comfortable feel in any member -
No shade, no shine, no butterflies, no bees,
No fruits, no flowers, no leaves, no birds! -
November!

Advent

In the midst of the winter darkness, Advent comes like a chink of light. The liturgy is full of longing and expectation, and in sync with what is going in nature. Each evening, having praised the 'kind maker of the stars of night', we walk out into the night air and see the Milky Way stretched over our heads. Each week, another lighted candle on the Advent wreath suspended at the back of the church intensifies the sense of anticipation.

In the school, too, the atmosphere heightens as exams loom and the round of Christmas dinners begin. The boys know that release and freedom are just around the corner. The annual Advent carol service takes place on the second Sunday of Advent. This is one of the highlights of the school year, demanding immense patience and preparation from all involved. There is a running debate between the purists who favour an Advent theme and those who prefer something more 'Christmassy'. Regardless, the end result never fails to hit the right note.

The mood shifts again from December 17th onwards as we begin singing the great O Antiphons each evening at Vespers. These seven verses address Christ with a messianic title drawn from the prophet Isaiah, and have been sung in the liturgy since at least the sixth century. Traditionally, certain officeholders in the monastery are assigned the antiphon appropriate to their role.

Thus, the bursar normally sings *O Clavis David* – O Key of David on December 20th, while *O Emmanuel*, sung on December 23rd, is reserved for the abbot. Read in reverse order, the first letters of each title form an acrostic: *Ero cras* – 'I will be there tomorrow....'

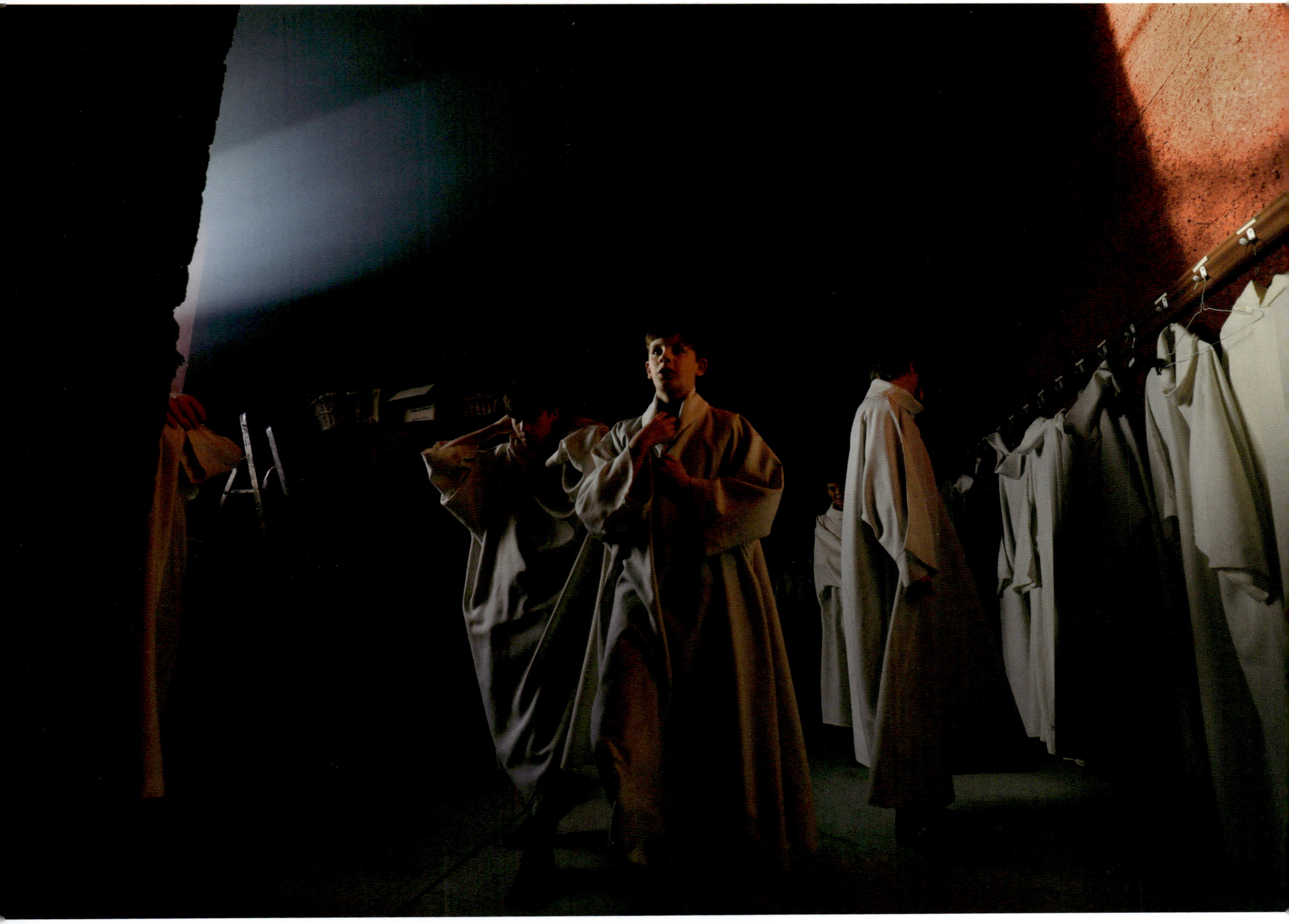

Choristers at Christmas... members of the School Choir prepare to sing at the annual Advent carol service in Glenstal Abbey Church

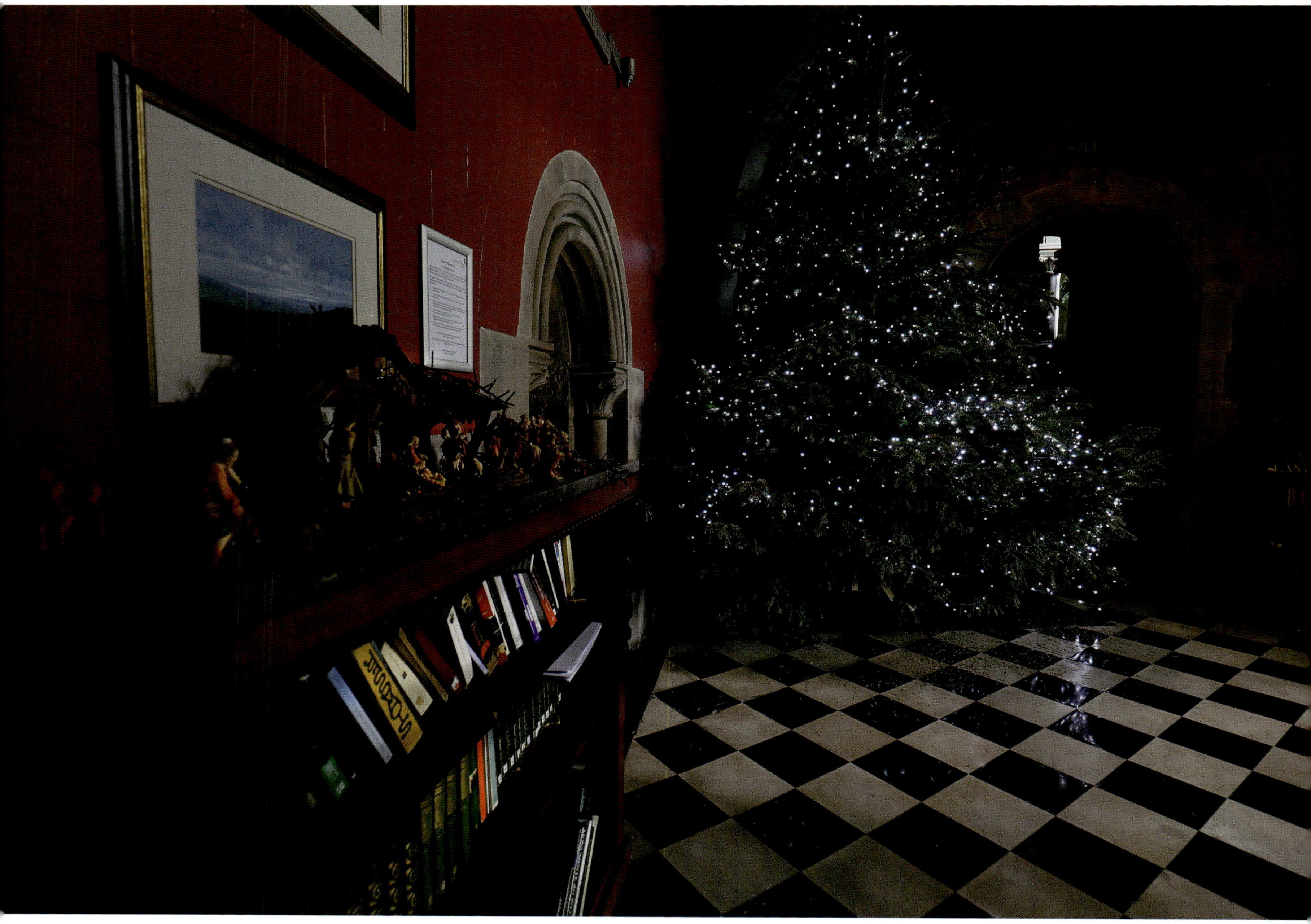

A Glenstal Christmas

The emphasis on waiting and expectation in the Advent liturgy means that Christmas bursts on the scene in a blaze of colour and light. Everywhere else Christmas decorations have been up since Hallowe'en and look a bit jaded. In the monastery there is a flurry of activity on the afternoon of Christmas Eve to set the house in order for the festivities.

With the exception of the Christmas tree in the school, the decorations around the place are, for the most part, whatever evergreen material is available locally. There is the annual 'berries are for birds' debate when it comes to putting up holly, but some compromise is reached and as we process into church for the first Vespers of Christmas, the place is aglow with candles, colour and greenery.

After Vespers, we move in procession to one of the side chapels for the blessing of the crib. The design each year is entrusted to the novices and junior members of the community and the end results can vary from Zen minimalism to something like a set from Zeffirelli's *Jesus of Nazareth*. Occasionally, the theme will reflect contemporary or social concerns like homelessness or the political situation in the Middle East.

From 10pm, people begin to gather in the church for the Christmas Vigil and Midnight Mass at which the abbot presides. This is the most popular of the church services celebrated in the monastery, and by 11.20pm the church is packed. The vigil consists of psalms, hymns and readings, and lasts approximately 40 minutes.

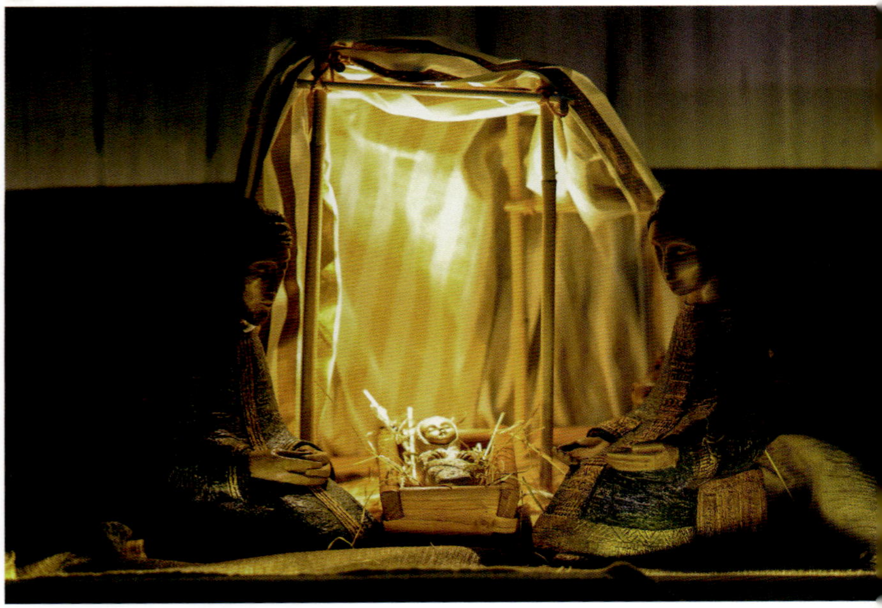

After a short pause, with the church bells ringing in celebration, Mass begins at the stroke of Midnight as the community processes into church, singing the opening antiphon of the feast: *Dominus dixit ad me* – the Lord said to me, 'You are my Son, today I have begotten you.' In addition to the Latin chants for the Mass, we also sing some traditional Christmas carols in which everyone joins. Many of the congregation are employees, former students, family members and other friends of the community, and the tea and mince pies that follow provide an opportunity to catch up.

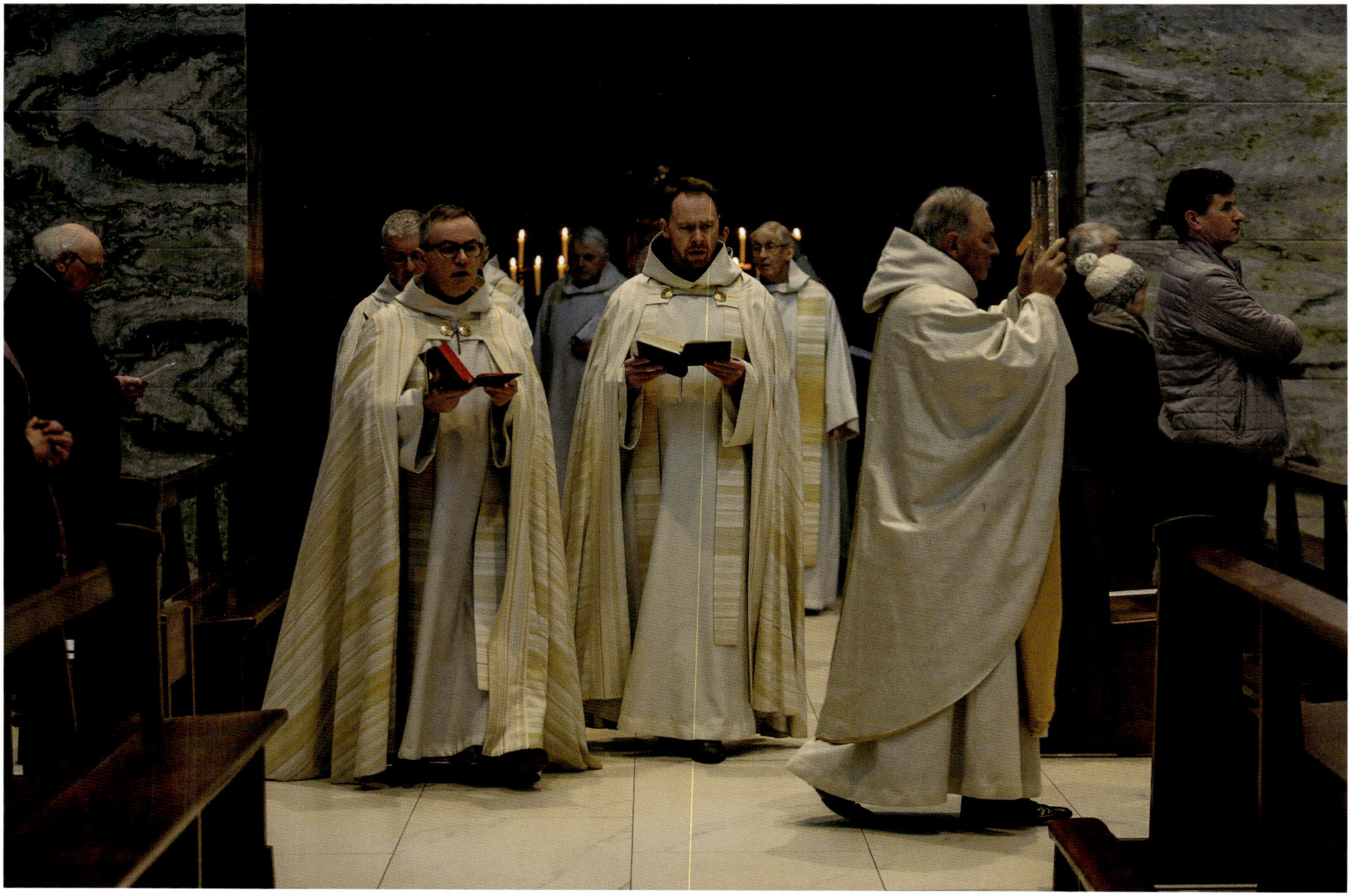

Christmas morning begins at 8am with the celebration of the Office of Lauds. At this time the church is generally empty, and yet we celebrate it with full solemnity: procession, vestments, incense. It's a reminder that the liturgy is first and foremost an act of worship for God. At 10am, the second Mass of Christmas is celebrated. This is a *missa lecta*, celebrated without chant and with only organ music to accompany the celebration. After the solemnity of the earlier liturgies, it offers a quieter, contemplative pause.

A small group of neighbours attend this, as they have for years, and afterwards an annual get-together takes place in the church porch. At midday, the prior celebrates the third and final Mass of the day. This is another solemn celebration with procession and incense, and opens with the hauntingly beautiful chant *Puer natus est nobis* – 'A child is born for us, a son given to us'.

Although the liturgical pace is slower on Christmas morning, there is a still a lot to do in the kitchen. The main meal takes place in the evening and so lunch is a light buffet, but delicious nonetheless with a selection of pickled products from the poly-tunnel and home-cooked crusty bread. A popular addition to the festivities in recent years has been the gift of some bottles of Belgian Trappist beer that for some of the senior brethren bring back memories of their time as novices and students at our motherhouse at Maredsous Abbey in Belgium.

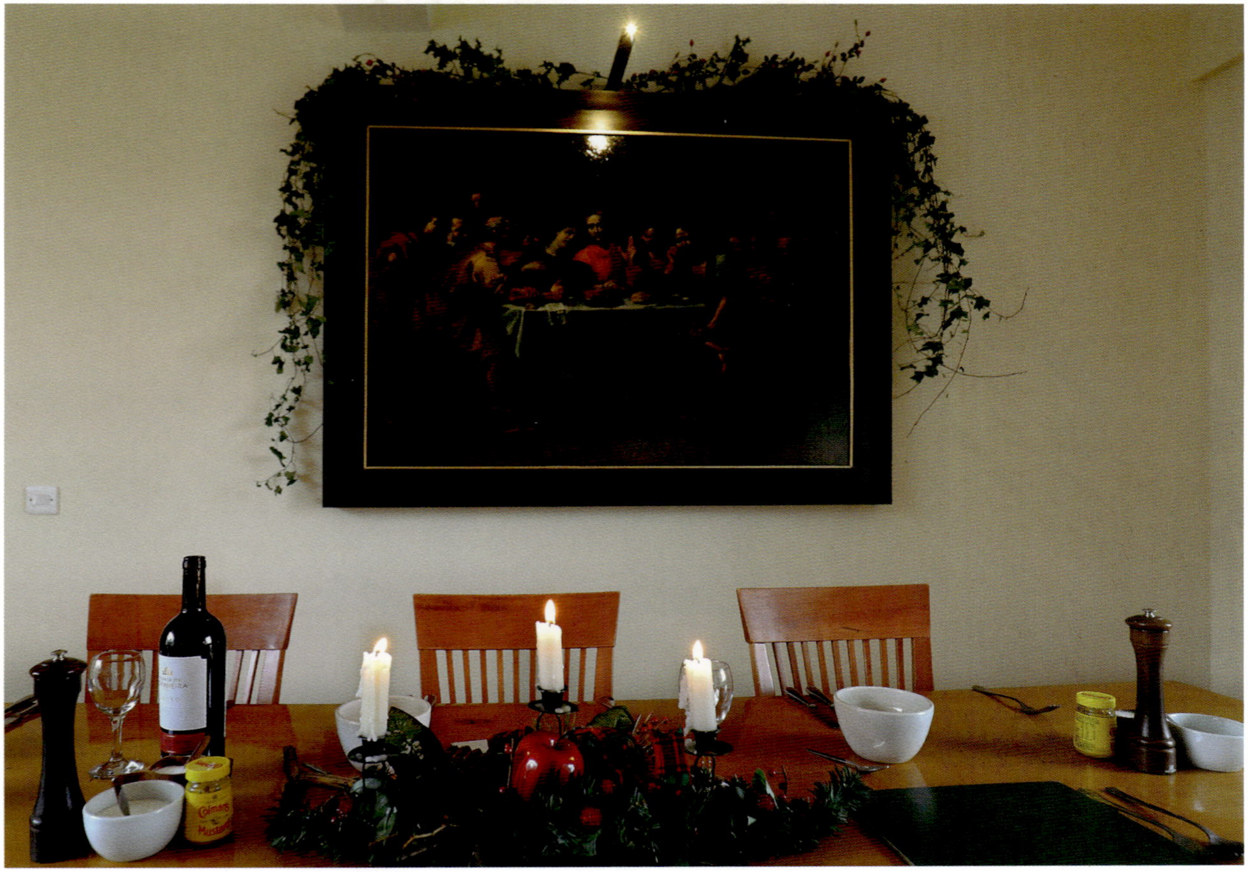

After lunch, those few not involved in the preparations for dinner either catch up on sleep or go for a hike. The second Vespers of Christmas takes place in the candlelit church at a slightly earlier time, and afterwards the community processes around the church, singing the festive chant *Puer natus est in Bethlehem, Alleluia!* – A boy is born for us in Bethlehem, Alleluia!

After a short pause for refreshments, the community assembles in the refectory for dinner. For this occasion the tables are pushed together and covered with tablecloths and the whole scene is lit by candlelight. The generosity of friends and benefactors means that most of what we enjoy has been donated to us, and it is with a sense of gratitude and appreciation that we sit down to eat.

The meal is the traditional Christmas fare: turkey and ham followed by plum pudding. This is made to an ancient Kerry recipe and glows an eerie electric blue in the darkened room as the brandy dressing is set alight. After tidying up, we recite Compline in the chapter room and, having finished the wash-up, we retire for an early night.

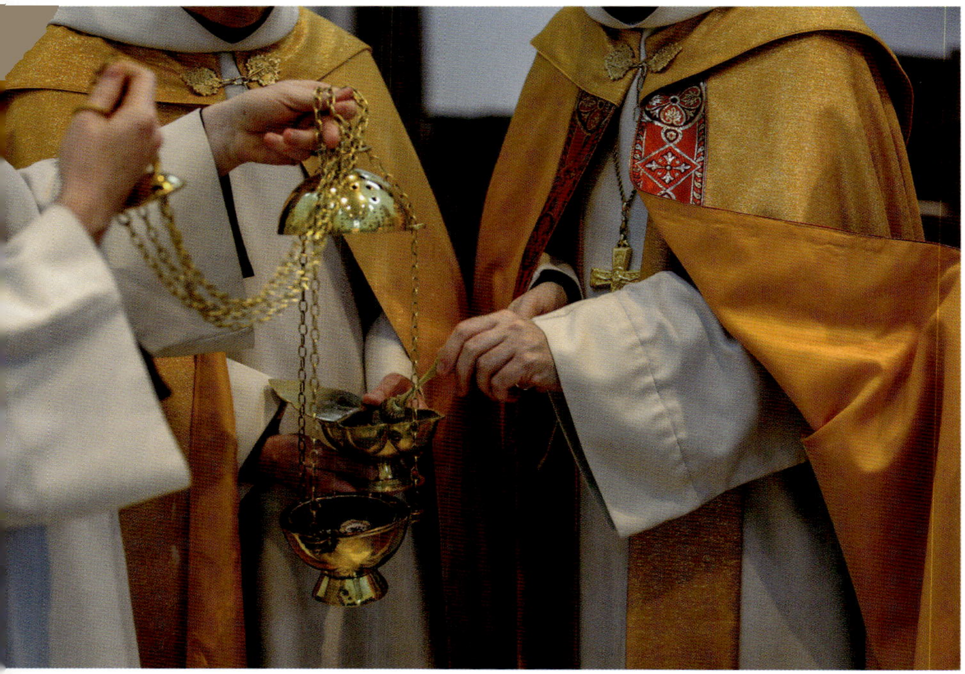

Christmastide

Because our celebration of Christmas only begins on December 24th, the days that follow have a special resonance. While everyone else is dismantling their decorations, the liturgy explores the significance of the Christ child's incarnation. In the days immediately following Christmas, we find gathered around the manger the martyrs Stephen, Thomas Becket and the Holy Innocents - a reminder of the cost of discipleship even in the midst of celebration.

On January 1st, we place the New Year under the protection of Mary, the Mother of God, and this is followed on January 6th by celebration of the Epiphany, the Lord's revelation of his glory to all the peoples of the earth. This, too, is a solemn celebration, and with it the holiday period draws to a close and, with the return of the school, life settles back into its normal pattern.

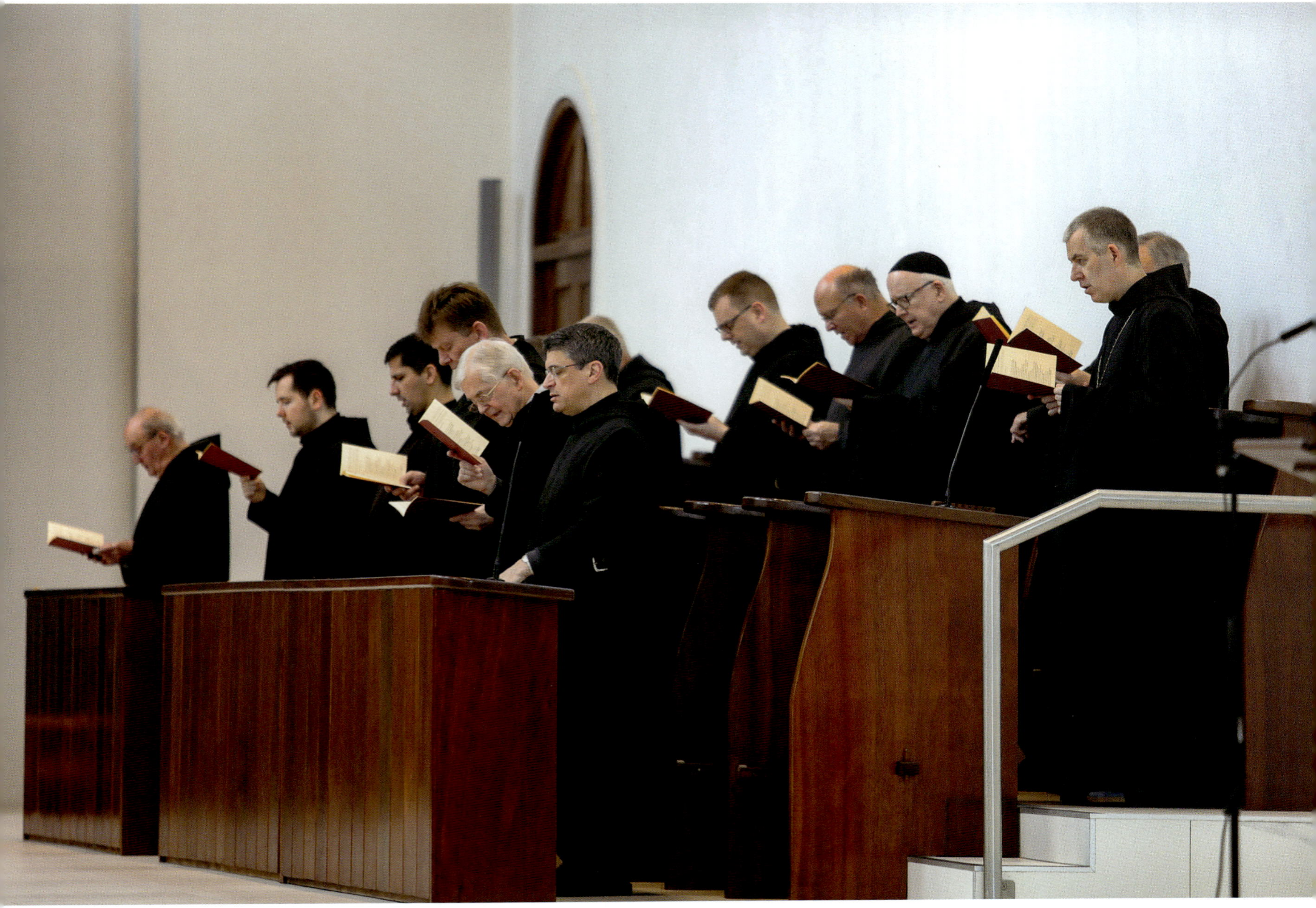

A Monk's Recipe:

Crusty Bread

The aroma of warm baking wafting through the cloister means all is well; bread, butter and homemade jam will be a feast this evening.

To be honest, bread is just mixing 'stuff' and after a while the hands feel what to do. I have many recipes, but I offer this one as a simple staple from the monastery.

This makes one large, or two small loaves

INGREDIENTS

560g	strong white flour
10g	salt
300ml	tepid water
15 ml	rapeseed oil
5g	dried yeast

Add the yeast to the water and let sit until it bubbles. Pour into the dry ingredients and then add the oil.

At this stage you can either mix it by hand (a great workout!), or use a mixer with a dough hook. I deal in large volumes, so I use a mixer.

Hand knead for 15 minutes or in the mixer for about 10.

This stage completed, let sit in the bowl for an hour covered with a towel or some clingfilm.

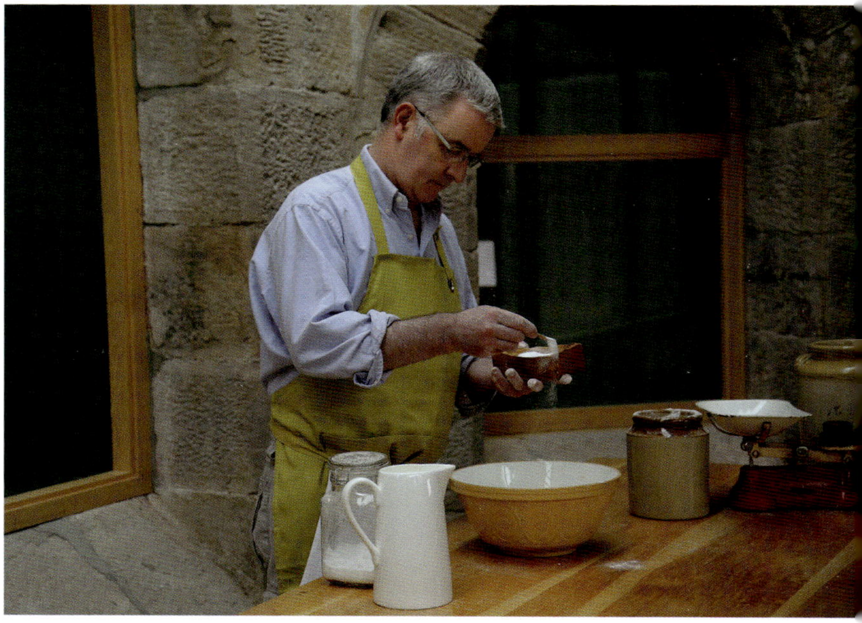

After an hour (though you can skip this stage), move the dough around the bowl so that it deflates and leave it sit for another hour.

At the end of the hour, scrape out onto lightly floured surface and shape into a 'sausage' shape that fits neatly into a well oiled or parchment lined tin (900g tin)

Once in the tin, leave covered in a warm place for another hour.

When ready, dust the loaf, score the top and place in oven at 220 degree for 10 minutes then at 180 degrees for 20 minutes. It is good to have a pan of boiling water in the oven at the beginning to produce steam.

When completed, tap the base which should sound hollow, and let cool on a wire rack.

Br Pádraig

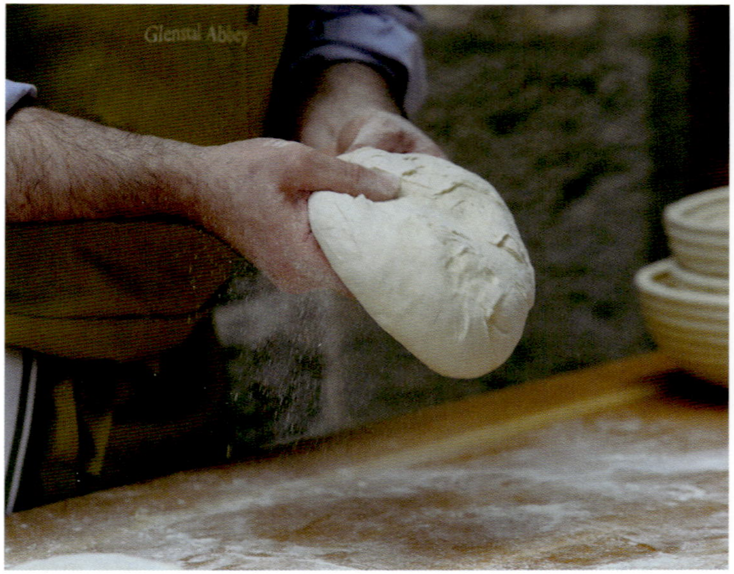
Glenstal Abbey

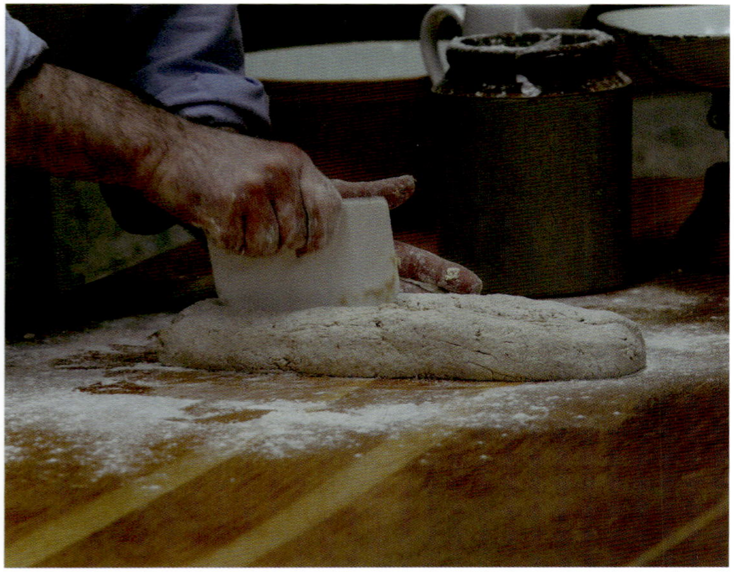

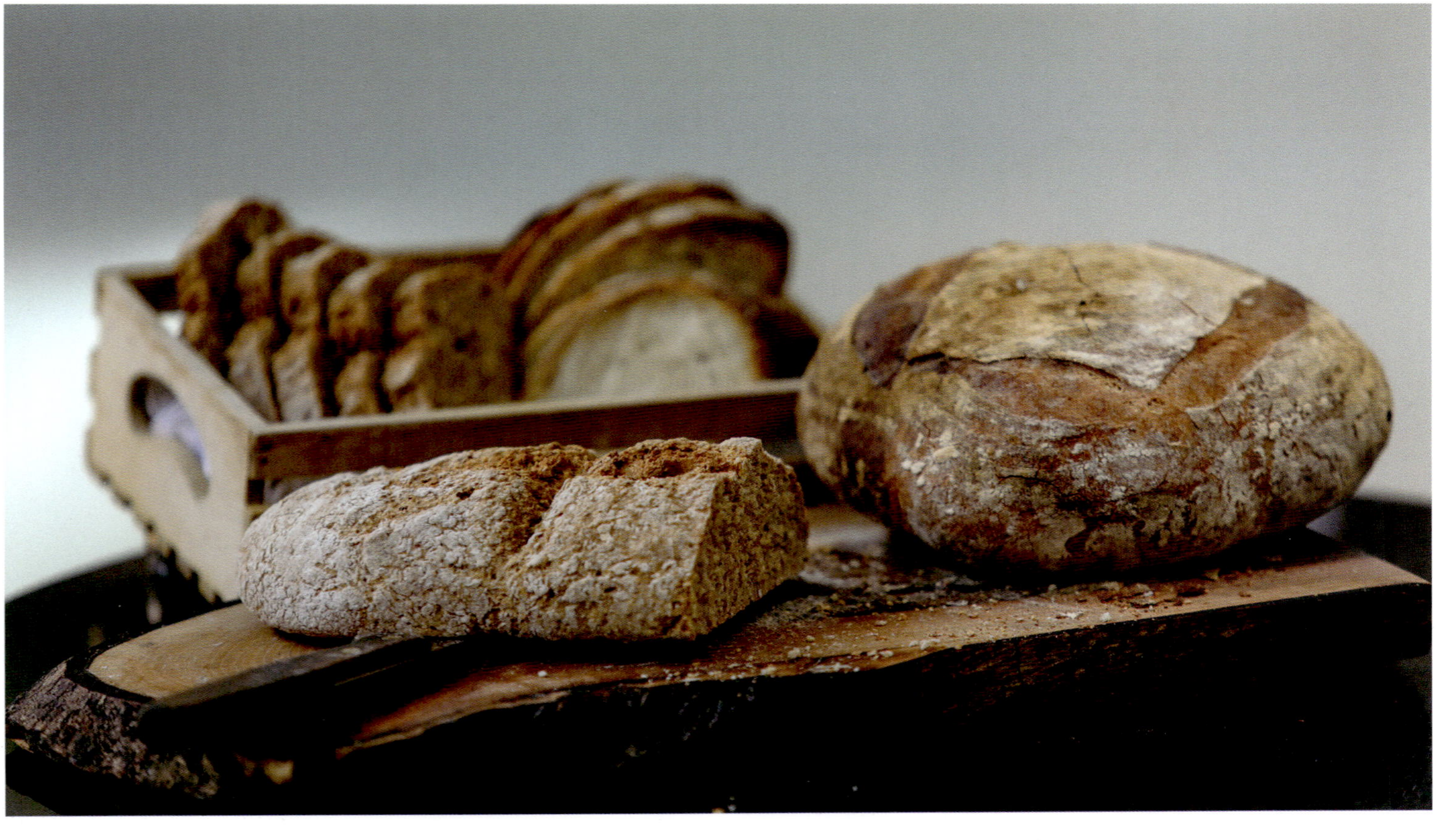

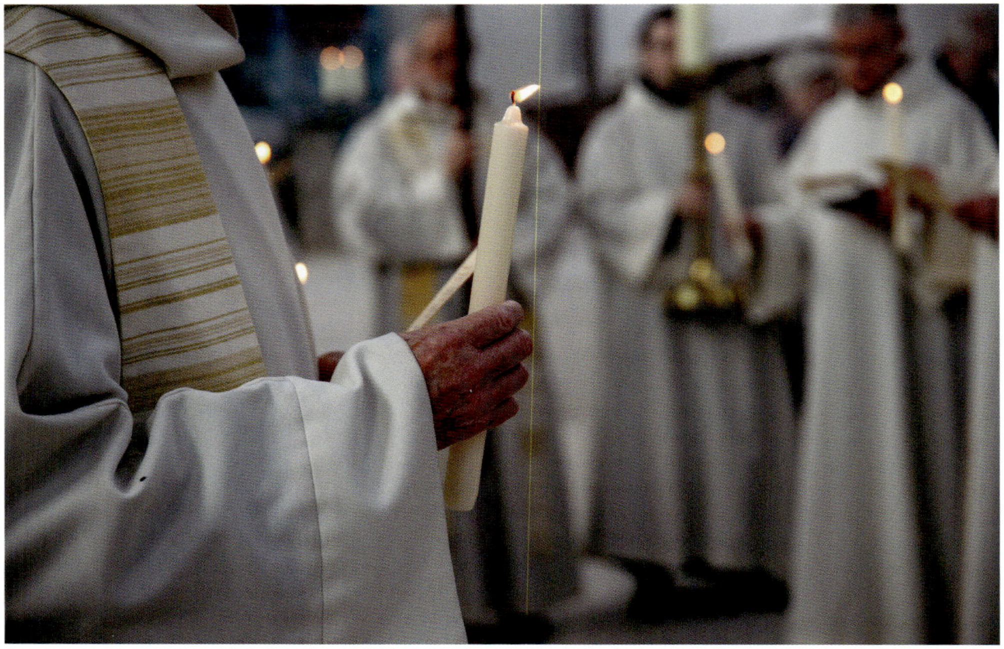

Candlemas

The Presentation of the Lord on February 2nd is the last of the Christmas celebrations. Commemorating Christ's parents' decision to do 'what the law required for him', it is a low key, but very beautiful, feast. Before Mass we gather at the back of the church for the blessing of the candles that will be used throughout the year. Once lit, we bear these in procession to the altar, commemorating the one who is 'a light to enlighten the Gentiles and the glory of God's people Israel.'

This is also the day in which the Church celebrates those called to religious life and we remember all our brothers and sisters who share the monastic vocation. It is also a time to remember the elderly, who like the prophets Simeon and Anna, faithfully see in Jesus the hope for which they long.

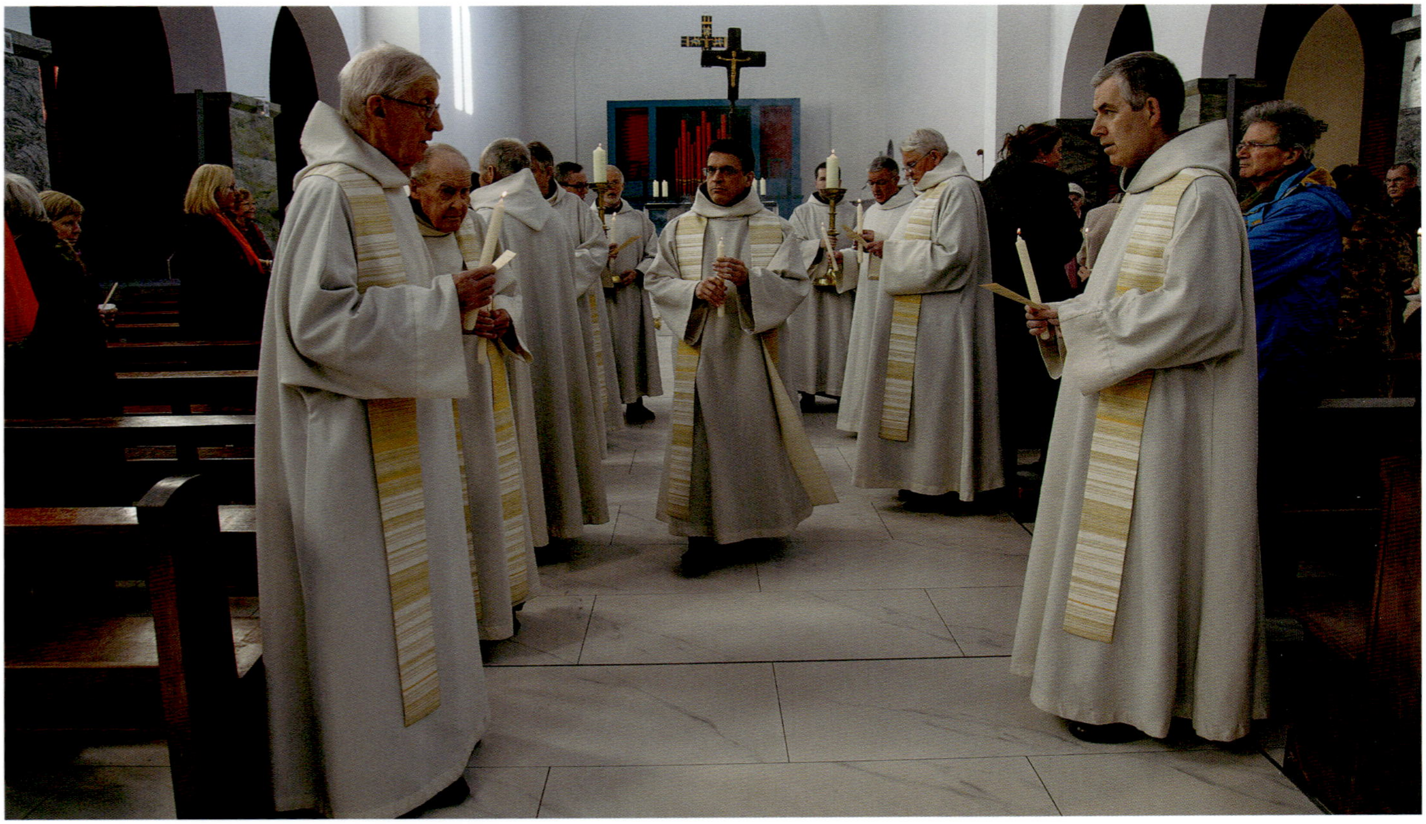

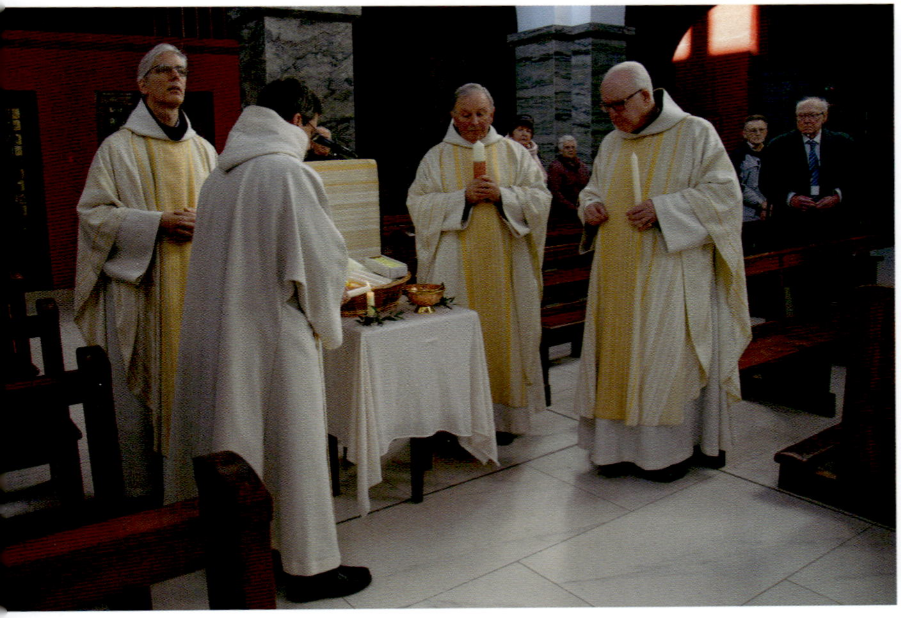

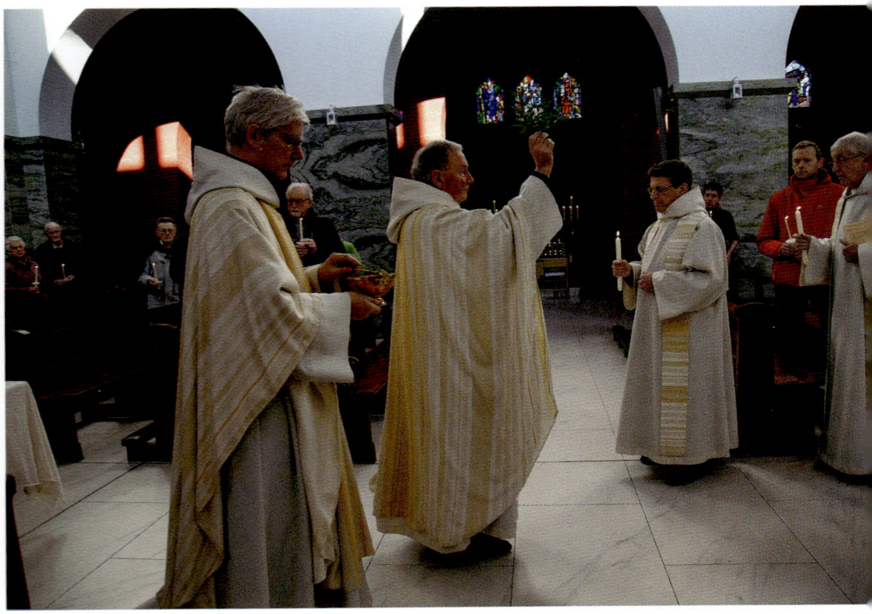

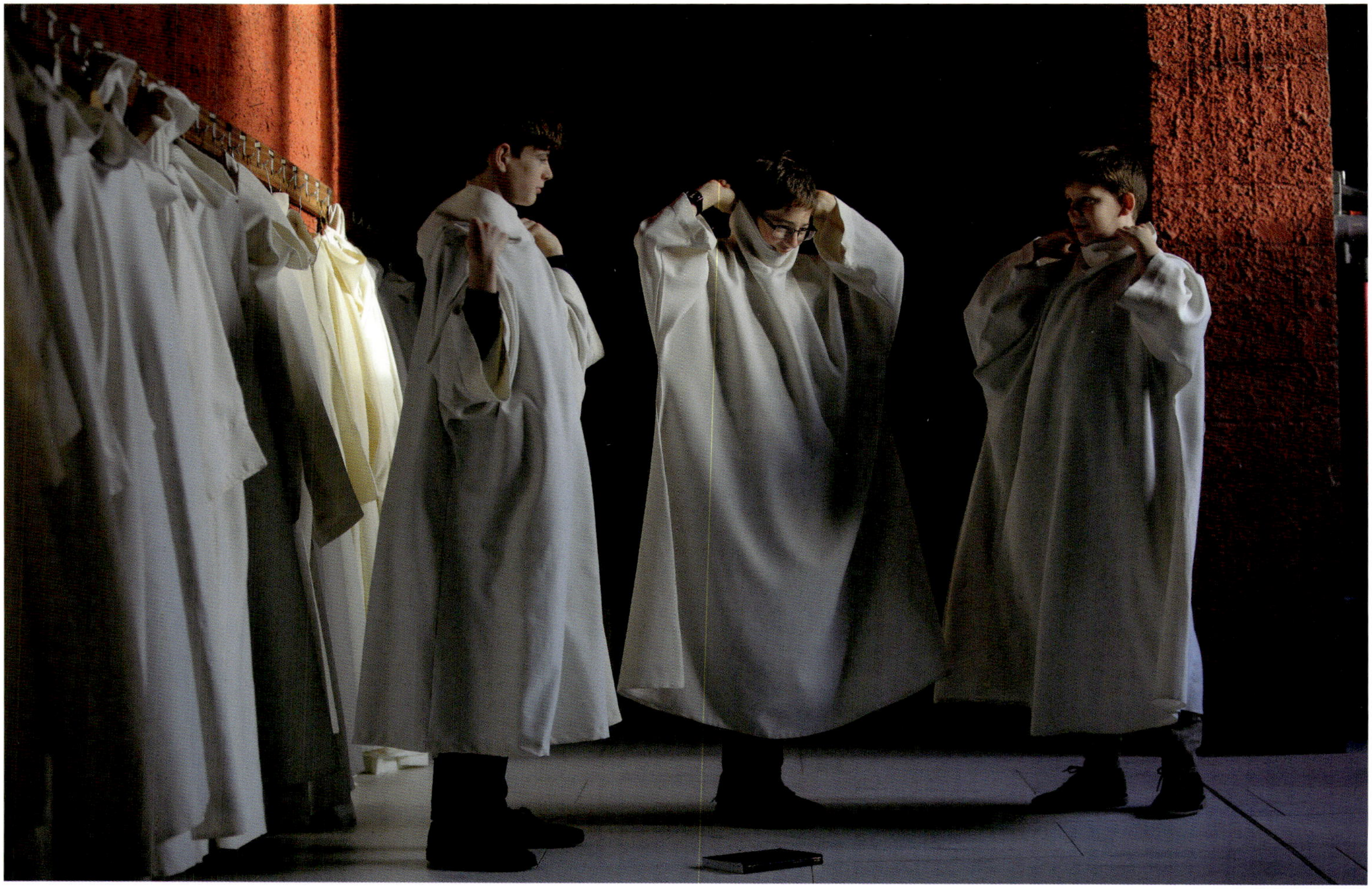

The School Choir

Glenstal Abbey School choir sings at the Sunday liturgies during term time. Music, and singing in particular, can make such a difference. St Augustine once said, 'Singing is for one who loves,' and an ancient proverb also affirms 'One who sings well prays twice.'

Glenstal Abbey School has many attractions, and music is one of them. Aside from the spiritual benefits, research has shown that, from a less explicitly religious perspective, singing is good for you. It uses the whole brain to an extent which is quite unusual compared to other activities; singing, especially in choirs, has been proven to be good for mental health; the benefits of music in education are well established, and some schools have found that the expansion of music within the life of the school has brought about a whole turnaround in overall results and excellence across the board.

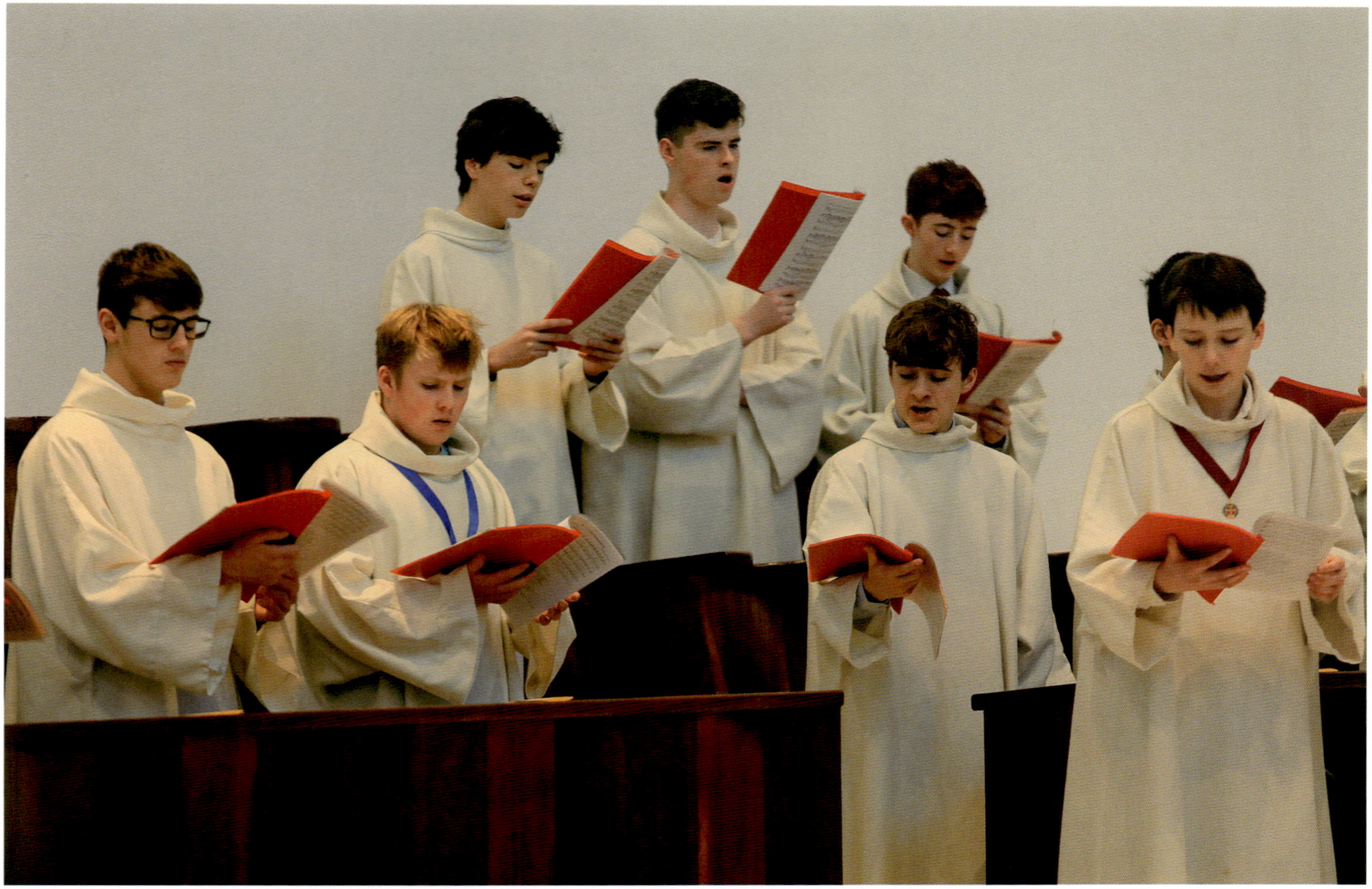

Beautiful music only comes with hard work. Those who are admitted to the choir forgo each week half an hour of the cherished Sunday-morning lie-on in order to arrive early for a warm-up before Mass. They also commit to two evening sessions, one in their own vocal line and one with the whole choir.

The annual Advent carol service is always a major event for the choir, with the emphasis very much on Advent, not Christmas. Newcomers to the choir generally ask 'Why aren't we learning lots of Christmas carols?', to which I generally reply, 'But Christmas doesn't come until December 25th!' There is a beauty to the poetic restraint of Advent that is so easily overlooked.

The choir also has other occasional outings: choral competitions (which they sometimes even win), public concerts, ecumenical services, the annual 'Darkness into Light' walk and occasionally even trips abroad.

Fr Columba

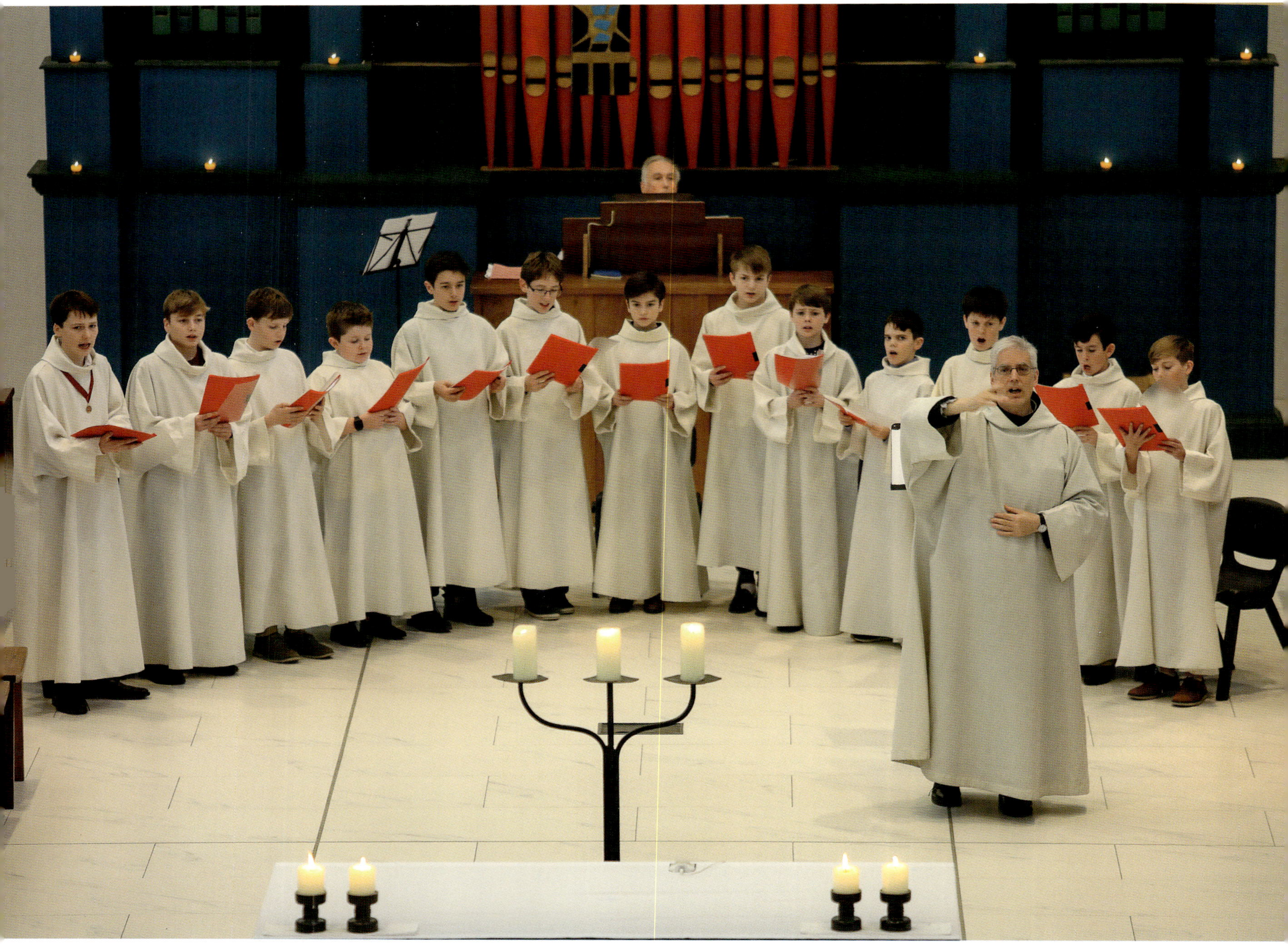

The Students Choir from Glenstal Abbey School, Murroe, Co. Limerick, getting ready to sing at the annual Advent Carol Service at the Abbey Church.

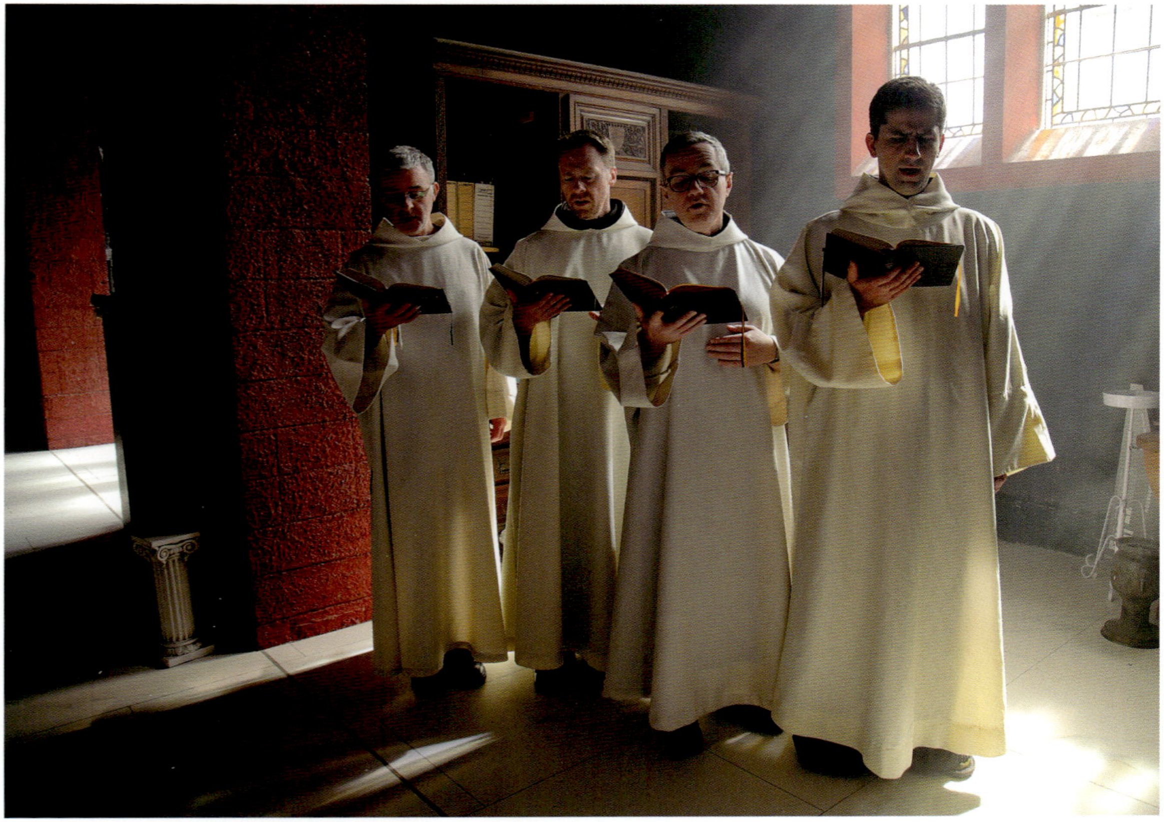

Glenstal Abbey Schola rehearsing for the Christmas liturgy: Br Pádraig, Fr Cuthbert, Fr Senan and Br Jarek.

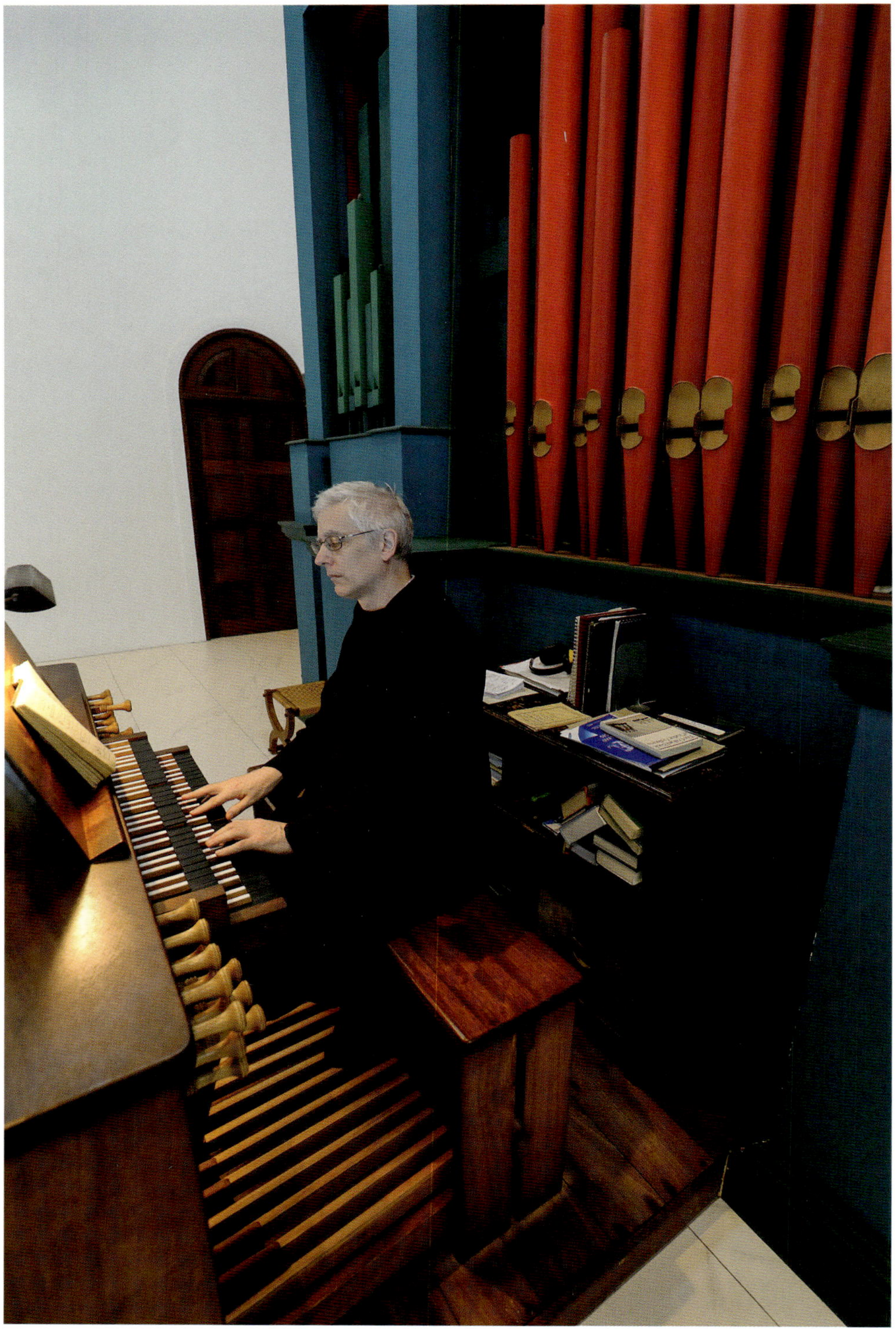

A Monk's Tale:

The School Choirmaster

How does someone educated by the Jesuits end up as a Benedictine monk? After school I studied music at University College, Dublin, but, while music has always been important to me, the question of a vocation to the priesthood had also arisen, even in my school years. After college I began my seminary training for priesthood in the Dublin diocese. But the seeds of a slightly different calling were also sown there.

Some Benedictine reading awoke my interest. Pre-ordination retreats at Glenstal and Mount Melleray gave me first-hand contact with monastic life and intensified that interest. I was advised not to follow this up and, in hindsight, I am convinced that the time was not ripe for a turn towards monastic life. Liturgical studies in Rome brought me to the Benedictine institute at Sant'Anselmo. Back in Ireland, my contact with Glenstal continued with annual retreats. The tipping point finally came when, after fourteen years of diocesan priesthood, a spiritual director suggested that maybe I should consider monastic life.

It was like a door opening. Being a diocesan priest was good, but monastic life now seemed far more attractive. What were the attractions? A very stable daily rhythm of community prayer, lectio divina, and life in common, with primacy given to the search for God at every turn. The attractions remain alive for me today.

I now treasure my opportunities to make music at Glenstal: accompanying the Divine Office on the organ, performing repertoire pieces and responding to the liturgical moment with organ improvisation, as well as composition of music for the liturgy.

I also work with the school choir which performs at Sunday Mass. Here the plainchant tradition of the monastery is complemented by some easy congregation-friendly music, as well as more elaborate choral music of a more specialised nature. Working with young people in the choir, and also as a religion teacher in the school, is a demanding but rewarding experience.

Fr Columba

A Monk's Tale:

The Librarian

Monks, especially in Ireland, have been associated with books. In the Dark Ages Ireland was library to forgotten European culture. Out of such vaults, buried traditions would rise again and spread throughout the early Middle Ages. Our monastery, in its turn, and especially in its library, would hope to be both storehouse and catalyst to a resurgence of specifically Celtic culture for future times.

Not that there is any programmed order or selection attached to the ninety or so thousand books housed within these recently constructed walls. Our library was started in September 1999 and handed over for occupation in January 2001. A turn of the century building, the books it contains are very much older: a copy of St Augustine's *De Civitate Dei* printed in 1522 is probably the oldest volume we have so far.

The provenance and profile of our library catalogue are haphazard. Whatever books come our way, through donations or bequests on the one hand; through areas of study or of interest to the monks of the community on the other; these make up the bulk of our collection. An expert on ornithology, a scholar of Celtic folklore, account for several volumes of interest in these areas. Such unwarranted stowaways share shelf space with more predictable liturgical and/or ecumenical standard works.

We are the repository and beneficiaries of many a personal library, where relatives of some deceased bibliophile donated, or even dumped, the treasure house of their departed in our care. Such benefaction makes of us receivers of large and small bundles of books, mostly worthless, but sometimes wonderful.

The result is a crazy alignment of most unlikely bedfellows: Aeschylus with Jane Austen; zoology and Zen Buddhism. During my novitiate I was sent to find for my spiritual reading Josef Jungmann's two volume history of *The Mass of the Roman Rite*. I ended up reading eighteen volumes of the *Complete Works of Carl Gustav Jung* which happened to be seductively prominent on an adjoining shelf. [This was a gift of the Bollingen Series to one of the earlier monks that would otherwise never have found its way to a Catholic monastery in Ireland of the 1940s].

Such eclectic mixum-gatherum allows scope to the Holy Spirit to drop on the heads of unwary searchers most unlikely 'spiritual' reading – a word too often understood as an adjective describing a certain predictable category of 'holy' book; whereas, more often and more effectively, it is an adverb qualifying whatever input is necessary for you, at this precise moment of your life, to stop you in your tracks and awaken you to the Divine, whether it be a treatise on heart disease or a story by Edgar Allan Poe.

A monastic library is a chamber of surprises; each of the sprightly books on the shelves has found its way to its position by some secret sat-nav system unknown to the finders or the keepers. Through coincidence, they say, God remains anonymous, and yet there can be no denying that the Holy Spirit is pseudonymous author of whatever book it takes to draw you into the net. Transformational as opposed to informational reading: you came for one book; another caught your eye; and you were hooked.

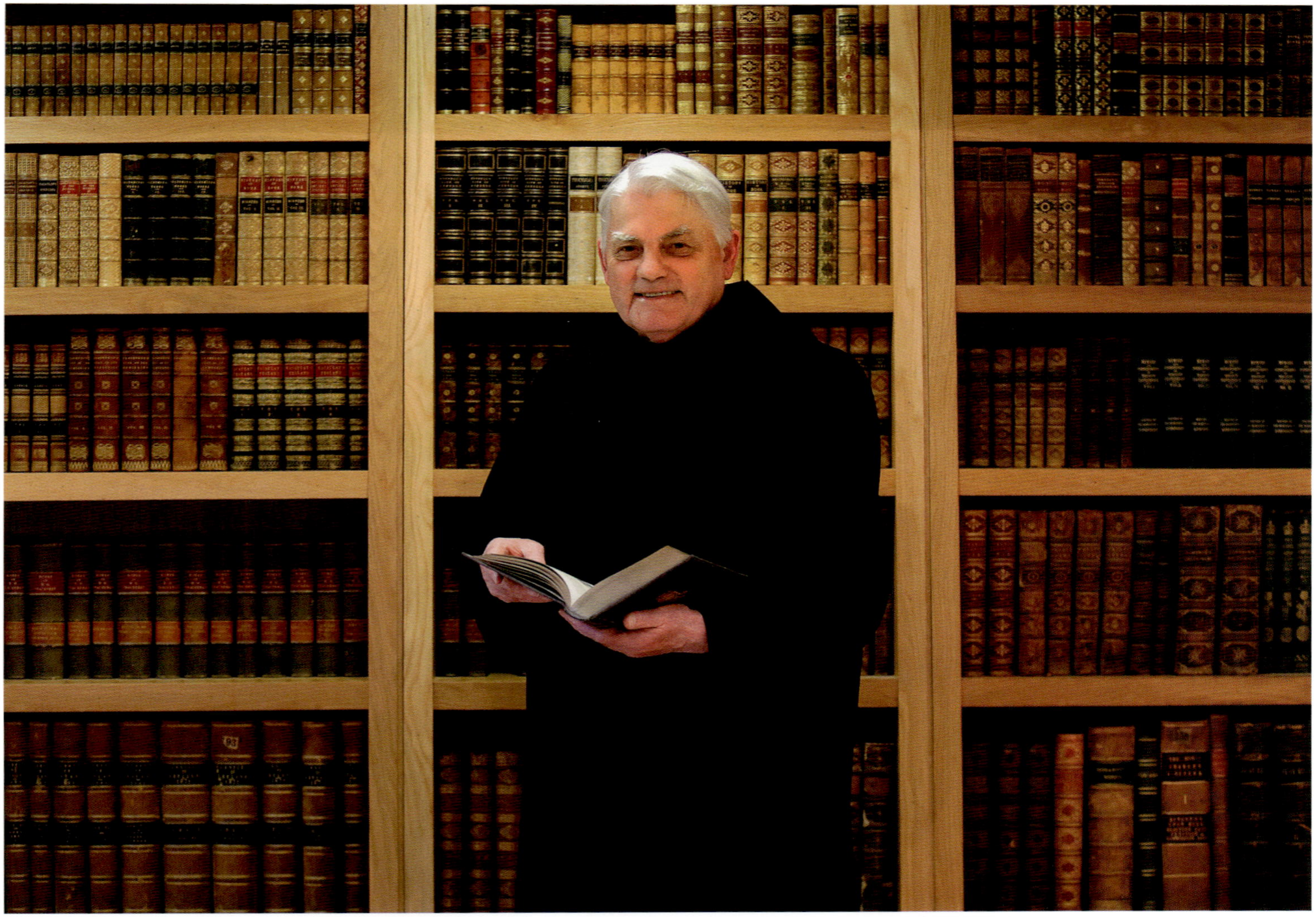

Modern technology coupled with scattergun selectivity produce miraculous identification systems. Up-to-date software for library cataloguing allied with a homespun version of Dewey's Decimal system [which, as Alberto Manguel observes, does turn books into rows of parked cars, each bearing a licence plate] provide almost fool-proof guidance to the exact location of every book, of whatever category or content.

Our library, built at the turn of the 21st century, housing lodgers from as far back as the 16th, harnesses wisdom from the ages to best provide identification, preservation, and dissemination of books:the noble and time-honoured task of the monastic library.

Fr Mark Patrick

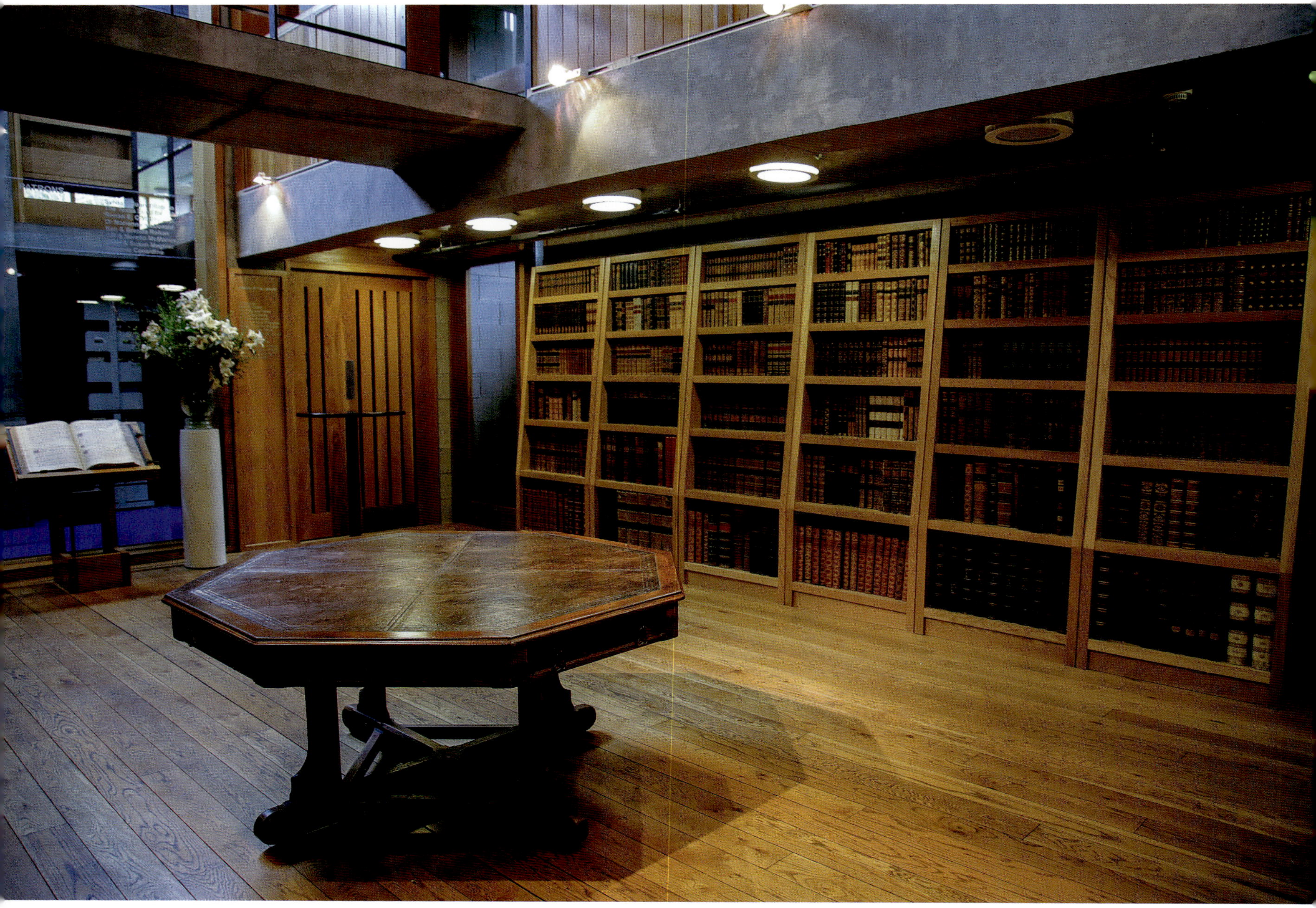

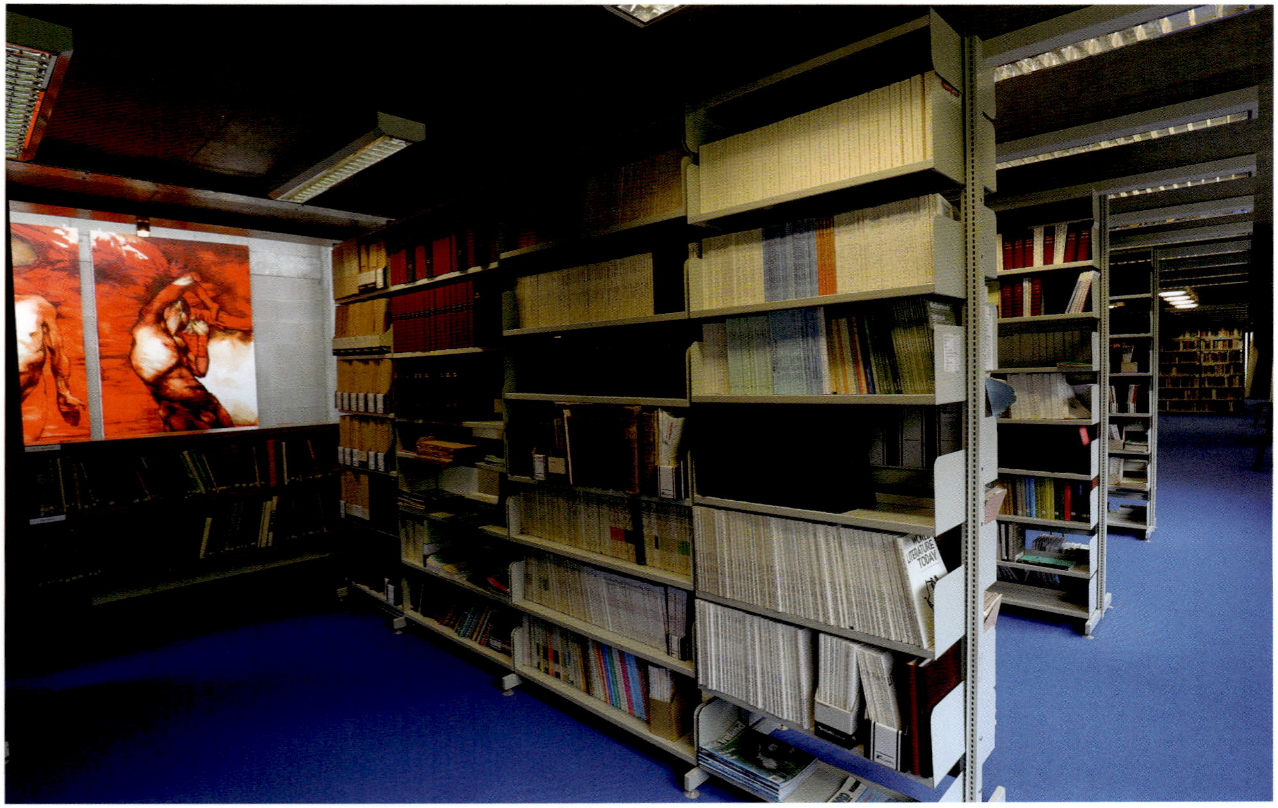

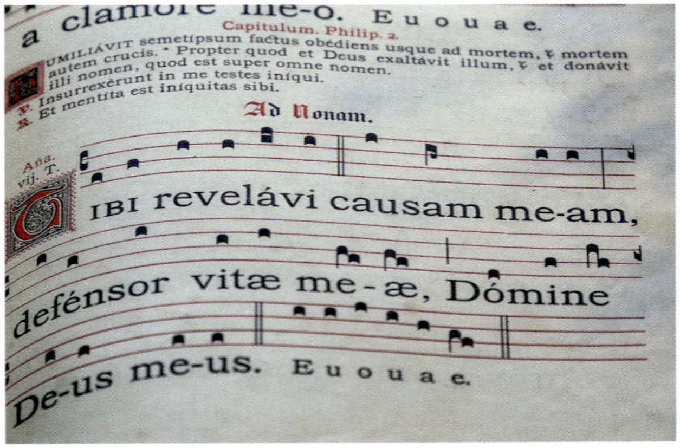
a clamore me-o. E u o u a e.
Capitulum. Philip. 2.
UMILIÁVIT semetípsum factus obédiens usque ad mortem, ℣ mortem autem crucis. * Propter quod et Deus exaltávit illum, ℣ et donávit illi nomen, quod est super omne nomen.
℣ Insurrexérunt in me testes iníqui.
℟ Et mentíta est iníquitas sibi.
Ad Nonam.
Aña. vij. T.
TIBI revelávi causam me-am,
defénsor vitæ me-æ, Dómine
De-us me-us. E u o u a e.

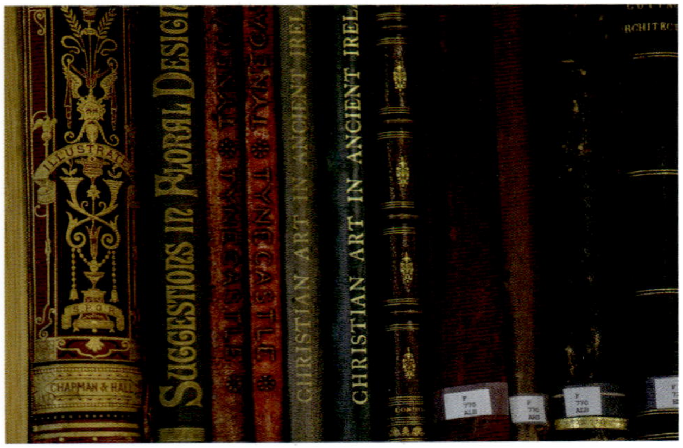
SUGGESTIONS IN FLORAL DESIG
CHRISTIAN ART IN ANCIENT IREL
CHRISTIAN ART IN ANCIENT IREL
CHAPMAN & HALL

A Monk's Task

Crib

The much-loved custom of making nativity scenes brings the story of Christ's birth into our hearts and homes, helping us to enter into the mystery and meaning of Christmas.

Saint Francis of Assisi created the first nativity scene in 1223, where he invited pilgrims to pray at a crib using real animals and actors in the Italian village of Greccio. This year, the nativity scene placed the 2000 year old Christmas story before the backdrop of modern-day Bethlehem to remind us of the conflict and injustice which afflicts the Holy Land today.

A lighted candle was taken from the Church of the Nativity there and carried around the world before being placed before the crib in Glenstal where visitors were invited to pray and act for justice and peace in Palestine, Israel and throughout the world.

Br Justin

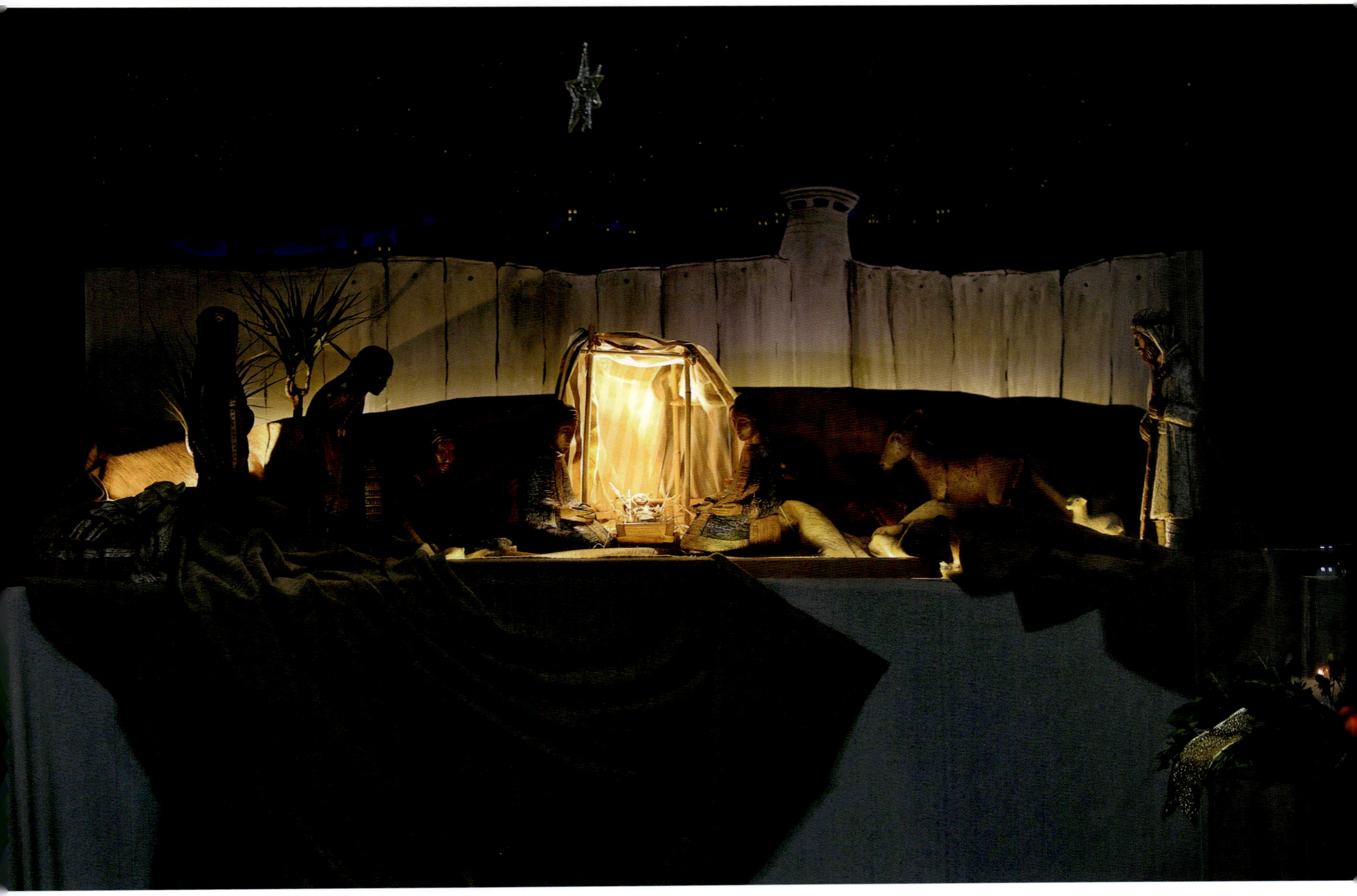

A Monk's Tale:

The Headmaster

St Benedict described the monastery as a 'School of the Lord's Service' and these words are displayed in block capitals on the wall in the school reception area. But it is another quote from the Rule that most catches the imagination of staff and students alike: 'that the strong may have something to strive after, and the weak may not fall back in dismay'. Benedict was writing for monks, but those words provide an inspirational charter for what we do in the school too.

Because the school is part of the abbey, community is profoundly important for us. This is true regardless of whether one adheres to the Catholic Church, another Christian tradition, a different faith, or has no religious affiliation at all. We have students and staff from all of those categories, but the school is a single community.

Lots of parents are attracted by the fact that our classes tend to be smaller than average. But for me, it is the scale of the school which is more significant. The castle is large, and the grounds are extensive, but the school is small and we wouldn't want it any other way. Nearly every student knows every other student's name as do the staff, even the ones they're not teaching. The place is small enough for that to happen and that, for me, really is very special indeed.

Fr Martin

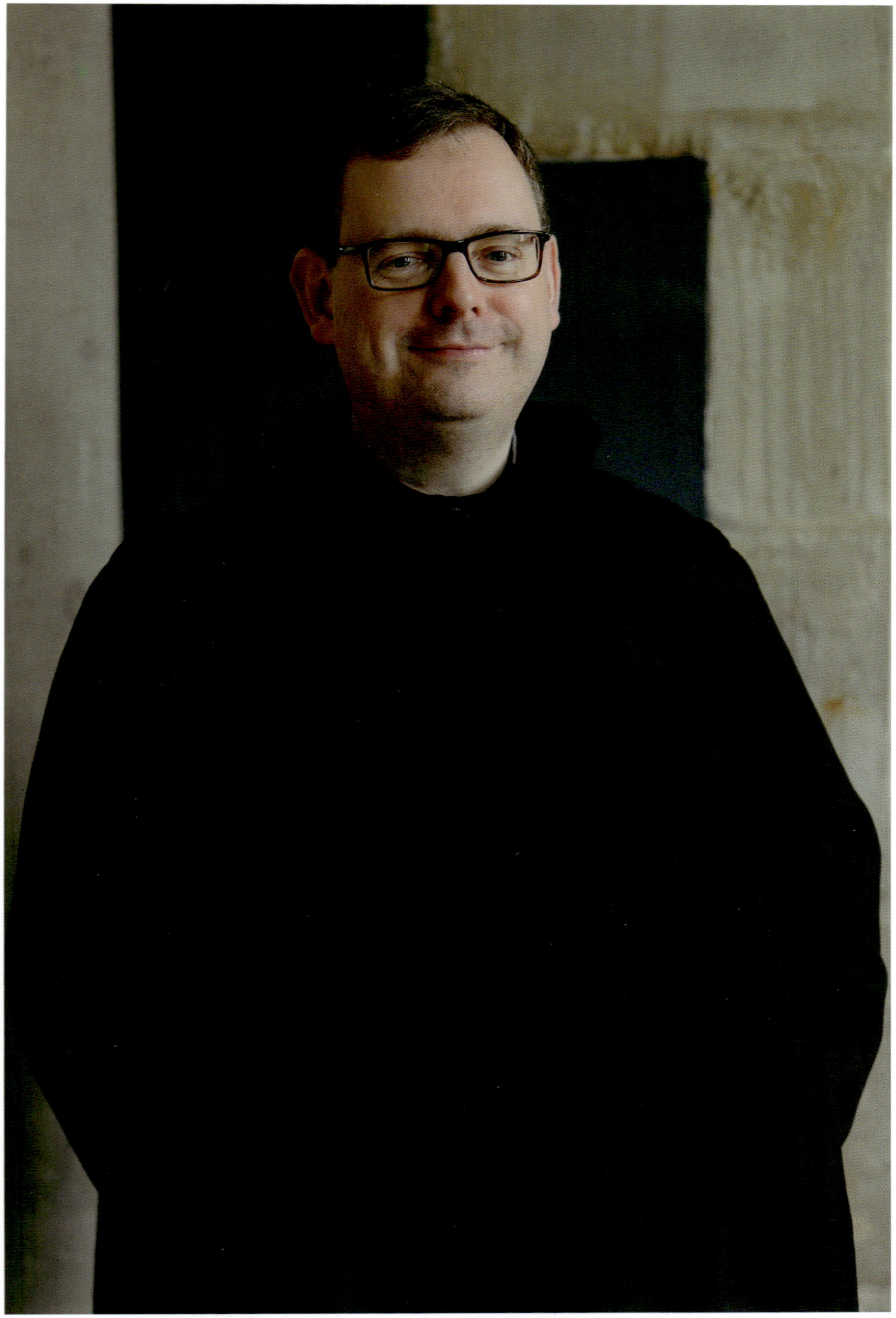

A Monk's Recipe:

Christmas Pudding

I make about 20kg of pudding mix, with our Christmas Day pudding weighing 7kg. I have tried to make these quantities more manageable for the home.

INGREDIENTS

150g	currants
150g	sultanas
100g	chopped figs
100g	chopped dates
50g	cranberries
50g	chopped apricots
50g	halved cocktail cherries
125g	self-raising flour
150g	fresh white breadcrumbs
125g	suet
125g	muscovado sugar
100g	toasted chopped nuts (almonds and hazlenuts)
2	large eggs
2 tblsp	chopped crystalised ginger
1	grated rind of orange & lemon
1	grated peeled apple
1tsp	cinnamon
¼ tsp	ground cloves & nutmeg
6 tblsp	Rum or brandy

I steam the fruit except the apricots and cherries for 30 seconds, or until barely softened. Let cool, and add alcohol and spices. I let sit in a sealed container in fridge for a week.

After the week, add all other ingredients and mix well. Leave in fridge for 24 hours. Bowl up and cook in a steamer oven or steamer.

My preferred alcohol is a drop of 'mountain dew', from a reliable source of course. We also like a brandy butter that has an orange liqueur base with zesty orange pieces added.

Br Pádraig

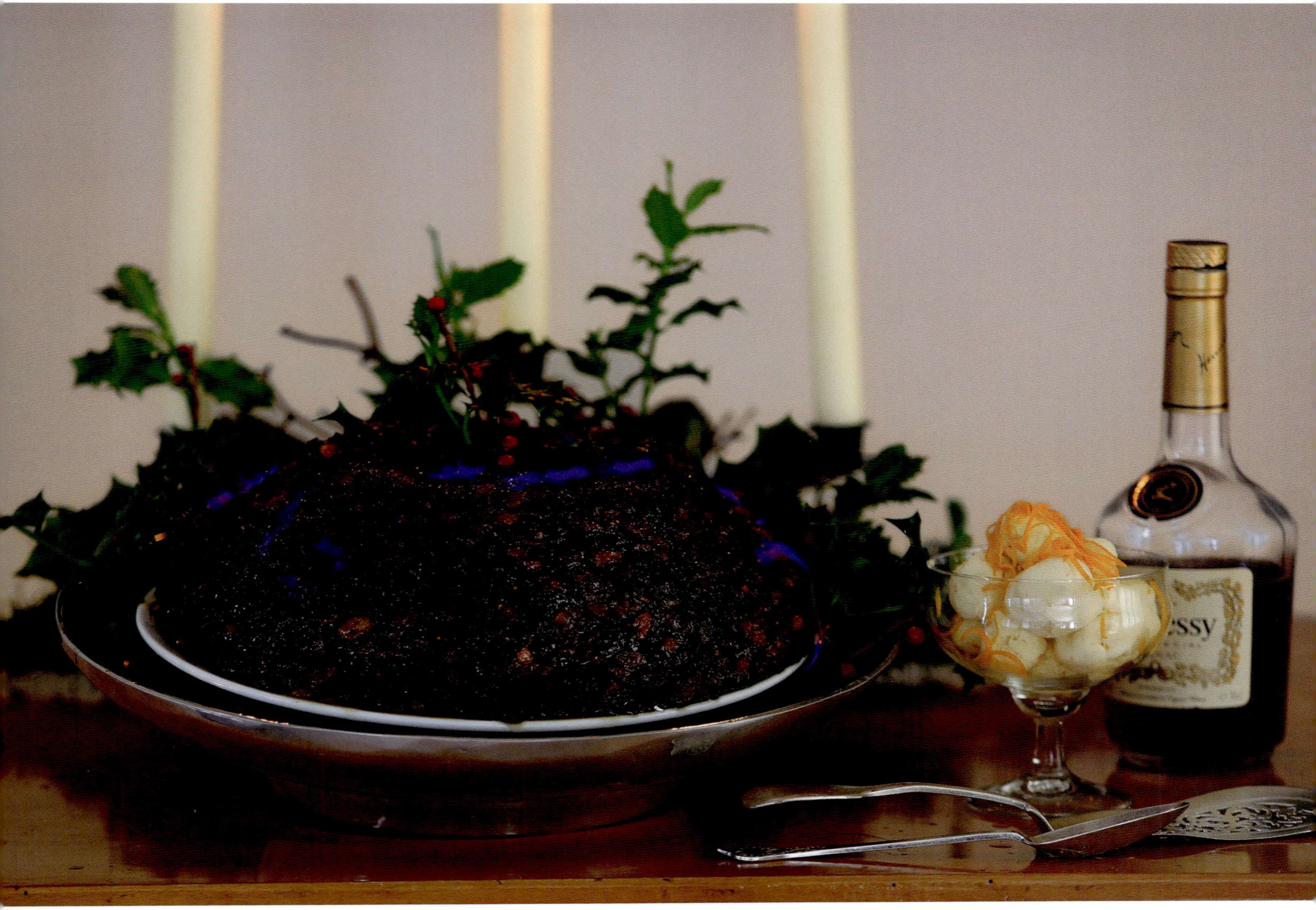

essy

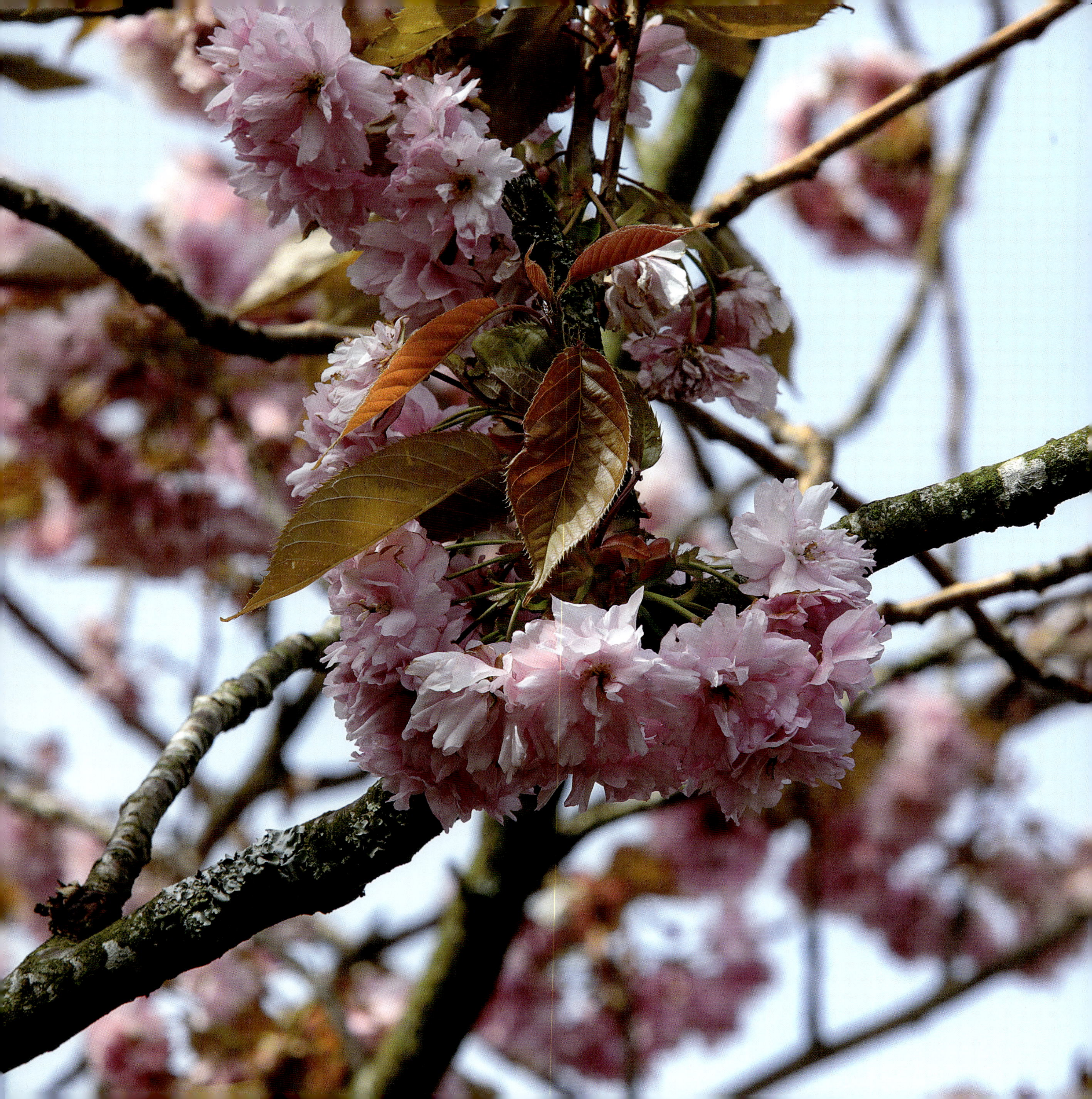

Spring

Snowdrops and a stretch in the evening are the first signs that Spring is upon us. On the farm, the cycle of life begins again with the arrival of the first new calves, while in the school excitement mounts as teams advance further in the various rugby competitions. Having reached the Munster final for two years in a row and actually winning it in 2018, hopes were high but, alas, hopes were dashed.

Ash Wednesday marks the beginning of Lent, and a period of more intense spiritual awareness. St Benedict urges monks to be especially diligent during this season and to devote more time and effort to the spiritual disciplines of prayer, fasting and silence. *Lectio Divina* is central to this programme. This consists of the slow, meditative reading of scripture or another inspirational text in the hope of being transformed by it.

Such reading has been a characteristic of monastic life since the beginning and we are fortunate to possess a well-stocked library to facilitate it. Sharing these insights is also important and the annual Lenten Sunday lecture series has become a popular and well-attended event. More recently it has been broadcast on the webcam and is now followed from as far afield as California and North Korea.

St Patrick's Day provides a welcome break in the Lenten programme. During the liturgy we use some of the traditional chants sung in his honour in medieval Irish monasteries and churches. His chapel in the abbey church contains a beautiful rendering in bronze lettering of his lúireach or breastplate designed by Fr Cornelius, along with three windows depicting scenes from his life by Patrick Pye. More recently we received the gift of a magnificent icon of the saint by the Greek iconwriter Maria Sigala-Spanopoulos.

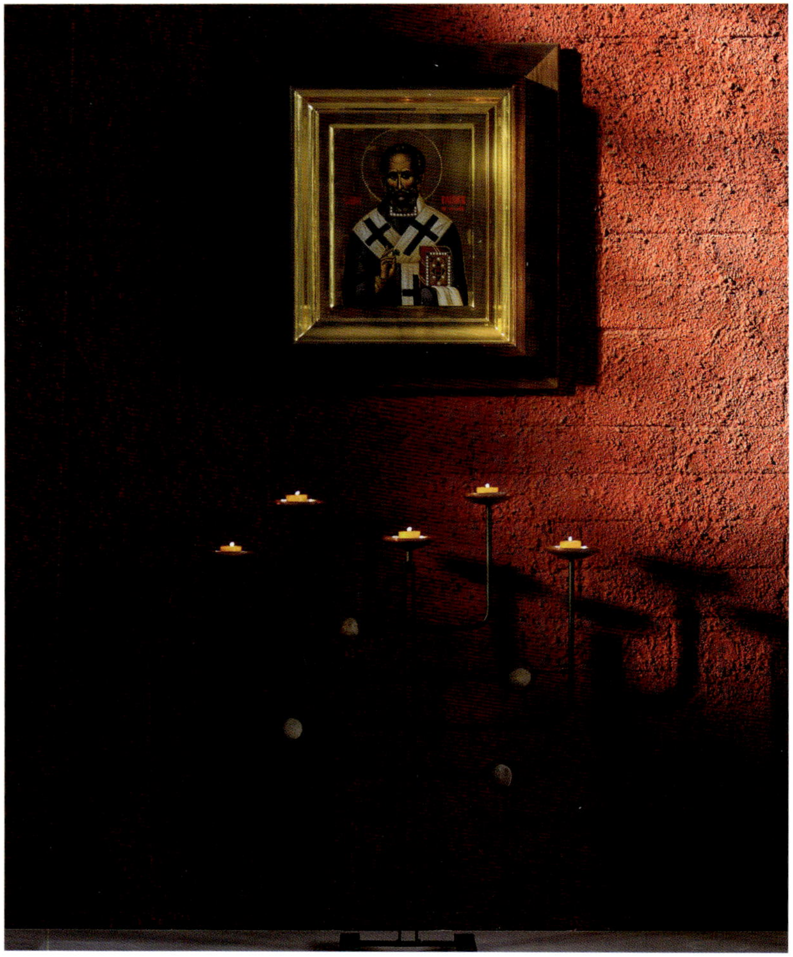

Icon of Saint Patrick, Glenstal Abbey Church.

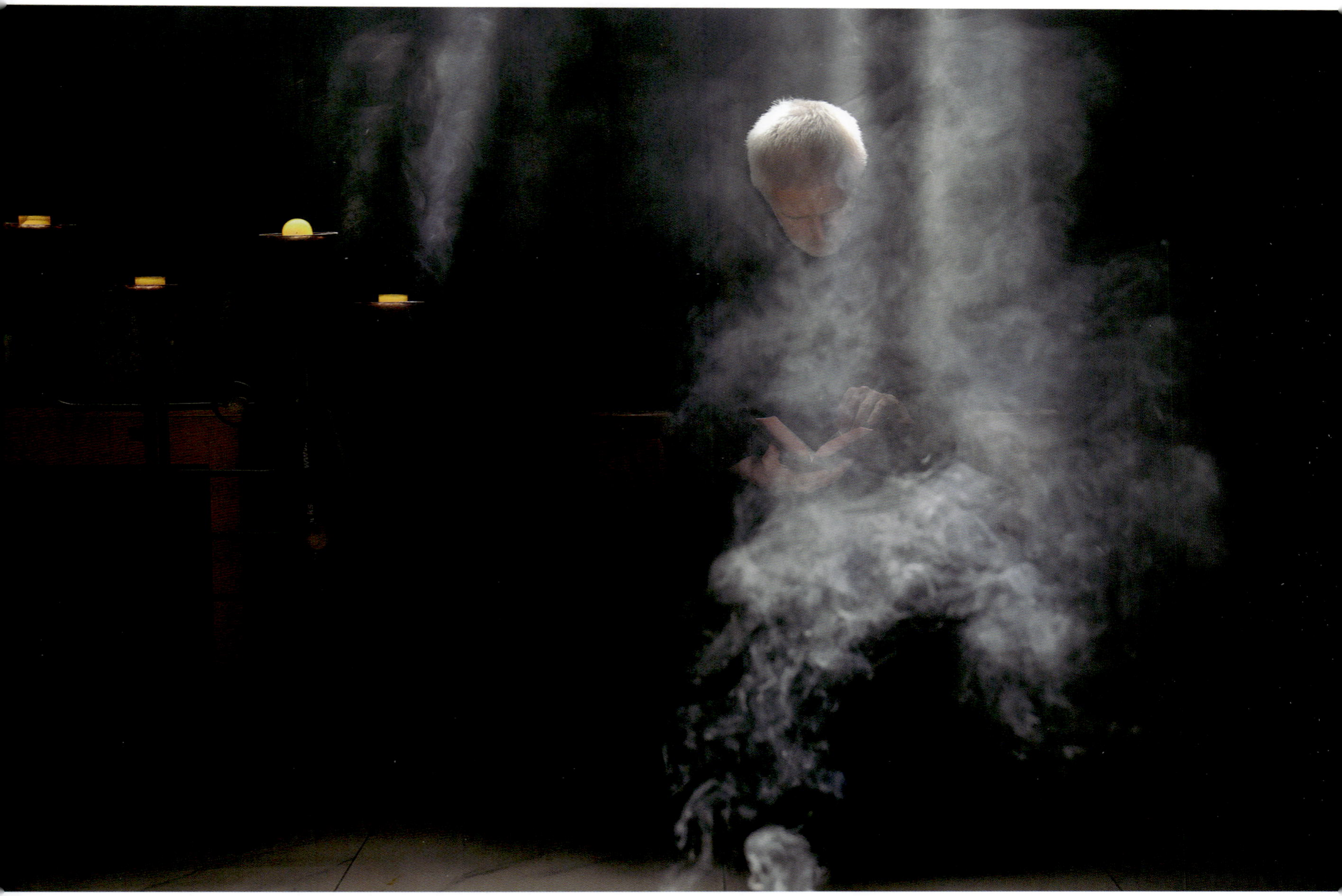

Lectio divina is the slow, repetitive and meditative murmuring of the Word of God in the Scriptures. The Word penetrates the innermost depths of the monk (Heb 4:12), while generous pauses allow the monk to respond with prayers shaped by the Word. Over time, the monk's subconscious, vocabulary, and even his speech become moulded to Christ who converses with him daily in the scriptures.

Fr Luke

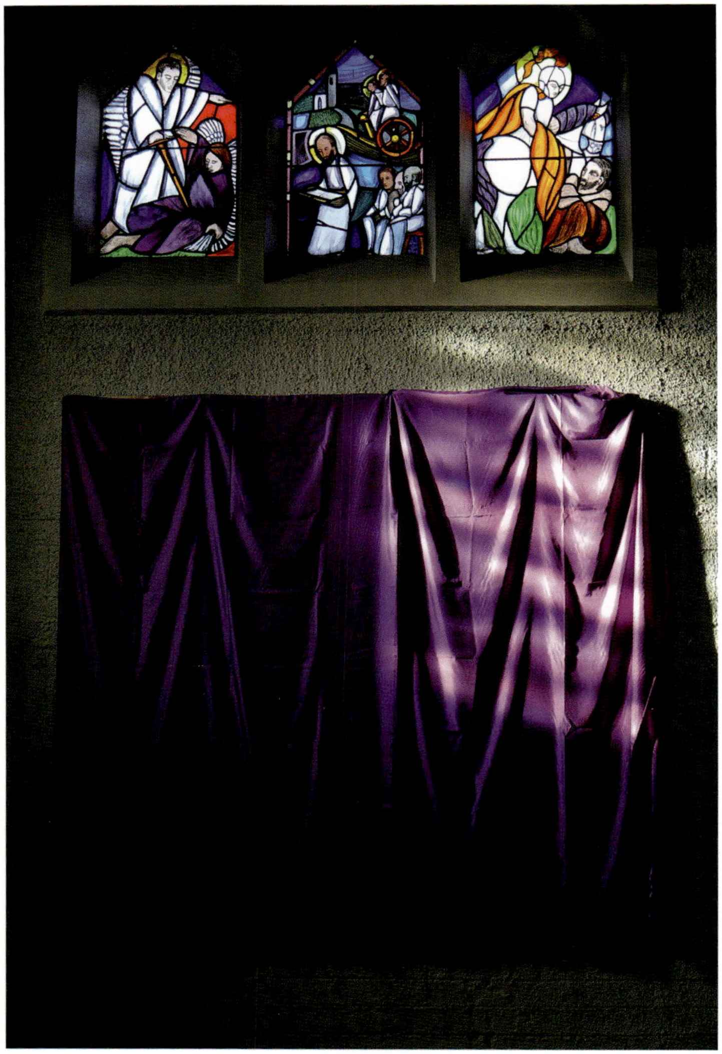

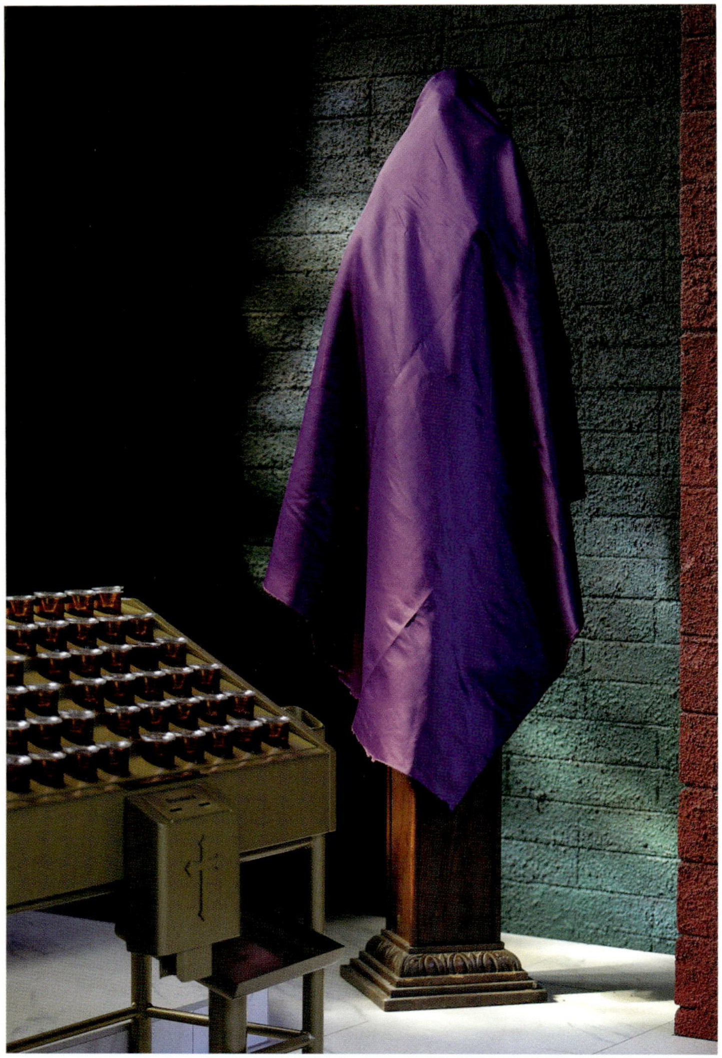

With the start of Passiontide, the mood becomes more sombre as we prepare for the celebration of Holy Week and the Sacred Triduum. In the church the images are draped in purple, and during Vespers we sing the ancient hymn *Vexilla Regis* – the banners of the King – composed in the 6th century by Venantius Fortunatus in honour of the Holy Cross. In it we hail Christ's cross as humanity's only hope, kneeling as we do so in a powerful union of voice and gesture.

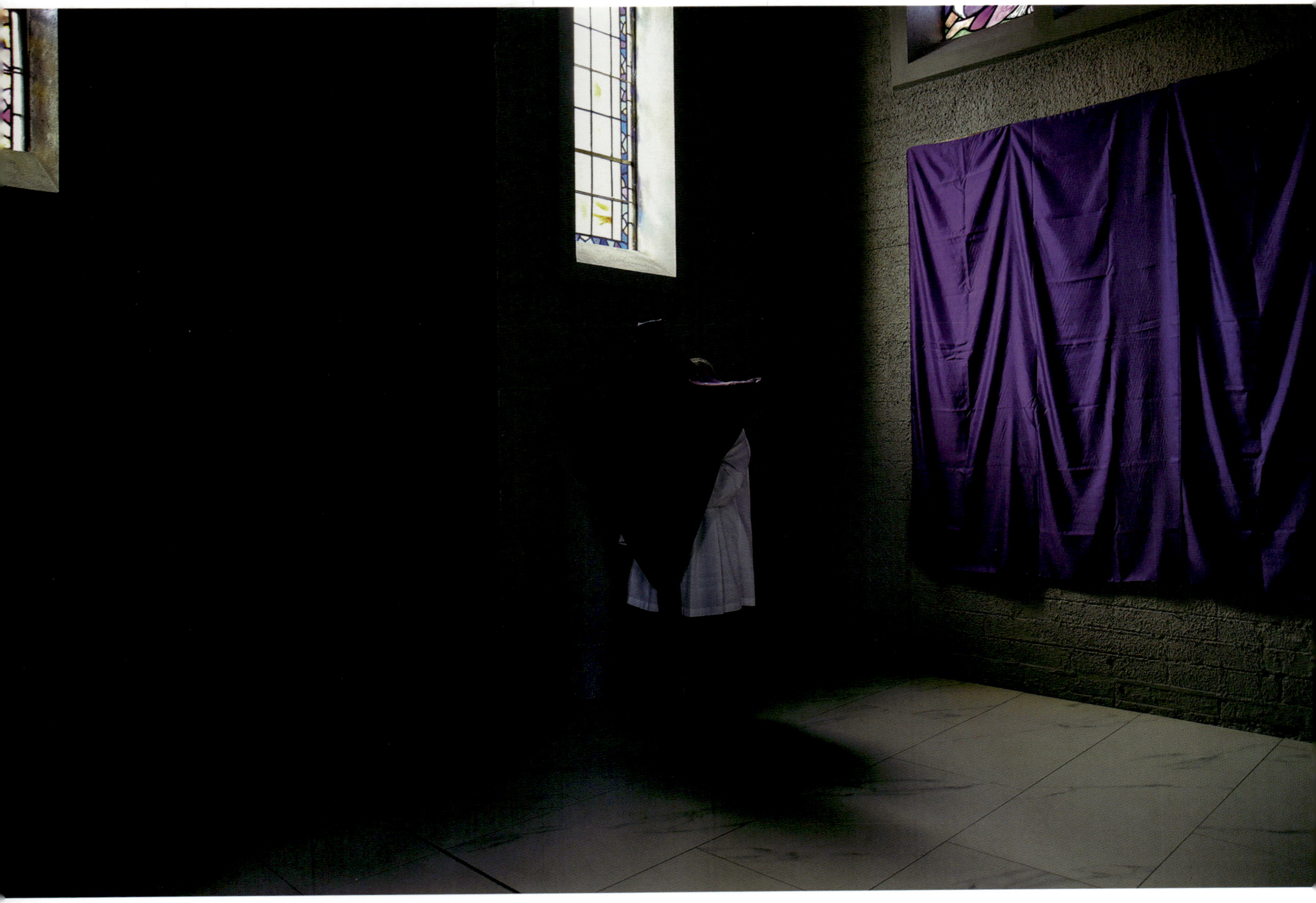

Holy Week

Holy Week begins with the solemn commemoration of the Lord's Passion on Palm Sunday. Weather permitting, the congregation assembles in the school atrium where, following the blessing of the palm fronds, we move in procession to the church where the abbot demands access by three times beating on the door with the processional cross. During Mass the account of the Passion is proclaimed by three monks taking the roles of the narrator, the crowd and of Christ. It is a dramatic start to the climax of the liturgical year and much of Holy Week is spent practising and preparing for the liturgies.

The Holy Week retreat is one of the busiest periods of the year during which up to 130 resident guests join us to celebrate the Sacred Triduum. Spanning all ages and occupations and hailing from all parts of the world, their presence is a great gift and fosters an atmosphere of prayer and devotion. Some of the sixth-year students also volunteer to serve at the liturgy and their contribution is likewise greatly appreciated. For some it will be their first opportunity to see the ceremonies celebrated with full solemnity, and for many of our guests Easter at Glenstal has become a fixture of their spiritual lives. In addition to the liturgical services, a full programme of talks and activities is also offered.

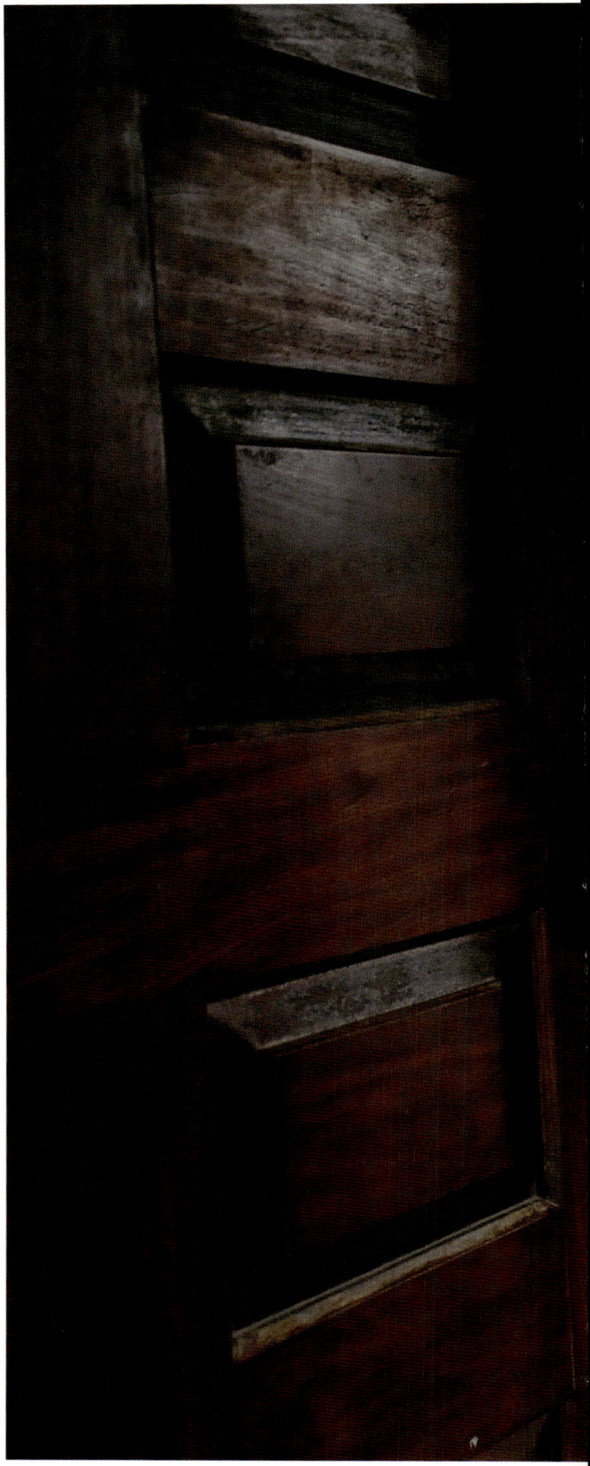

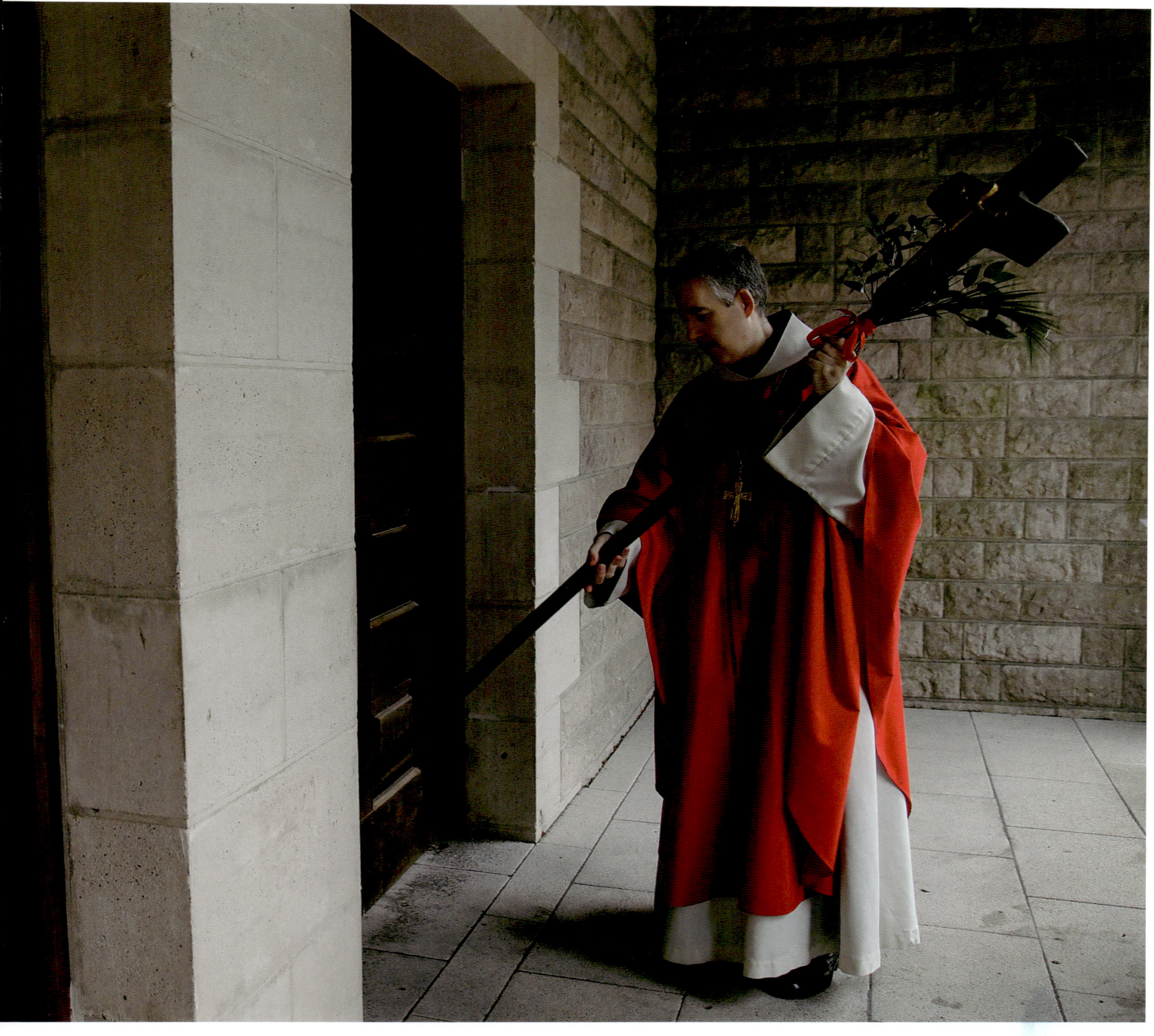

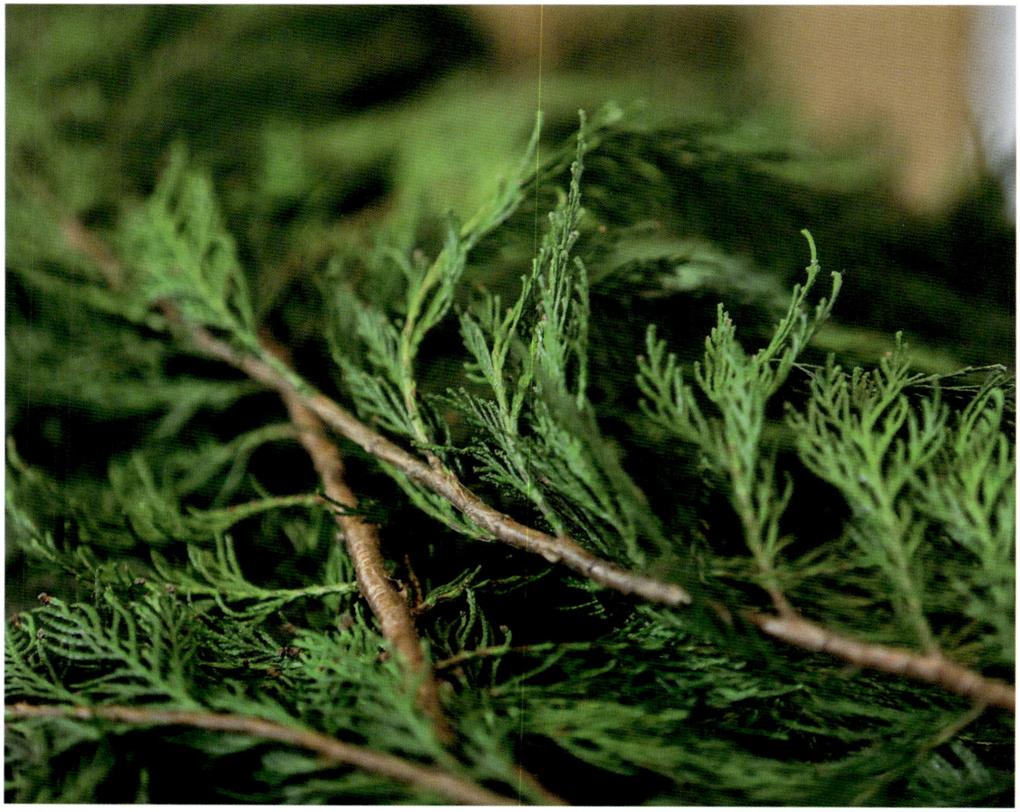

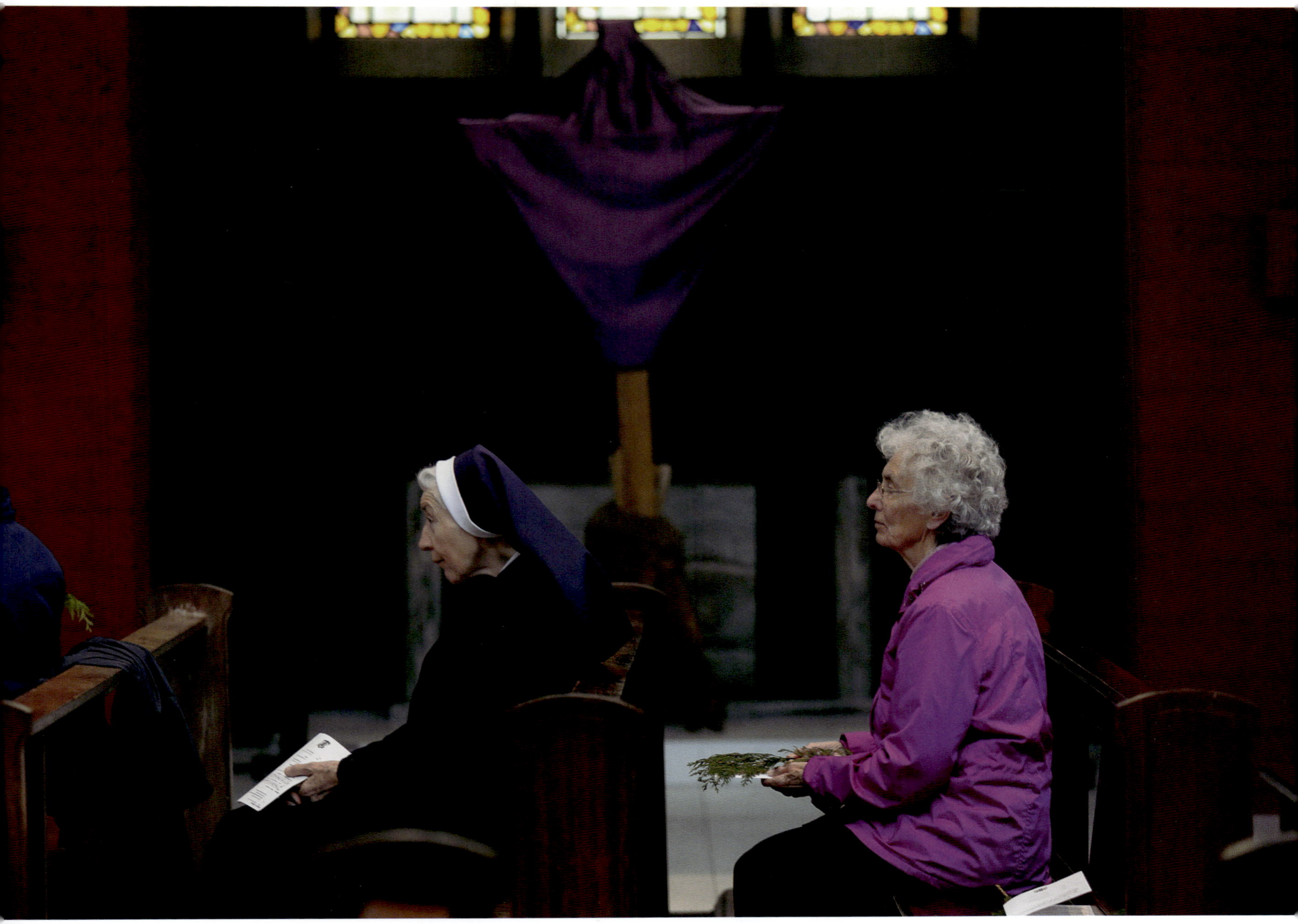

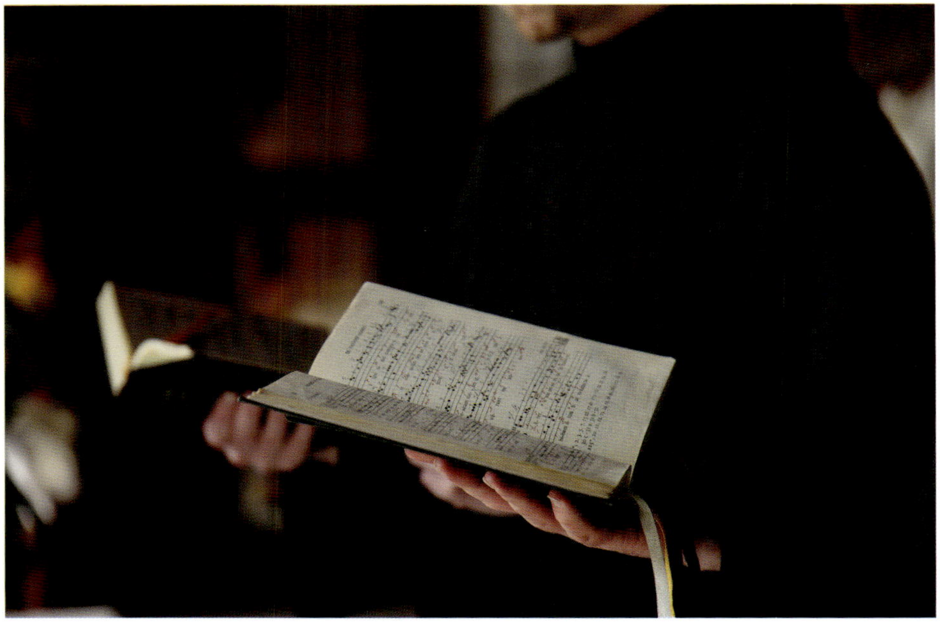

It is a particularly busy time for all involved behind the scenes: for the housekeeping staff who have to prepare accommodation; for the catering department who provide sustenance, and for the choirmaster, schola and sacristans who prepare for the liturgy and decorate the church.

Below: Glenstal Schola: Br Jarek, Fr Senan, Fr Cuthbert and Br Pádraig, rehearse the chants of the Easter Triduum.

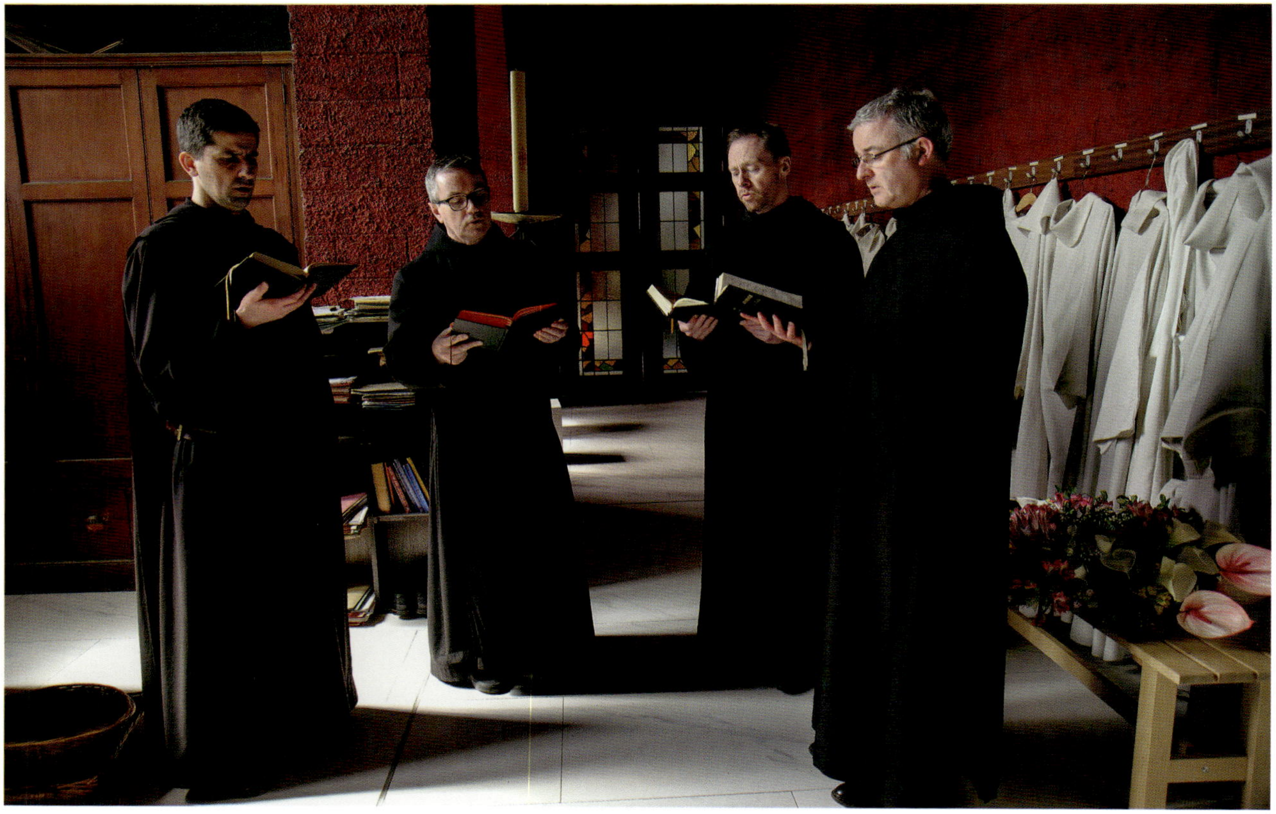

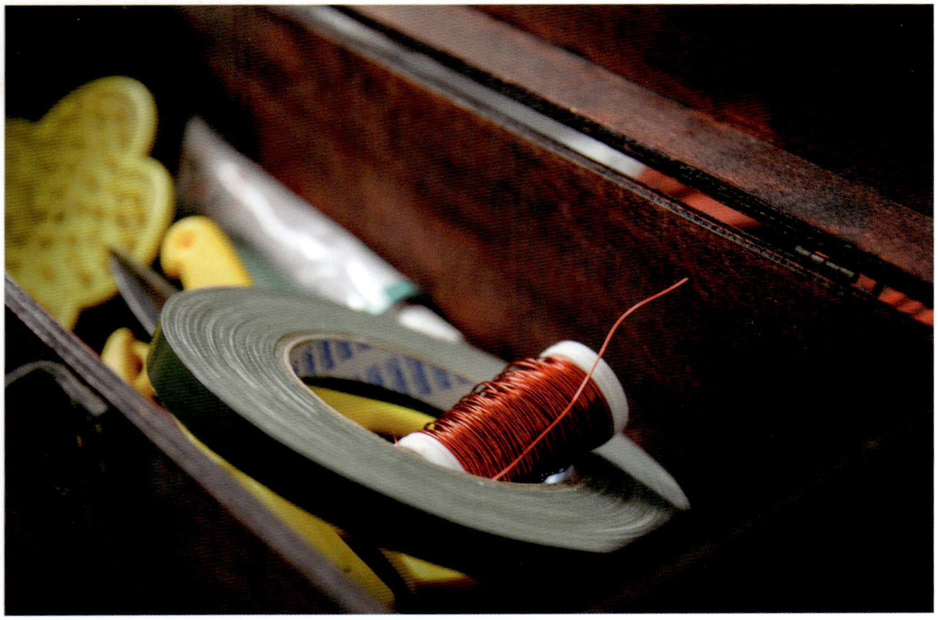

Below: Fr Martin prepares the flowers for the Easter Vigil.

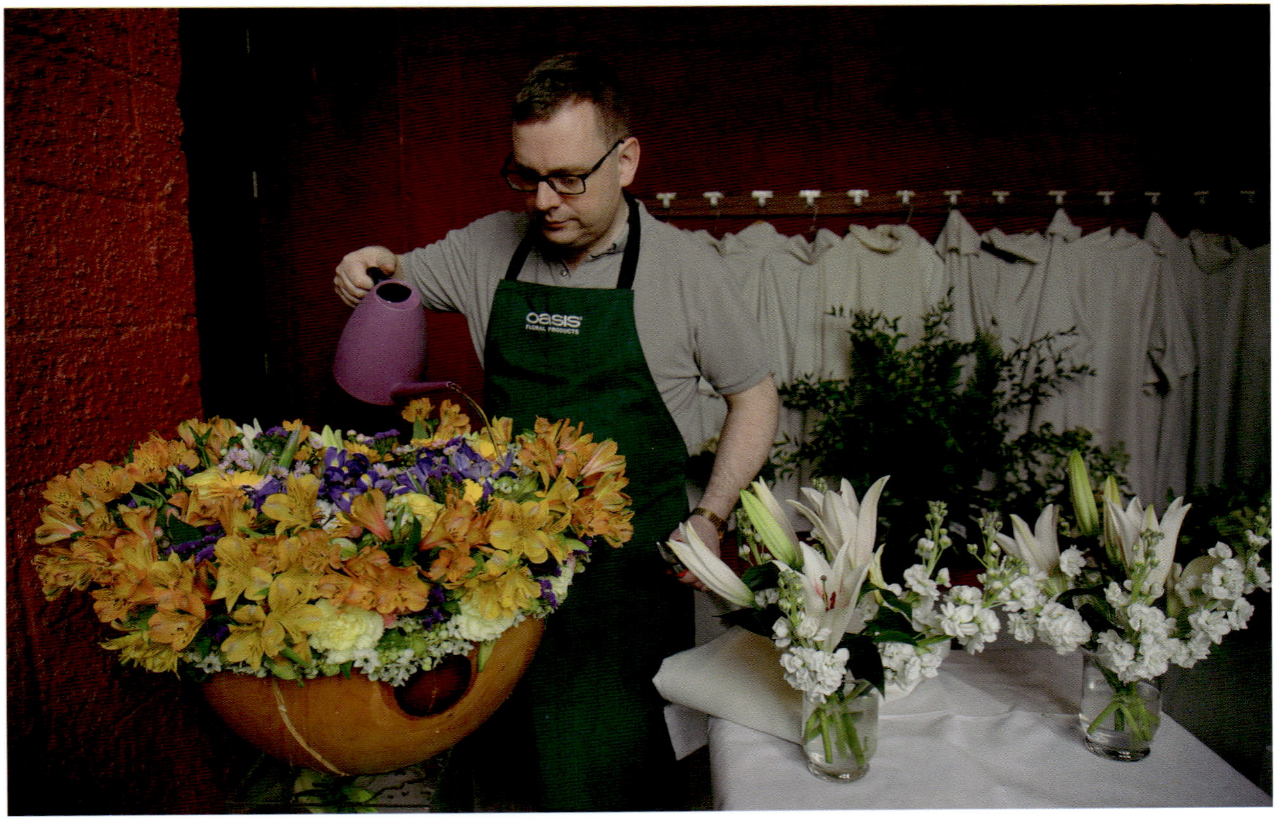

Holy Thursday

The Easter Triduum opens on Holy Thursday with the solemn celebration of the Mass of the Lord's Supper. Commemorating the institution of the Eucharist, the abbot presides and one of the most striking moments of the liturgy occurs when, in imitation of Christ's example, he washes the feet of twelve men and women after which the choir sings the chant *Ubi caritas est vera, Deus ibi est* – Where true charity is found, God is there. This model of humble service is a reminder of the task of discipleship to which all followers of Christ are called.

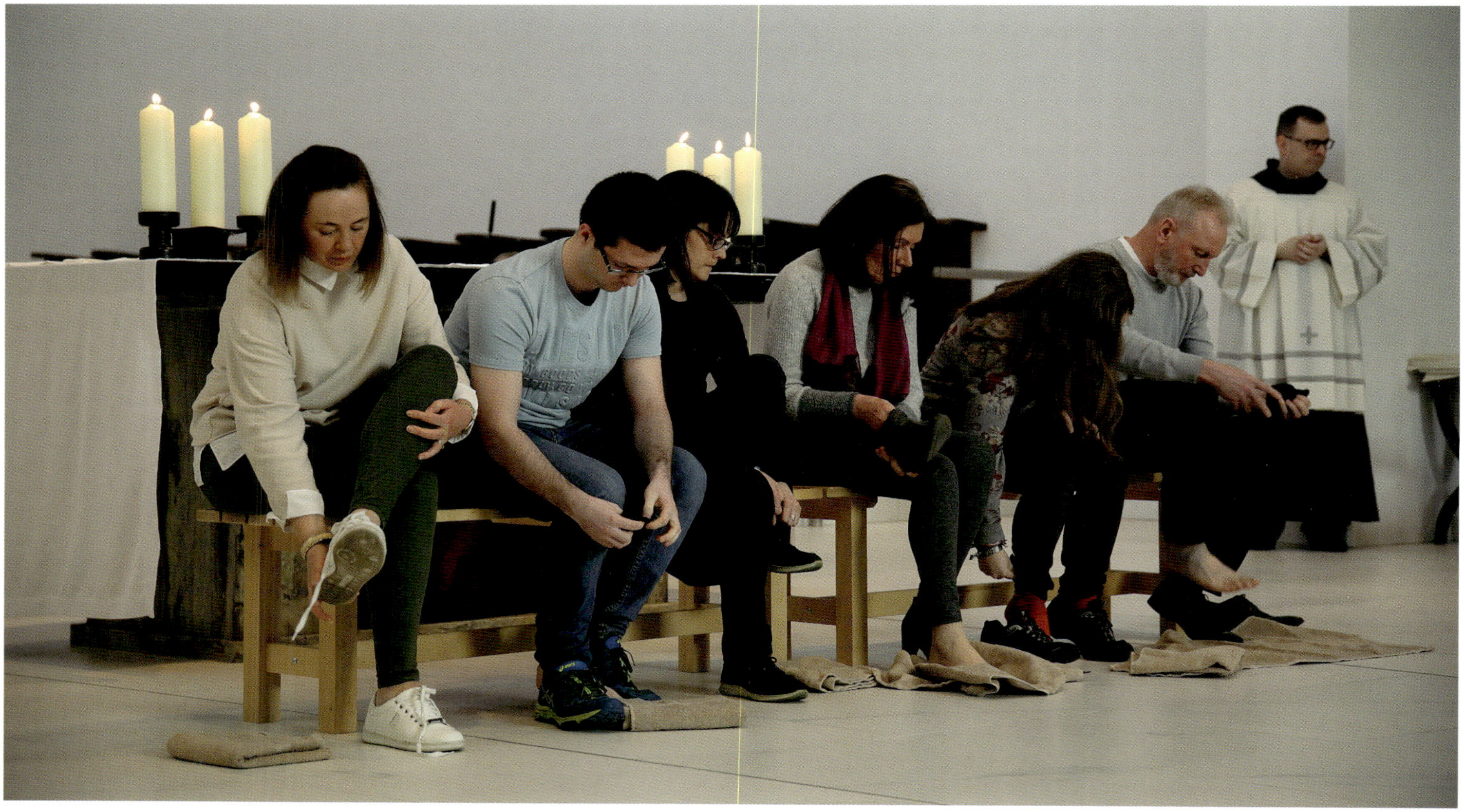

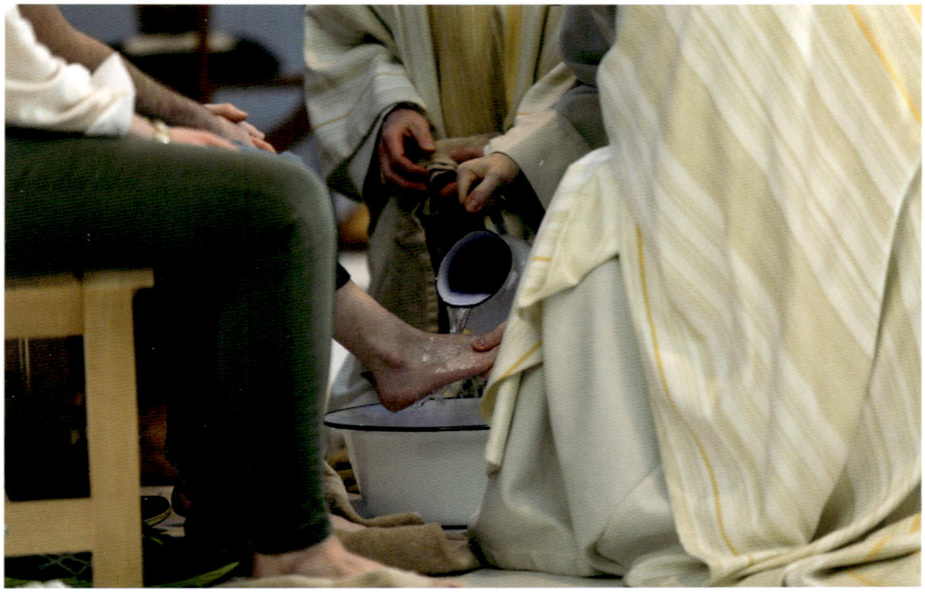

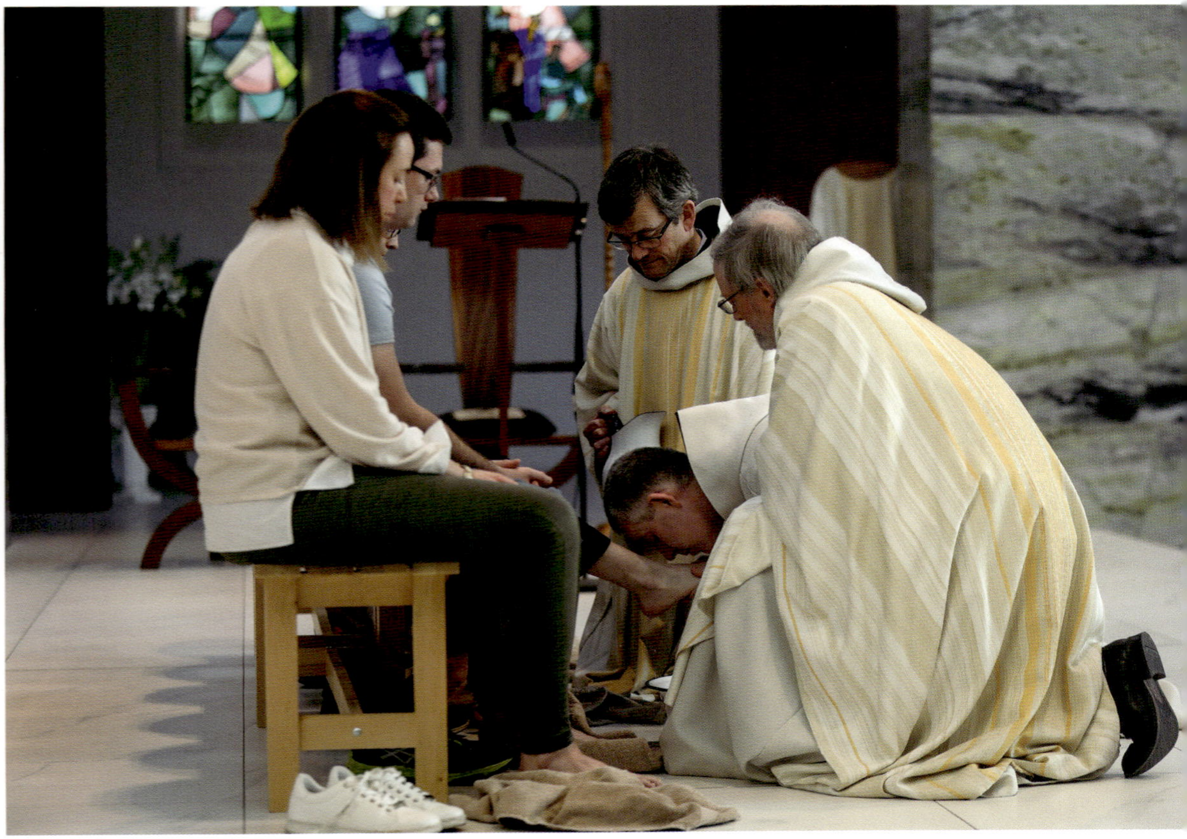

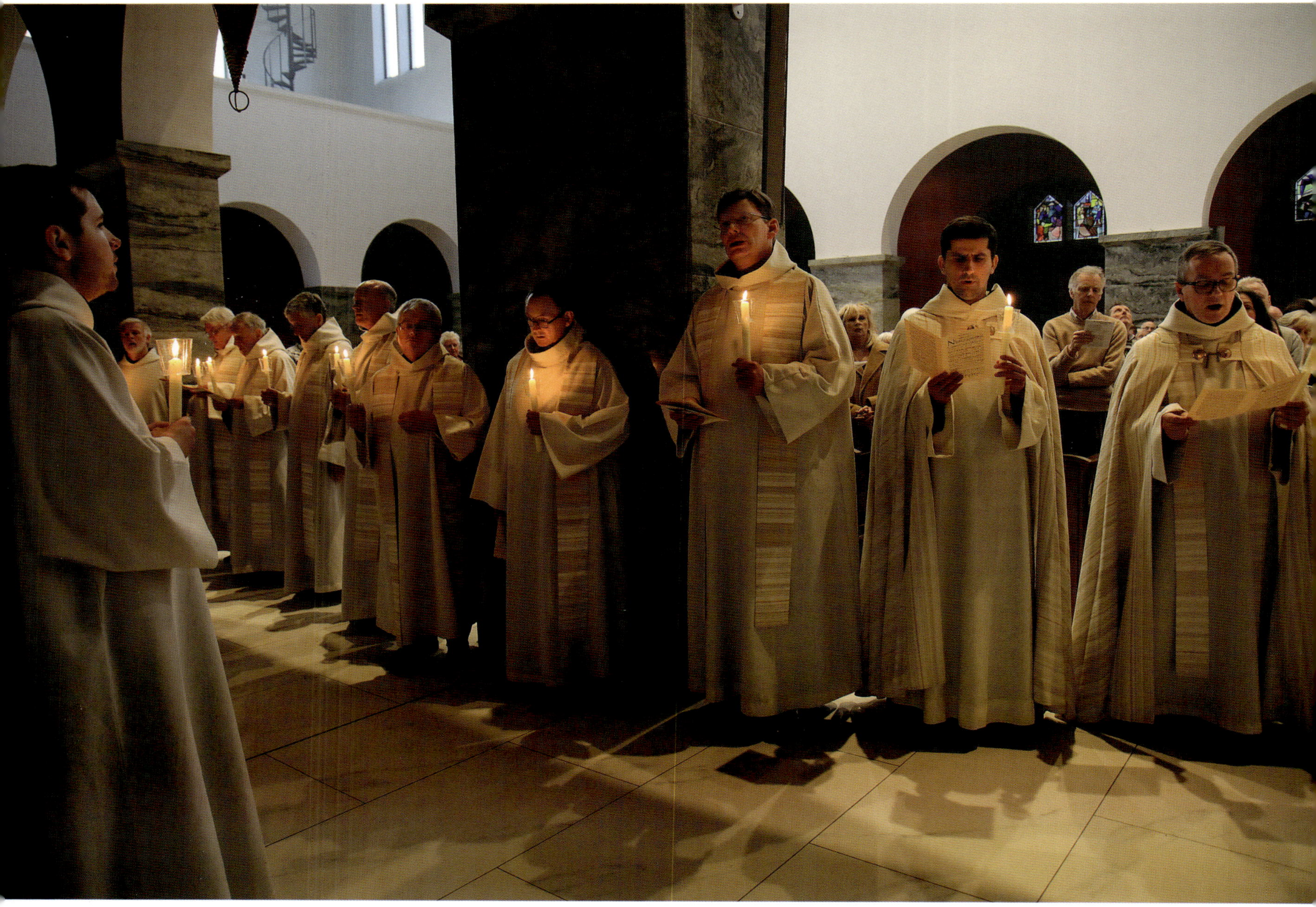

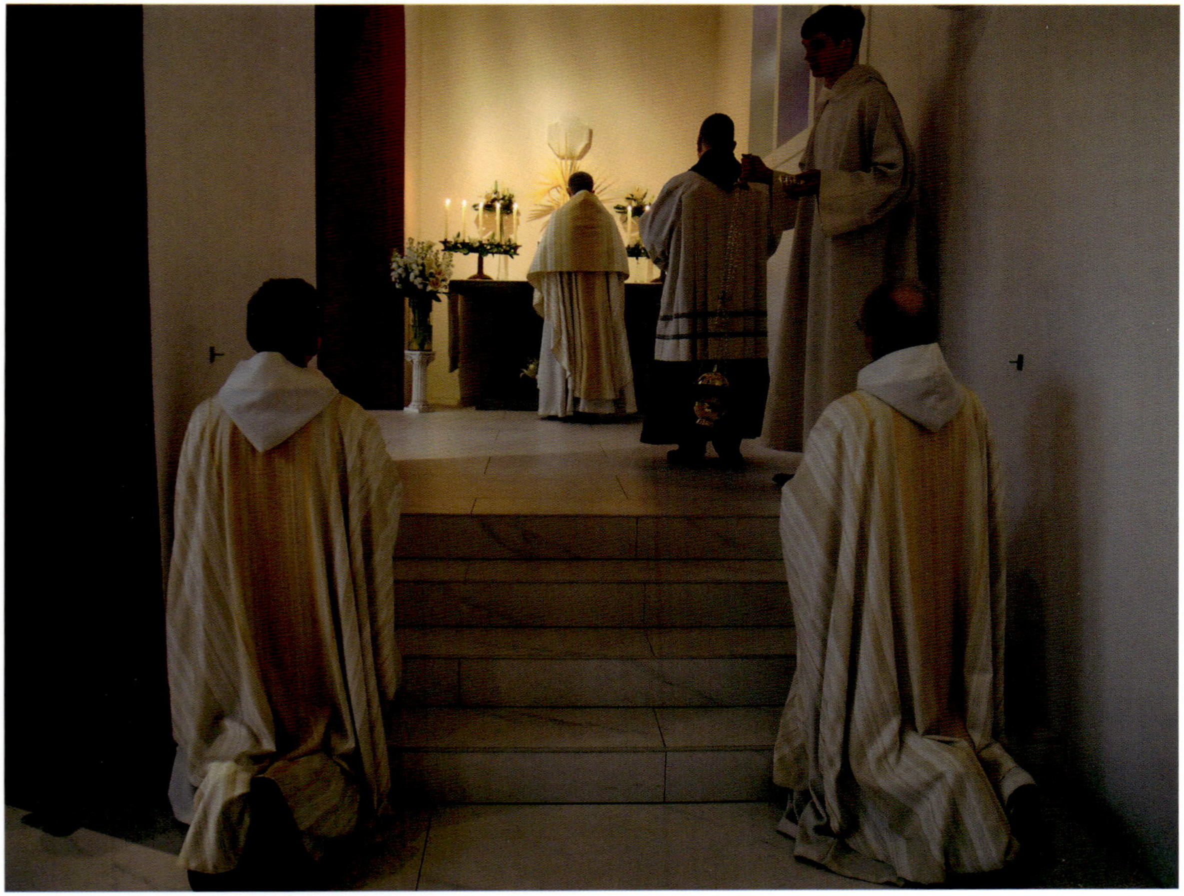

At the end of Mass, the Blessed Sacrament is borne in procession to the altar of repose as the community, bearing lighted candles, sing the great Eucharistic hymn of St Thomas Aquinas, *Pange lingua*. The altar remains a focus for prayer and adoration until midnight, while in the refectory there is a festive meal and a chance for the guests to renew acquaintances. During Compline we sing the haunting chant *Christus factus est*. Taken from St Paul's Letter to the Philippians, it expresses wonder at Christ's humility in accepting death on the cross and awe at the Father's raising him from death. Afterwards, the church is stripped of all ornaments and decorations in preparation for Good Friday.

Good Friday

The atmosphere during Good Friday is stripped back, stark and reflective. During the morning office prayer, we sing sections from the Lamentations of Jeremiah bemoaning the destructive hard-heartedness of the people of Jerusalem. The commemoration of the Lord's Passion takes place at 3pm. The abbot and assistants enter in silence and prostrate before the altar in prayer. The account of the Passion is sung by three cantors and followed by the solemn intercessions for the needs of the church and of all humanity.

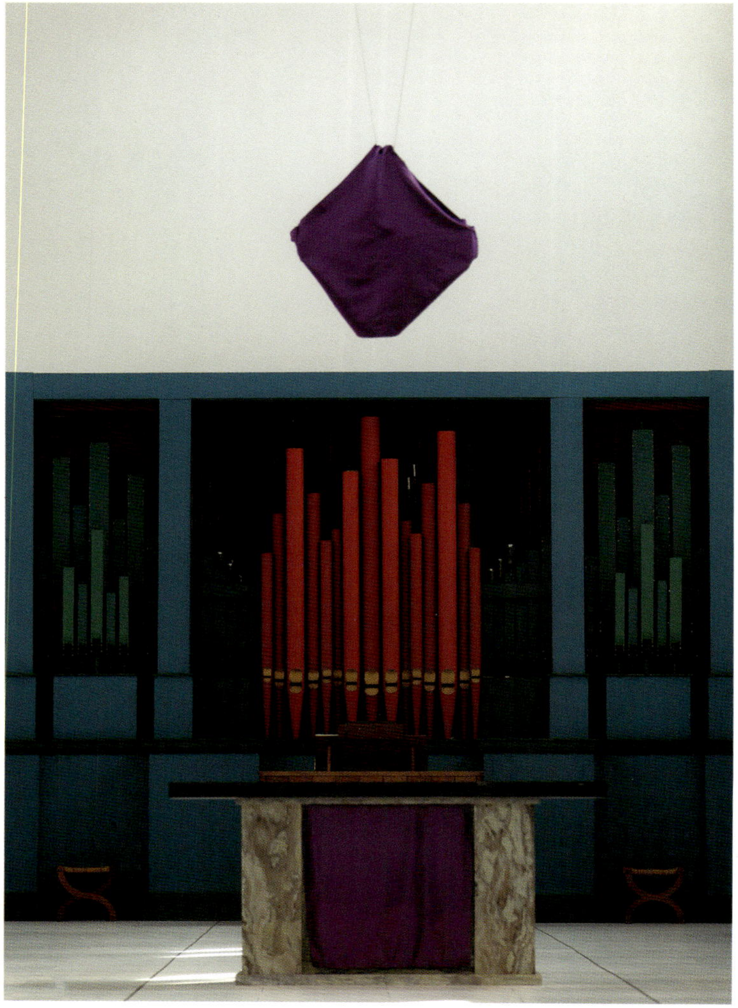

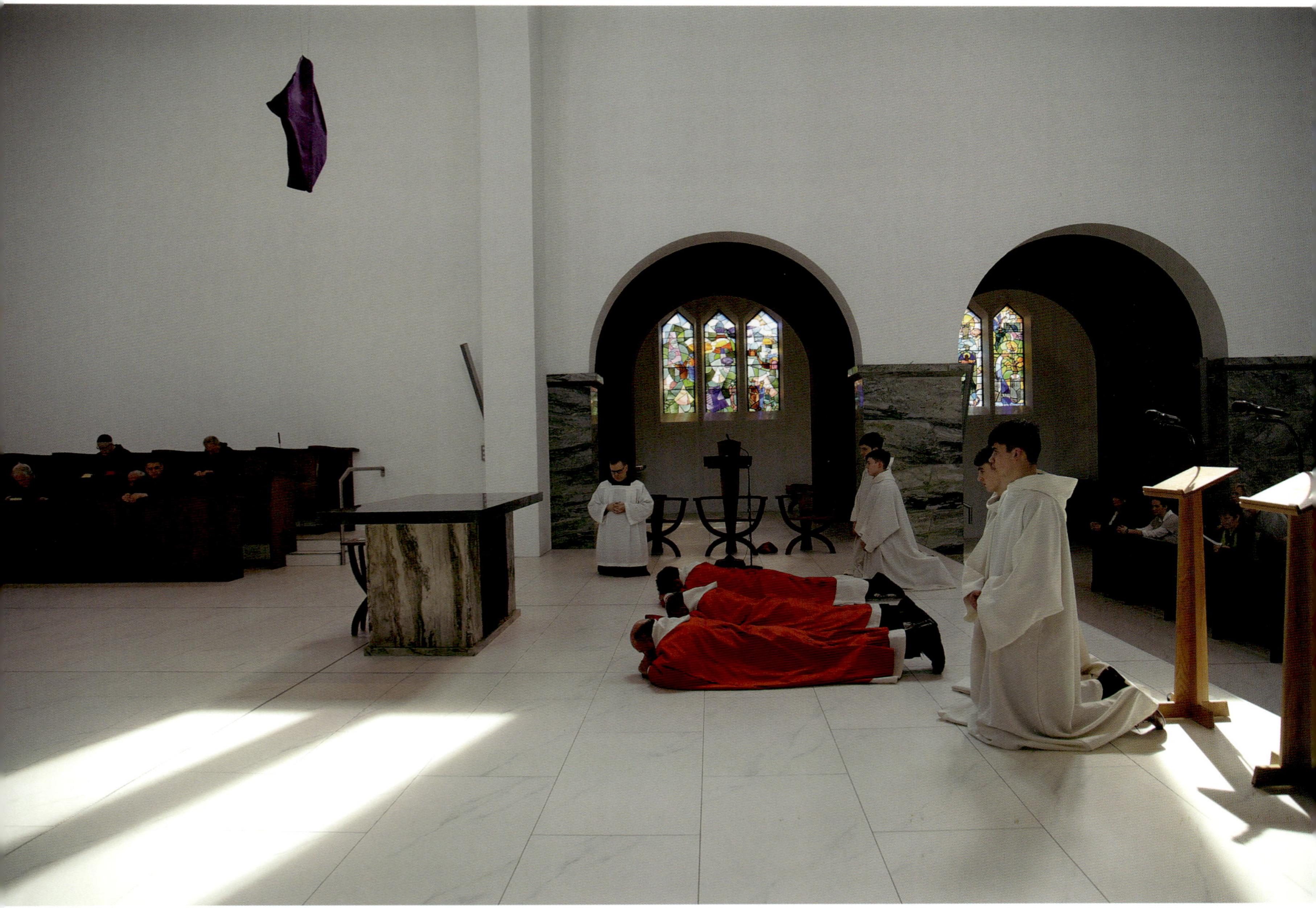

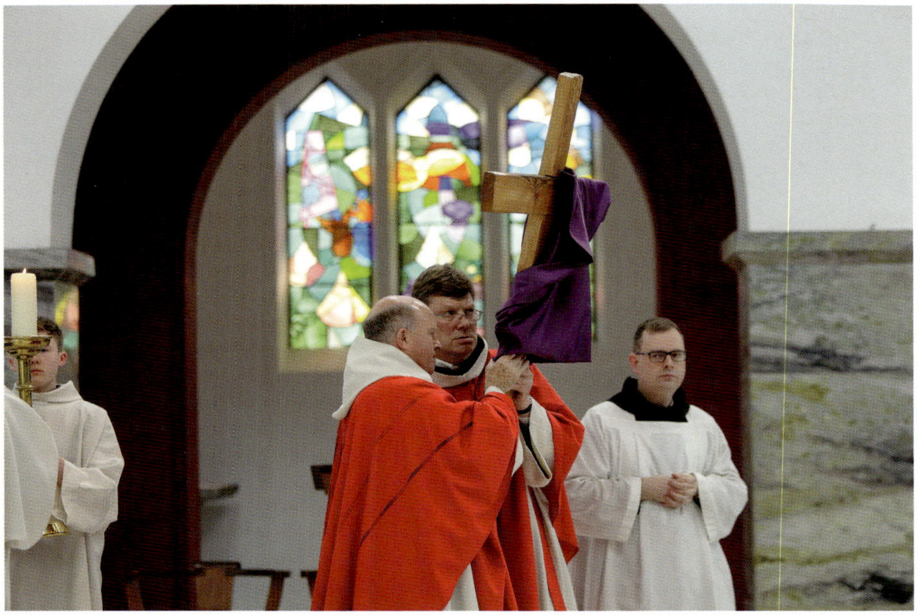

The unveiling and veneration of the Cross then follows. Made from wood grown in Glenstal, the Cross contains a relic of the True Cross and, as the abbot gradually unveils it, he three times hails 'the Wood of the Cross on which hung the Saviour of the World'. When fully exposed, the community and congregation venerate it by genuflecting and kissing it as the choir sing the reproaches and other hymns and antiphons in honour of the Holy Cross. The service concludes with the reception of Holy Communion.

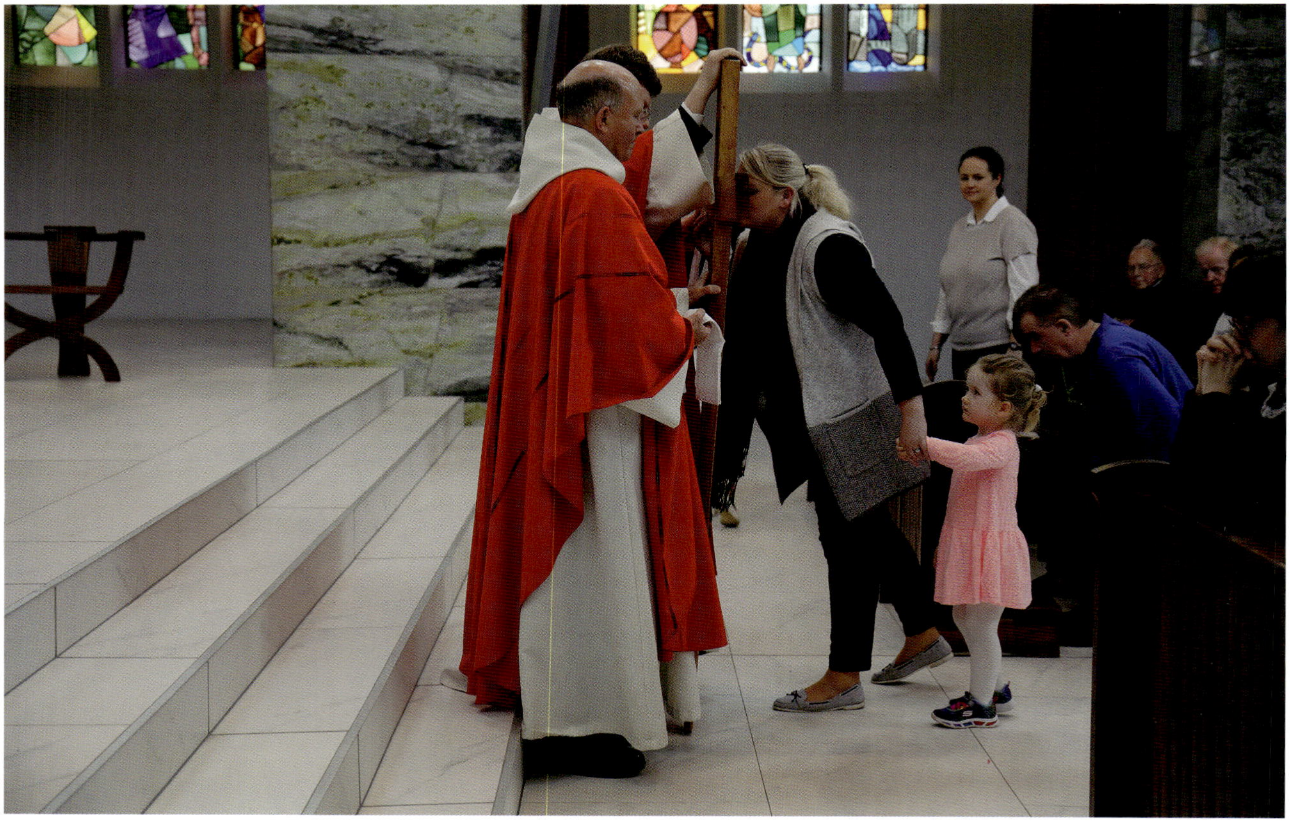

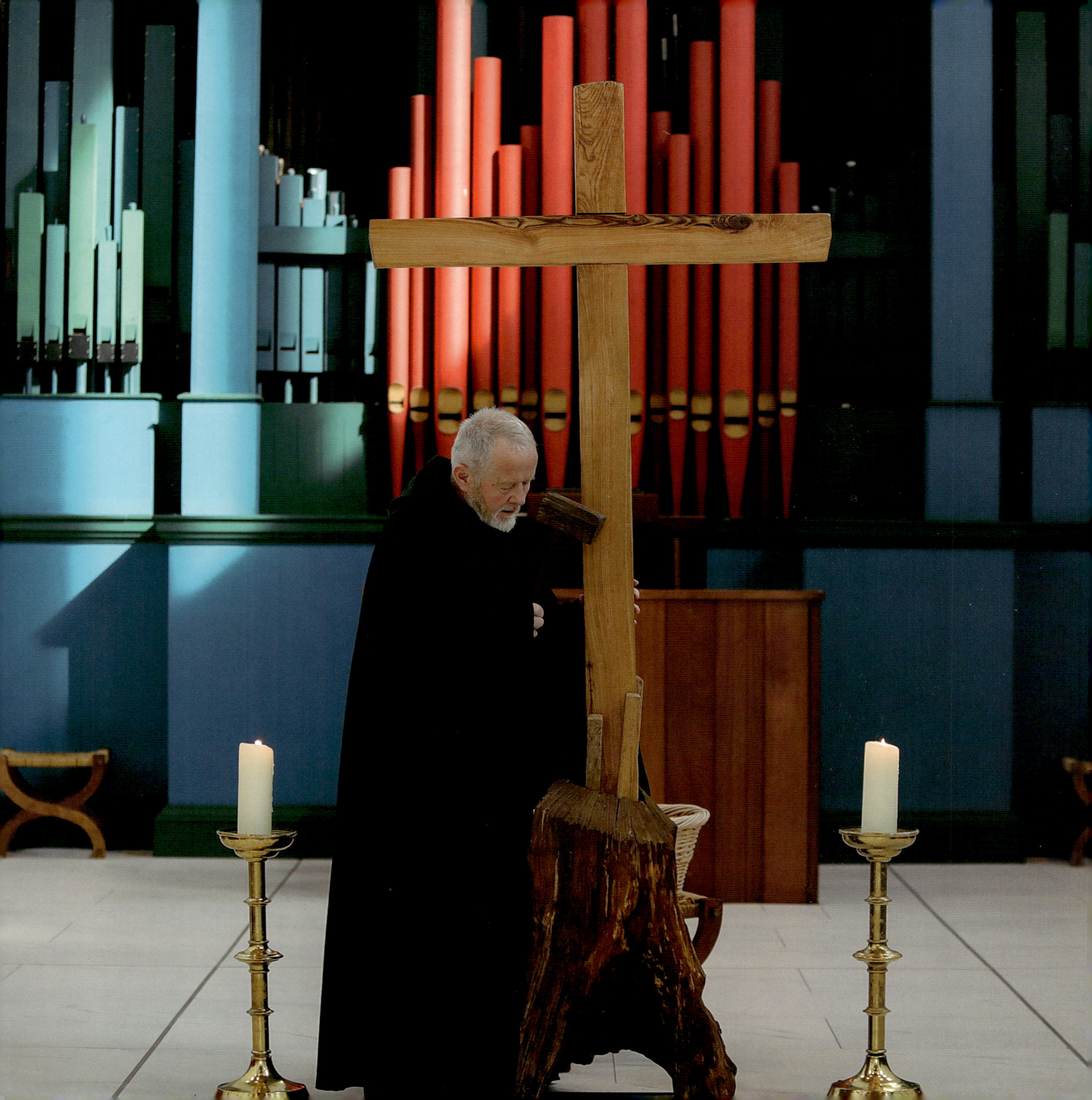

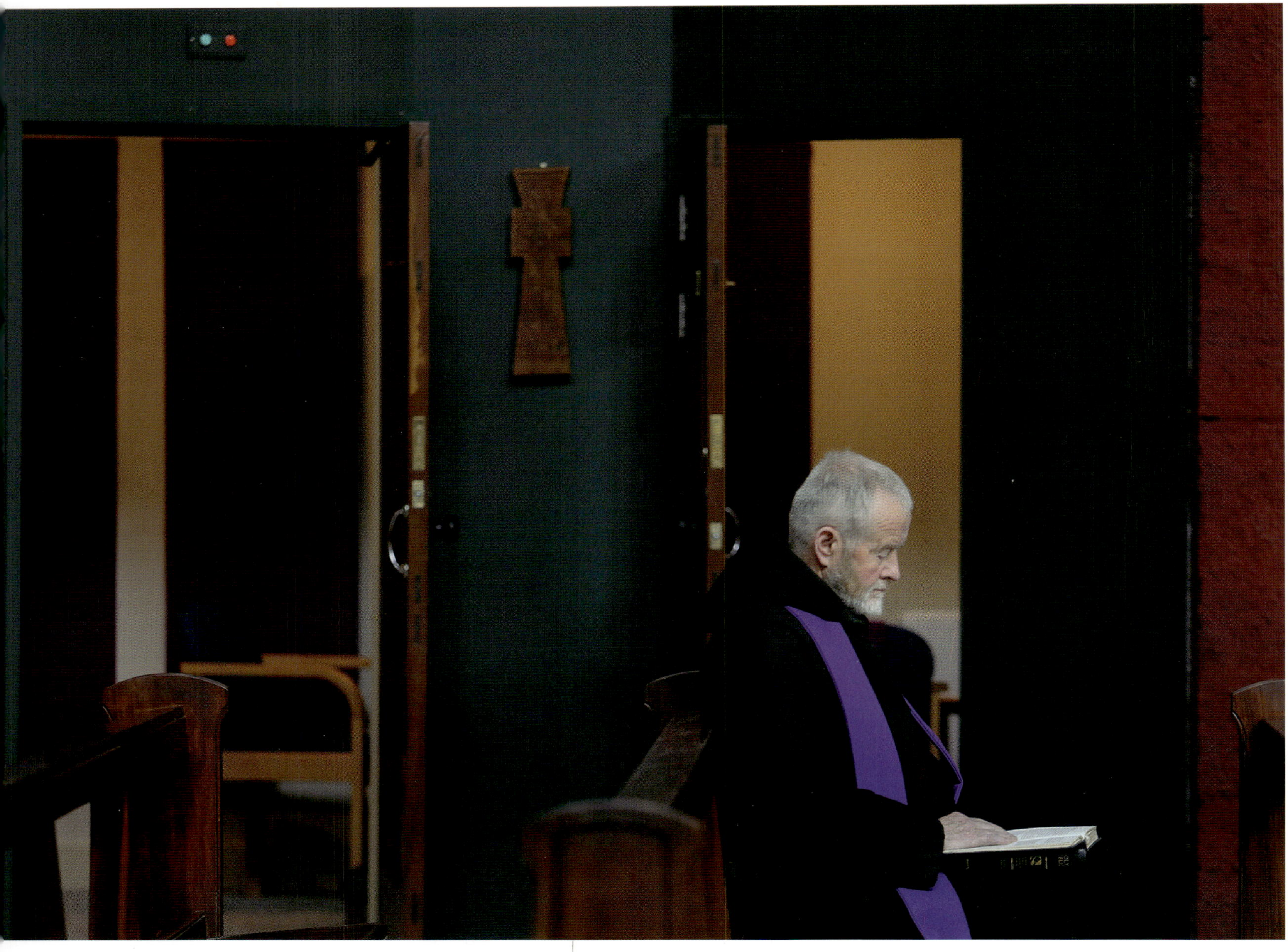

Paradoxically, Holy Saturday is a time of great calm and intense activity. Apart from the Divine Office, no other service takes place during the day, but much work has to be done in the sacristy and the kitchen to prepare for the coming feast of Easter.

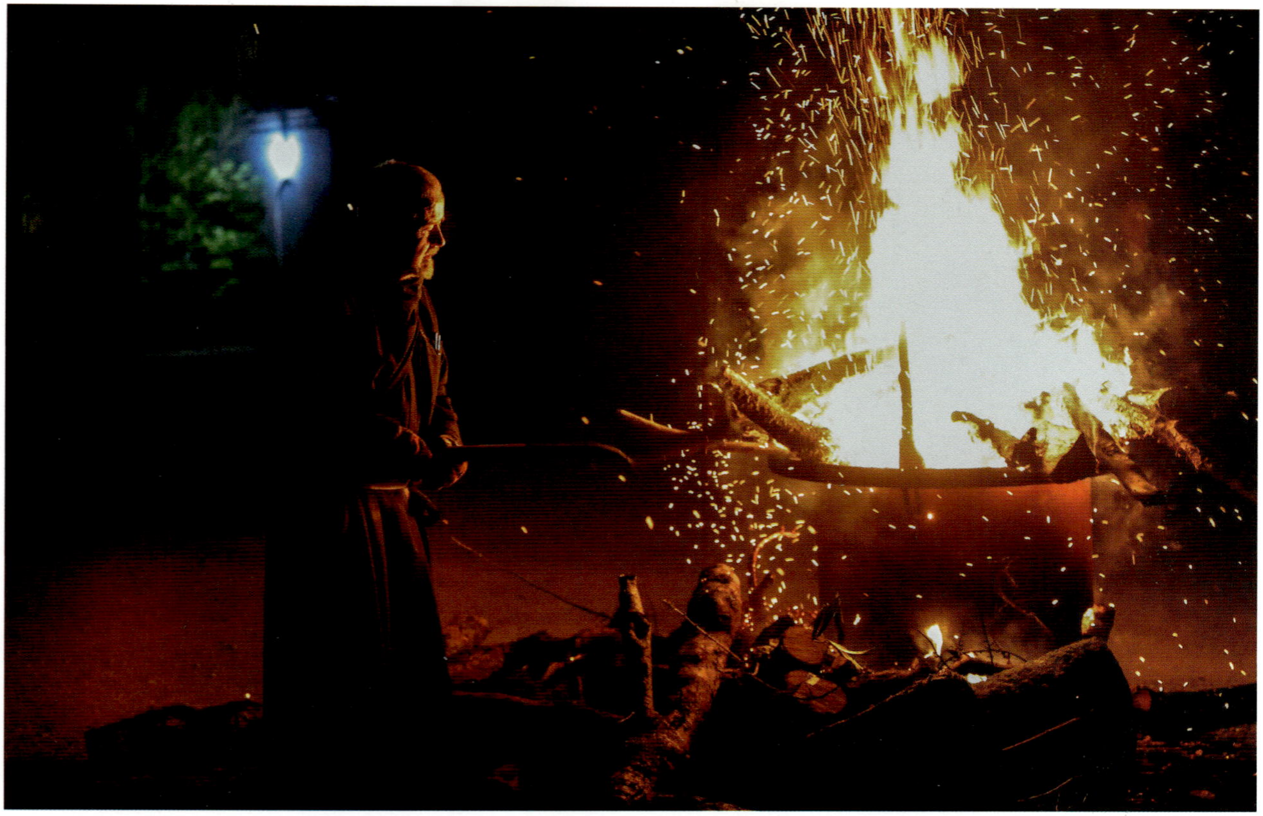

The Easter Vigil

Under a night sky the congregation gathers in front of the abbey church. The ceremony begins with the *Lucernarium* or service of light in which the Paschal Candle is lit from the newly blessed fire and carried in procession. As the flame is passed from person to person in the darkness, the church gradually fills with light, transformed into a symbol of hope and resurrection. With the singing of the *Exsultet*, the great, joyous proclamation of Easter all creation – from the angels to the bees – joins in hailing Christ's victory over death.

The scripture readings that follow trace God's saving work amongst his people and culminate in the singing of the Gloria, the pealing of the church bells and the singing of the Gospel of the Resurrection. In the baptismal liturgy that ensues, water is blessed and baptismal vows renewed. On occasion, adult candidates have been baptised or confirmed at this point, providing a powerful witness for all present. The liturgy culminates in the celebration of the Eucharist in which all participate in 'the wedding banquet of the Lamb once slain who lives for ever.'

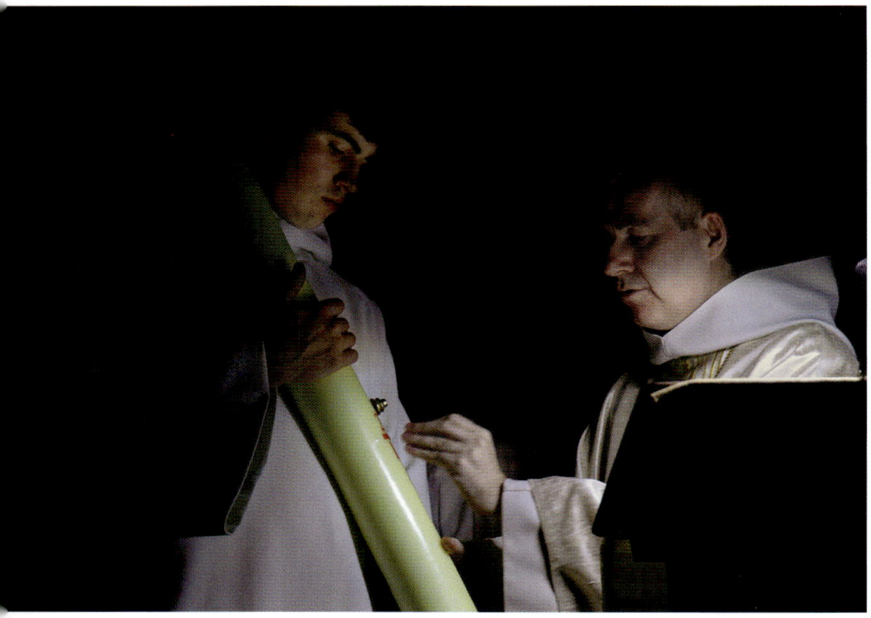

Left: Abbot Brendan inscribes the Paschal Candle with the year and with 'Alpha' and 'Omega', the first and last letters of the Greek alphabet.
Below: The candle is lit with flame from the newly kindled paschal fire.

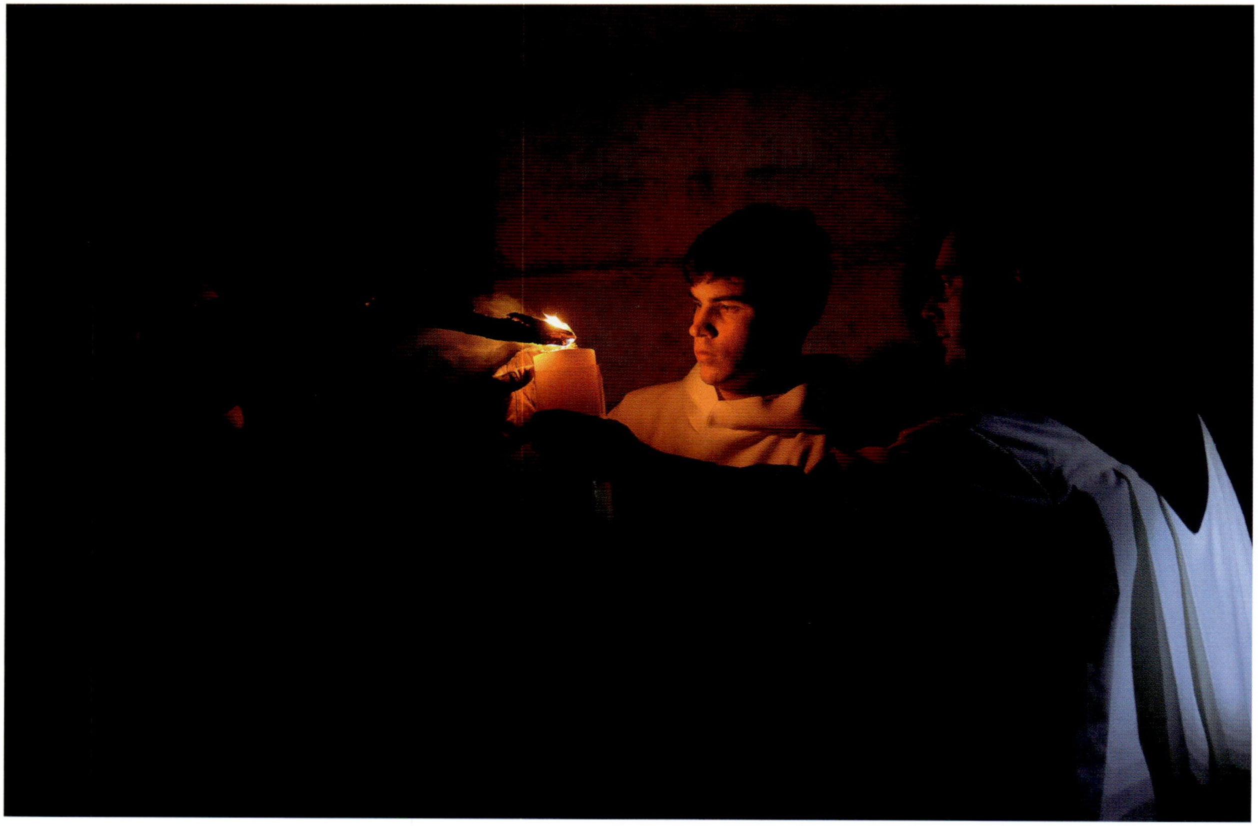

“

Christ yesterday and today,
the beginning and the end,
Alpha and Omega,
all time belongs to him,
and all ages;
to him be glory and power,
through every age and for ever. Amen

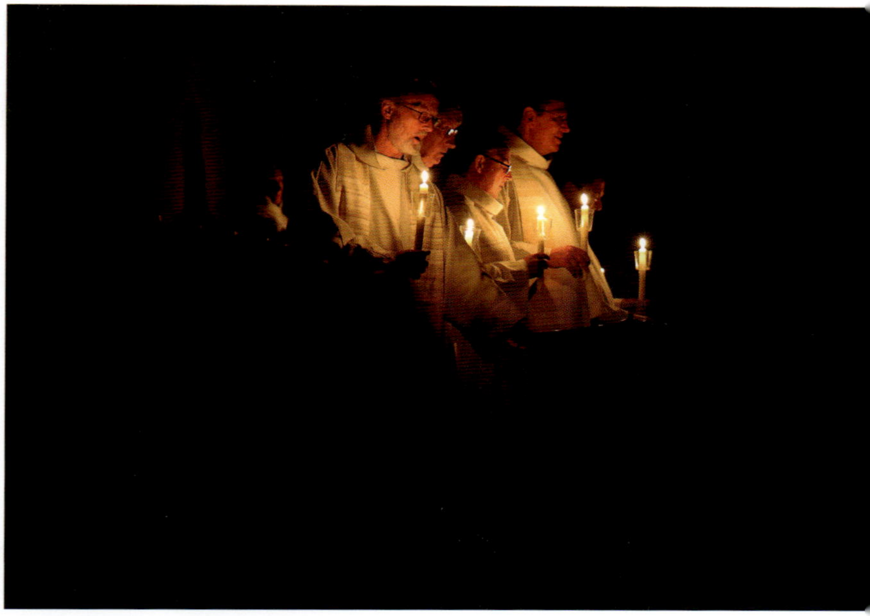

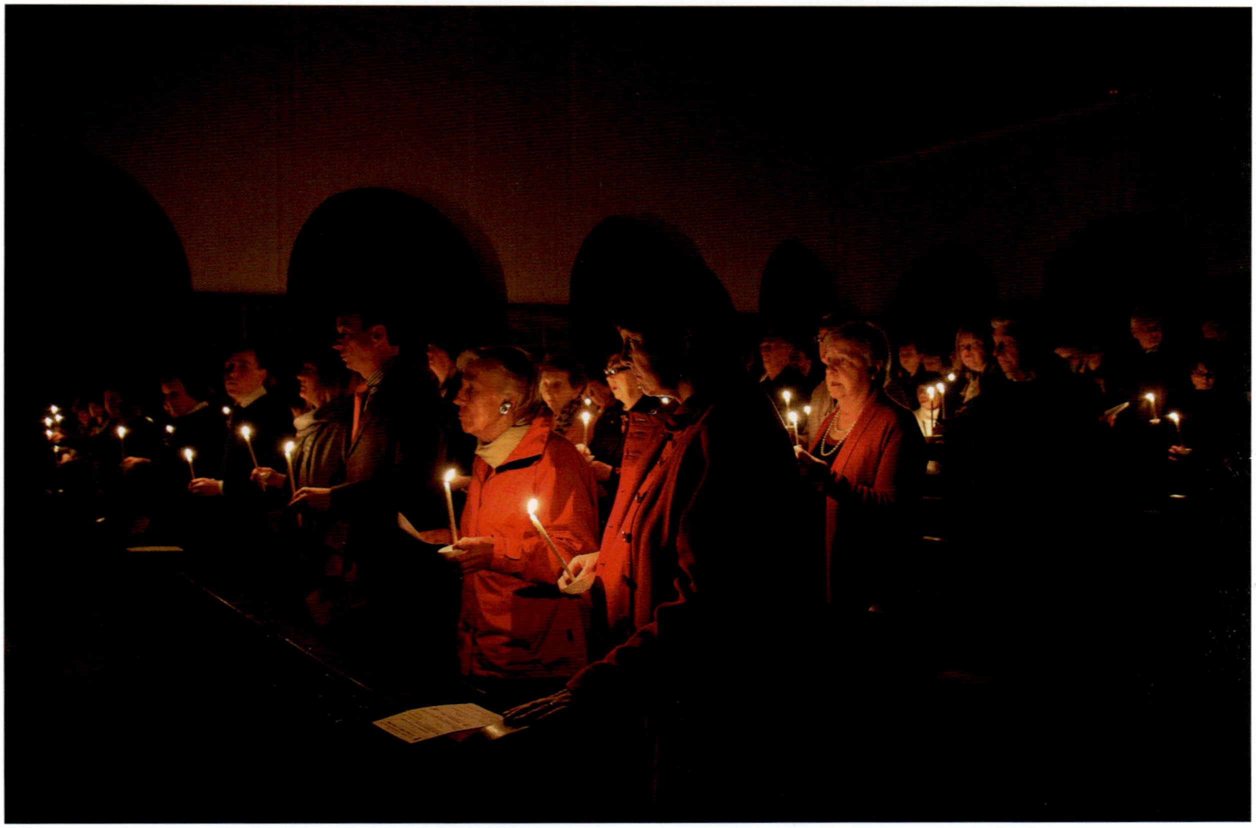

The Easter Sunday liturgy is also celebrated with full solemnity, beginning with Lauds at the later time of 8 am. After the celebration of the Conventual Mass at midday, the guests depart and the community settles down to enjoy a festive lunch. Vespers are followed by a procession around the church during which we sing the chants *Salve festa dies* and *Regnavit Dominus*. After that, for most it will be an early night.

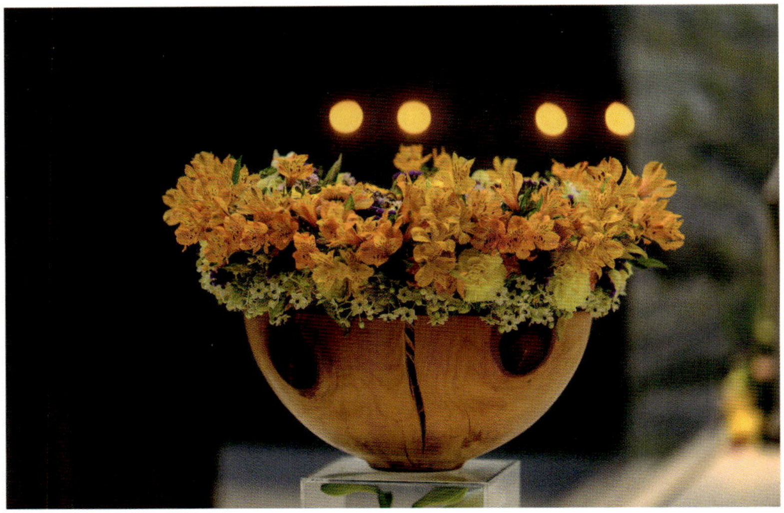

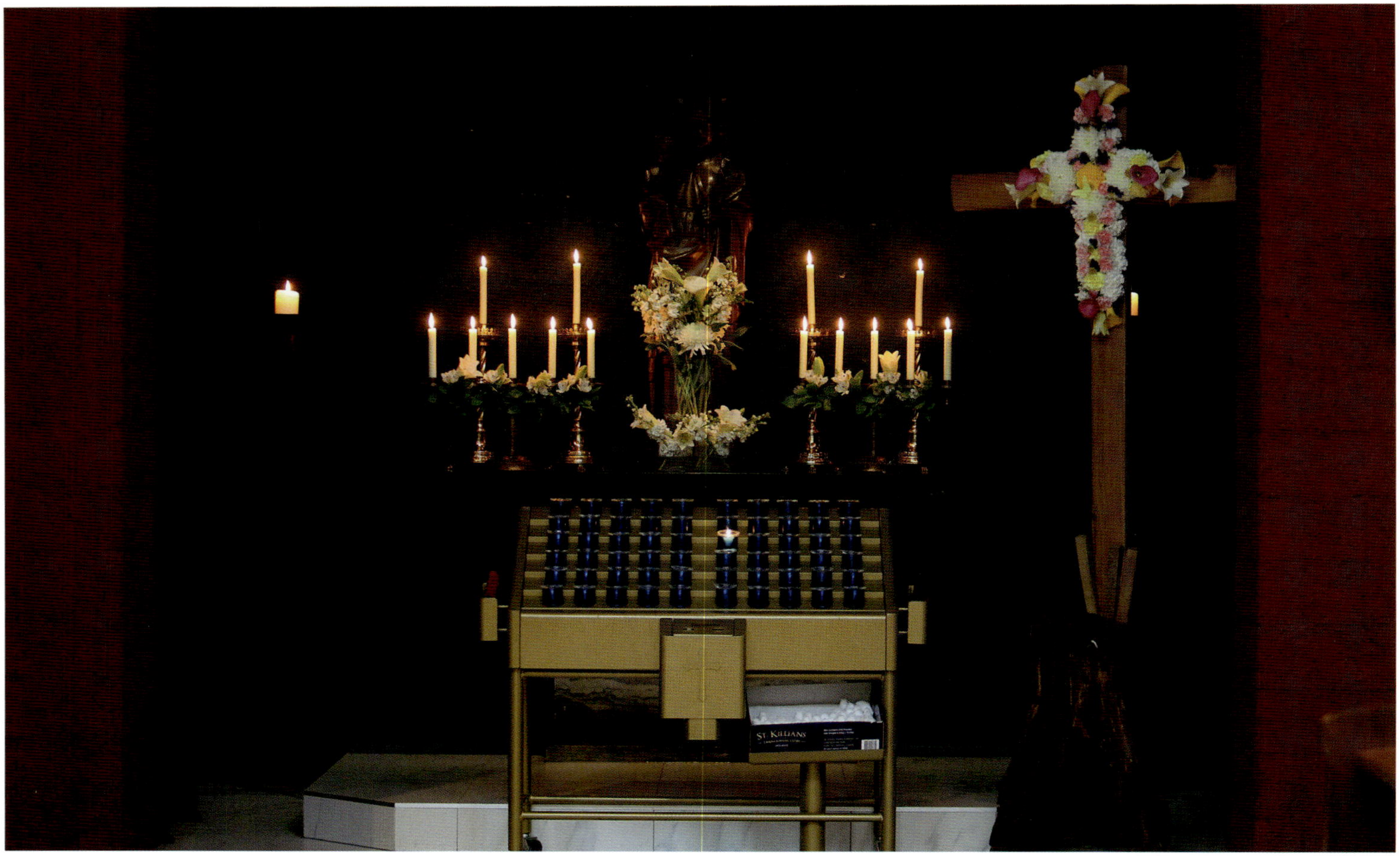

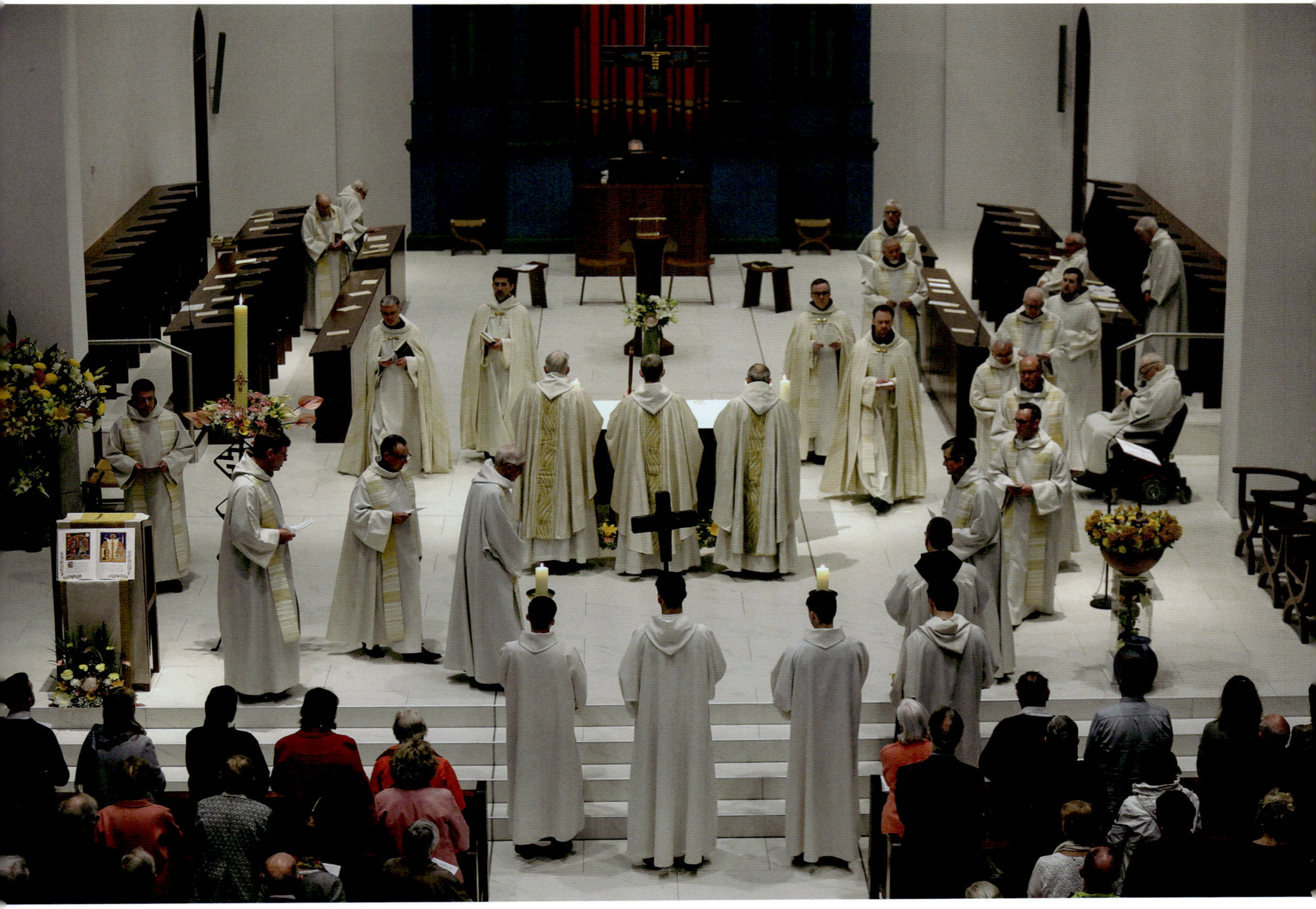

Spring in Glenstal

Two centuries of intensive planting and careful husbandry by the Barringtons and successive monk-foresters means that springtime in Glenstal is breathtakingly beautiful. Everywhere the shoots of new life are in evidence, that delicate shade of fresh green that Hildegard of Bingen called *viriditas* and which she interpreted as the colour of the Holy Spirit, the giver of life. As the season advances the flowers and colours increase and multiply. Snowdrops, crocuses and daffodils carpet the ground while overhead azaleas, rhododendron and cherry clothe the boughs. Occasionally, the bright red of a Chilean flame tree blazes against the green backdrop.

At such a time and in such a place it is easy to identify with Kavanagh's farmers in *The Great Hunger*:

Yet sometimes when the sun comes through a gap
These men know God the Father in a tree:
The Holy Spirit is the rising sap,
And Christ will be the green leaves that will come
At Easter from the sealed and guarded tomb.

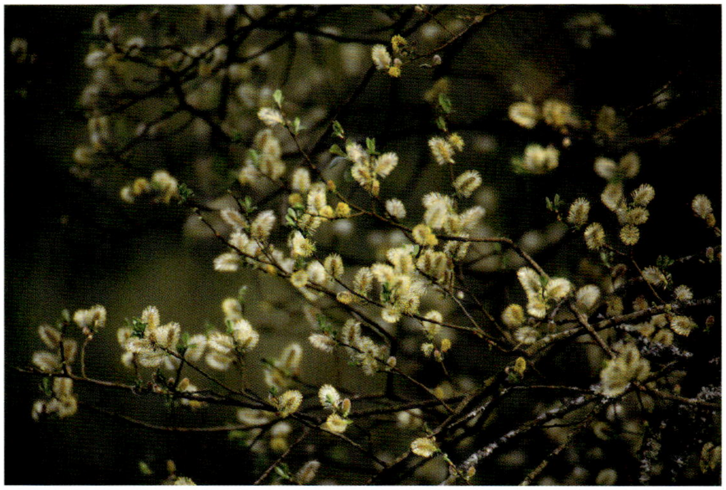

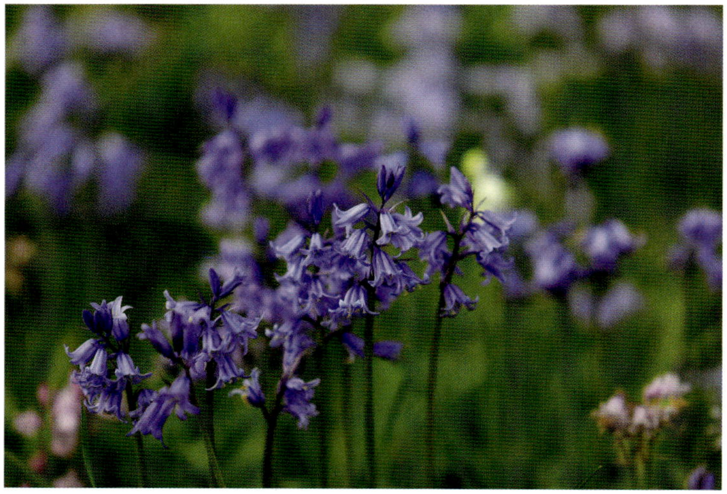

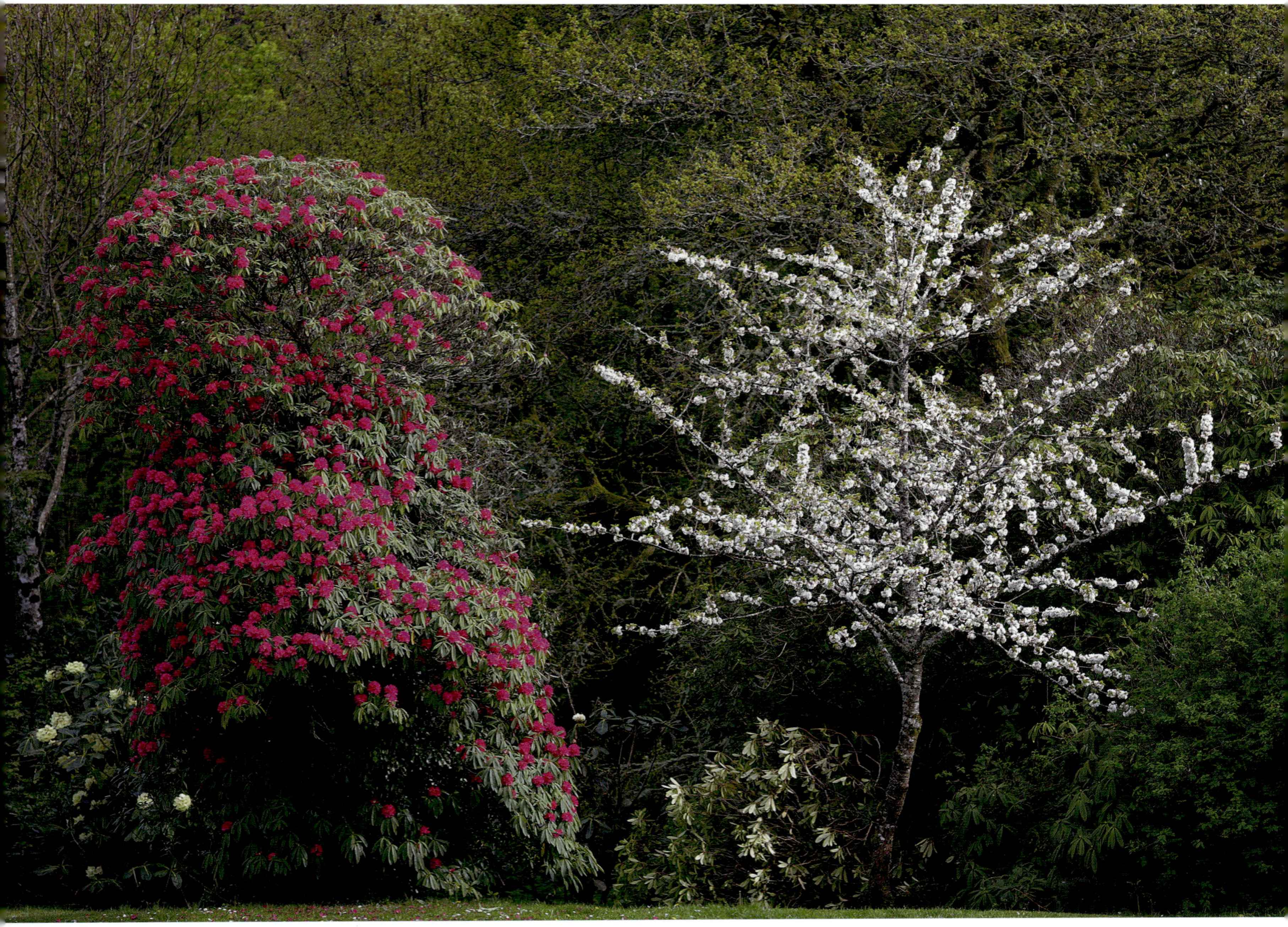

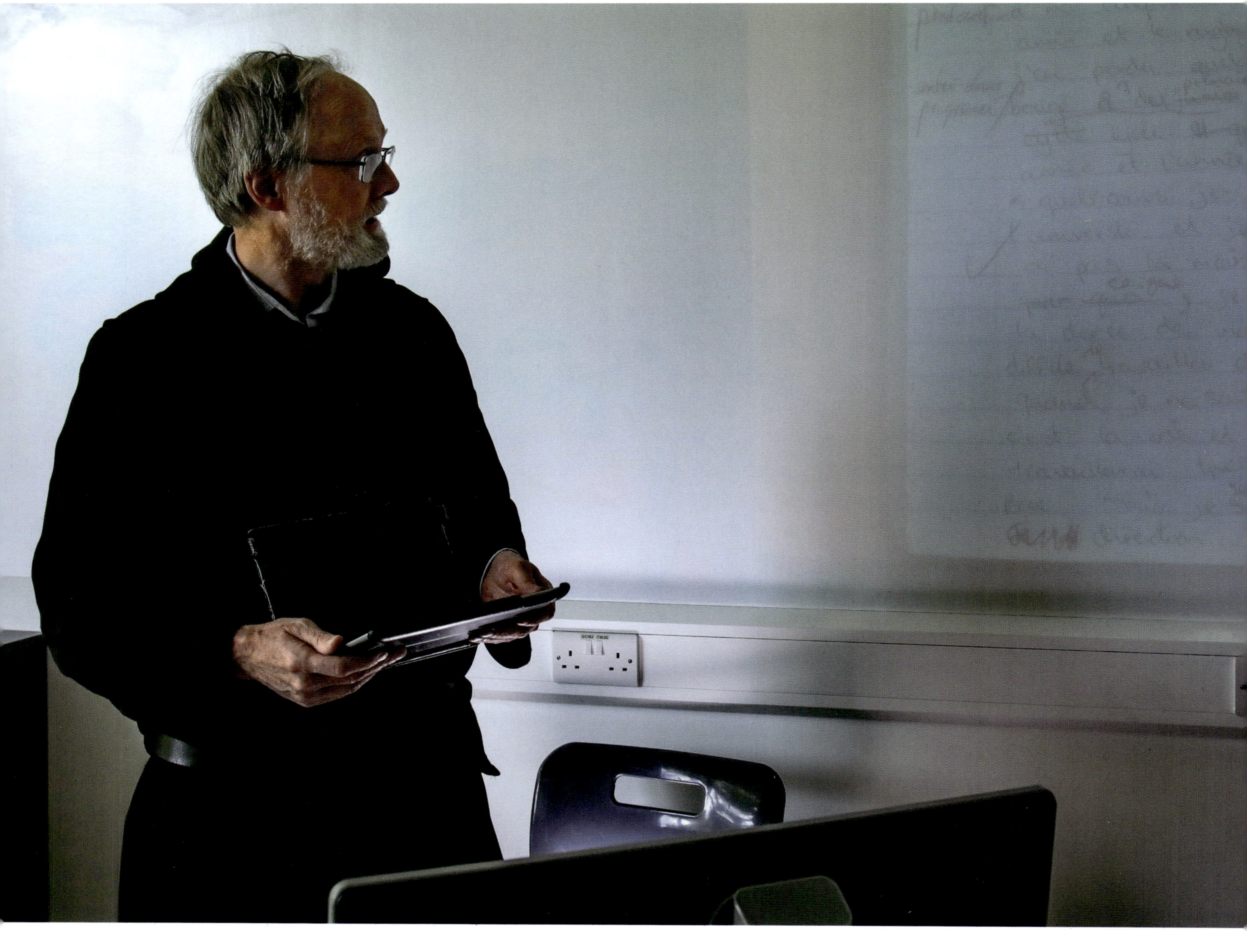

A Monk's Tale:

The Teacher

If you ask what brought me here, it's the life style. For years I thought one had to have a 'vocation' to be a monk, priest or whatever. I had a few friends who said they had one. I clearly didn't so, having qualified as a psychologist, I worked as one and prepared to 'get ahead' (in Canada, from where I come) and so on. Then someone told me that Glenstal is quite wary of people who claim to be 'called by God'. Their position is 'if the shoe fits, wear it'. I tried it for a year and got what I wanted. A God-centred existence with a rhythm of prayer, and a share in the ideals of the early Christian community. Perhaps, as some people say, that is a vocation, and I accept that, but my experience was from a secular point of view.

I teach French and Religious Education and I love it. It is primarily with the senior classes. In the former, the best technology is available in the classroom so the first thing we do some mornings is to check on the world news, thanks to a Francophone site. Then we might correct some written work. The students here know each other so well that they don't mind if I project their text on the wall with my Ipad and we correct the grammar together.

Organising exchanges has been a major and necessary addition to furthering fluency in the students. Religious Education is the best subject to teach if one has open-minded students who can see beyond the Leaving Certificate. For example, we read extracts from the Koran, sometimes with a Muslim in the class, and thus understand religions, their history and the questions which preoccupy us all the better. I give my view, like anyone else can; the bottom line is intellectual honesty! 'Social conscience' work is backed up by projects carried out in remote parts of Africa during the summer vacation.

Fr John

A Monk's Tale:

The Chaplain

'We'll call back for you after supper because you aren't going to last two hours in this place', joked the friend who had given me the lift to Glenstal. I was about to start what was called a 'Live-in'. Abbot Celestine thought I should give it a try before committing to a more permanent arrangement. I suspect he didn't hold out much hope for me getting much further so, what harm?

A month later I finished the 'Live-in' and headed home to prepare to return to Glenstal for a year's novitiate. The four weeks had ignited something in me that had been dormant. I wasn't quite sure what it was, but I had no choice except to pursue it. I could leave at any time.

The day arrived for me to join the novitiate. I took the train this time. The nearer I got to Limerick Junction, the more stressed I became. This was madness. Before the train arrived, I decided that this was the stupidest idea I had ever had. And I had come up with some crazy things for sure.

The train would stop in Limerick Junction where a Fr James was due to drive me on to Glenstal. I decided that I would not get off the train. I would go on to Cork instead and forget about this cracked idea. What was I thinking? This madness had gone too far.

The brakes of the train screeched their way into the Junction, bringing the train to a halt. I sat there while passengers got off. I wasn't budging. But then the train didn't move. Through the window I could see a monk frantically looking around for me. Still the train wasn't budging, for some reason it was delayed. After what seem like and eternity, there was nothing else for it. I had to get off.

'Hello, I'm Fr James', said the monk impatiently. He drove me to Glenstal. I kept thinking that I could high tail it out of the place at any time.

Some 37 years later, and I am still in Glenstal. What has kept me here throughout has been the place, the people and the presence of God in both. If I died tomorrow, I wouldn't regret a day of my time here.

I have lasted more than 'two hours in this place'. At least I have gotten this far. A day at a time. God has a great sense of humour. *Deo Gratias.*

Fr Denis

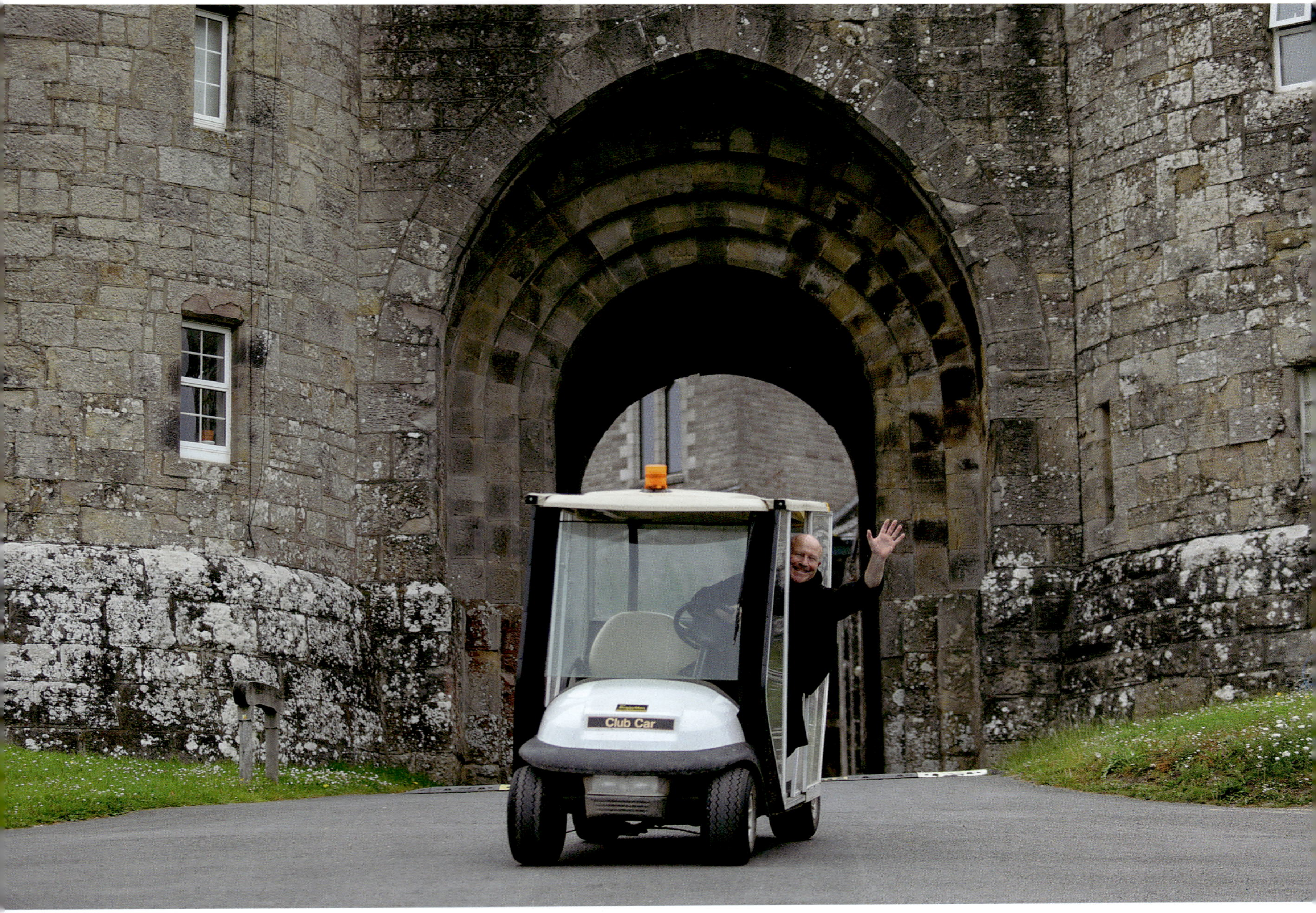
Club Car

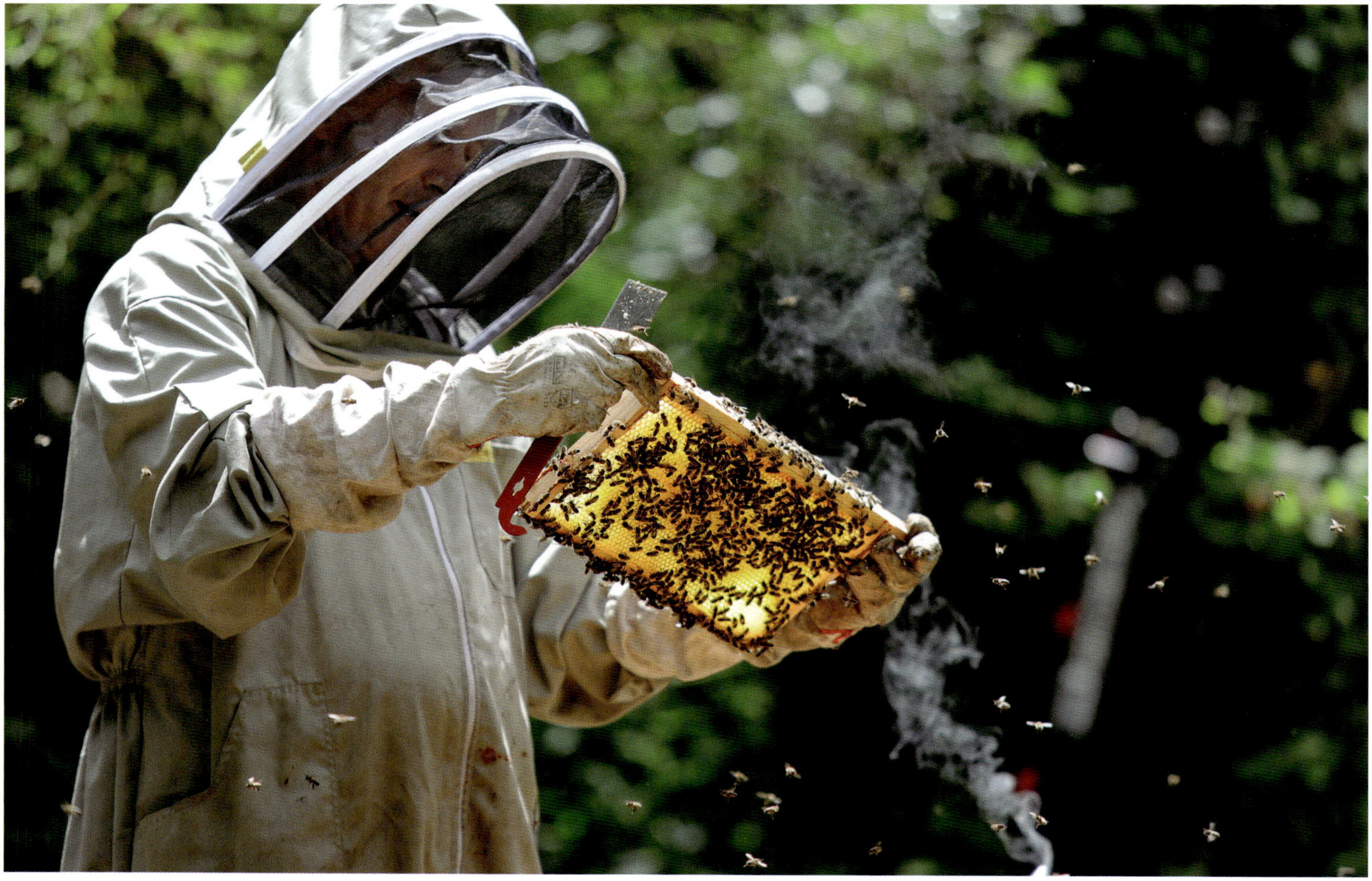

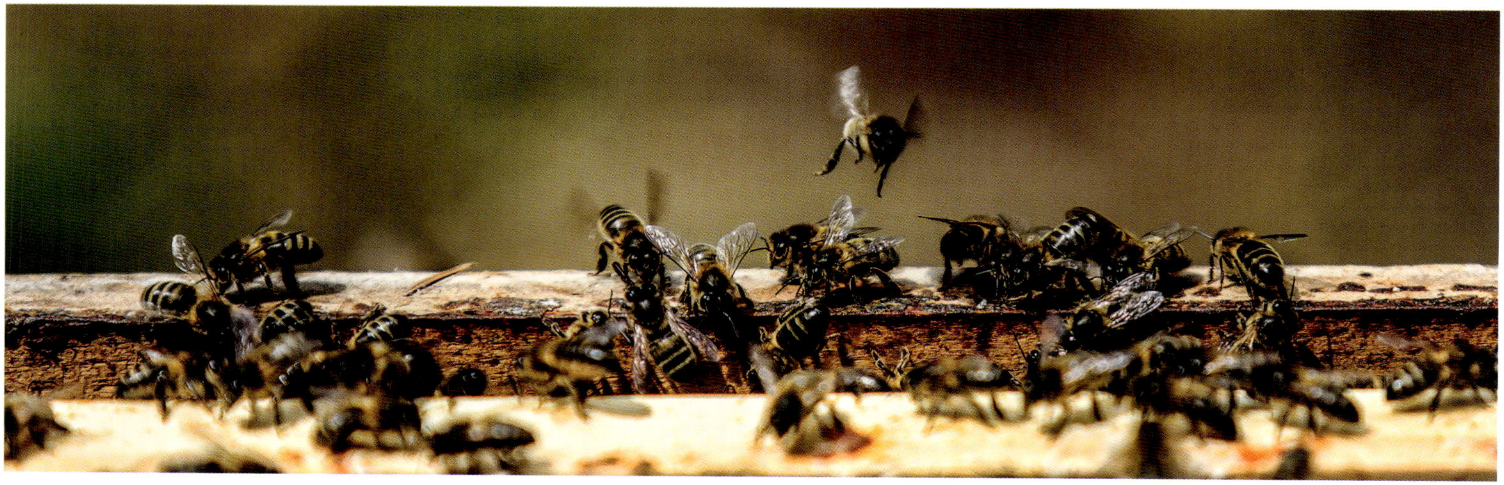

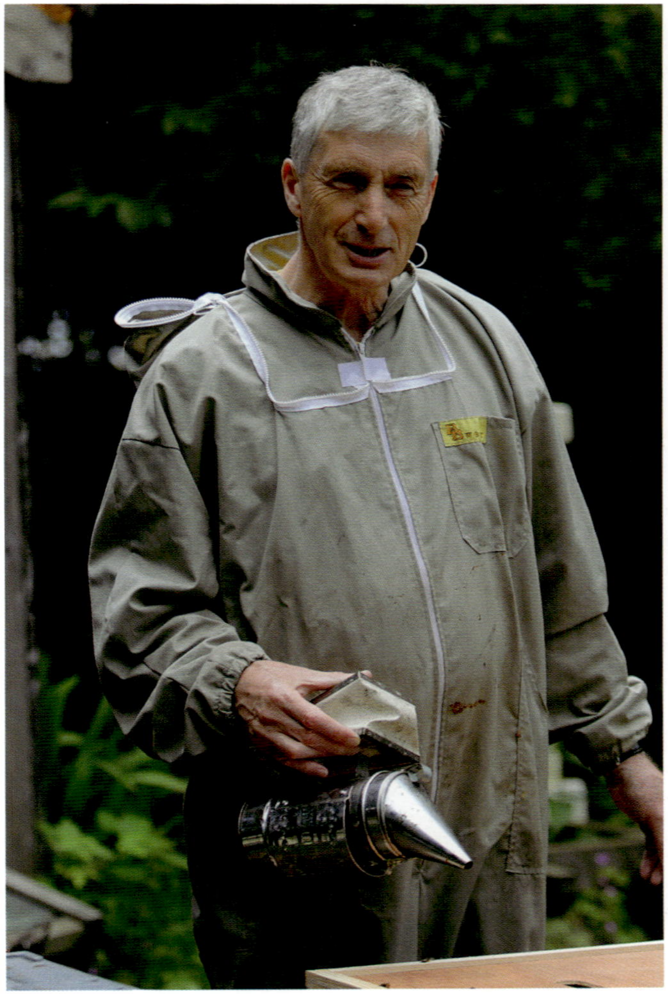

A Monk's Task:

The Beekeeper

I hesitate to single out bees for attention. They are important but so are so many other insects. Bees were always important in monasteries, as they provided much needed wax for making candles and honey as a sweetener.

As I get older I realise the bees are happier and probably do better with less management by me. They self-manage very well with skills developed over the last 35 million years.

Beekeeping has provided me with years of entertainment and fascination - you never know it all. I love to go out and watch the entrance of the hives and marvel at the industry of the bees as they fly in laden with brightly coloured pollen on their legs. Pollen is the fish of their fish and chips - the protein - while nectar is the chips, the carbohydrate or energy food.

The great thing about bees is that you don't have to look after them 24/7. You don't need to find a minder when you go away, as you do for your dog or the cat. But then they are not pets.

And bees are respectful of their environment. Saint Francis de Sales sums this up well when he says; "The bee collects honey from flowers in such a way as to do the least damage or destruction to them and she leaves them whole, undamaged and fresh, just as she found them."

Fr Simon

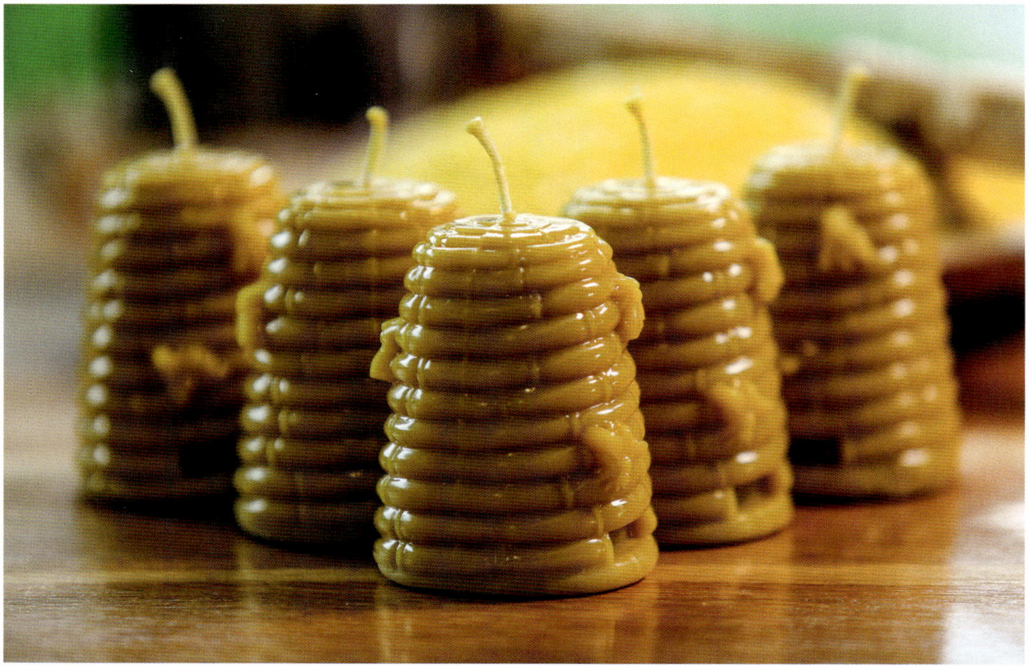

A Monk's Task:

Candles

A candle's flame symbolises Christ's light and presence dispelling the darkness of the world. Pure beeswax candles were long preferred for use in church worship, with bleached wax used for joyous celebrations and unbleached for more sombre occasions such as funerals.

Beeswax gift candles are made at Glenstal Abbey where, with the help of our bees, we are beginning to make altar candles for use in the liturgy. We are reminded by the Easter *Exsultet* of this sacred use of earth's gifts as the cantor implores God to 'accept this candle, a solemn offering, the work of bees and of your servants' hands, an evening sacrifice of praise, this gift from your most holy Church ... for it is fed by melting wax, drawn out by mother bees to build a torch so precious.'

Br Justin

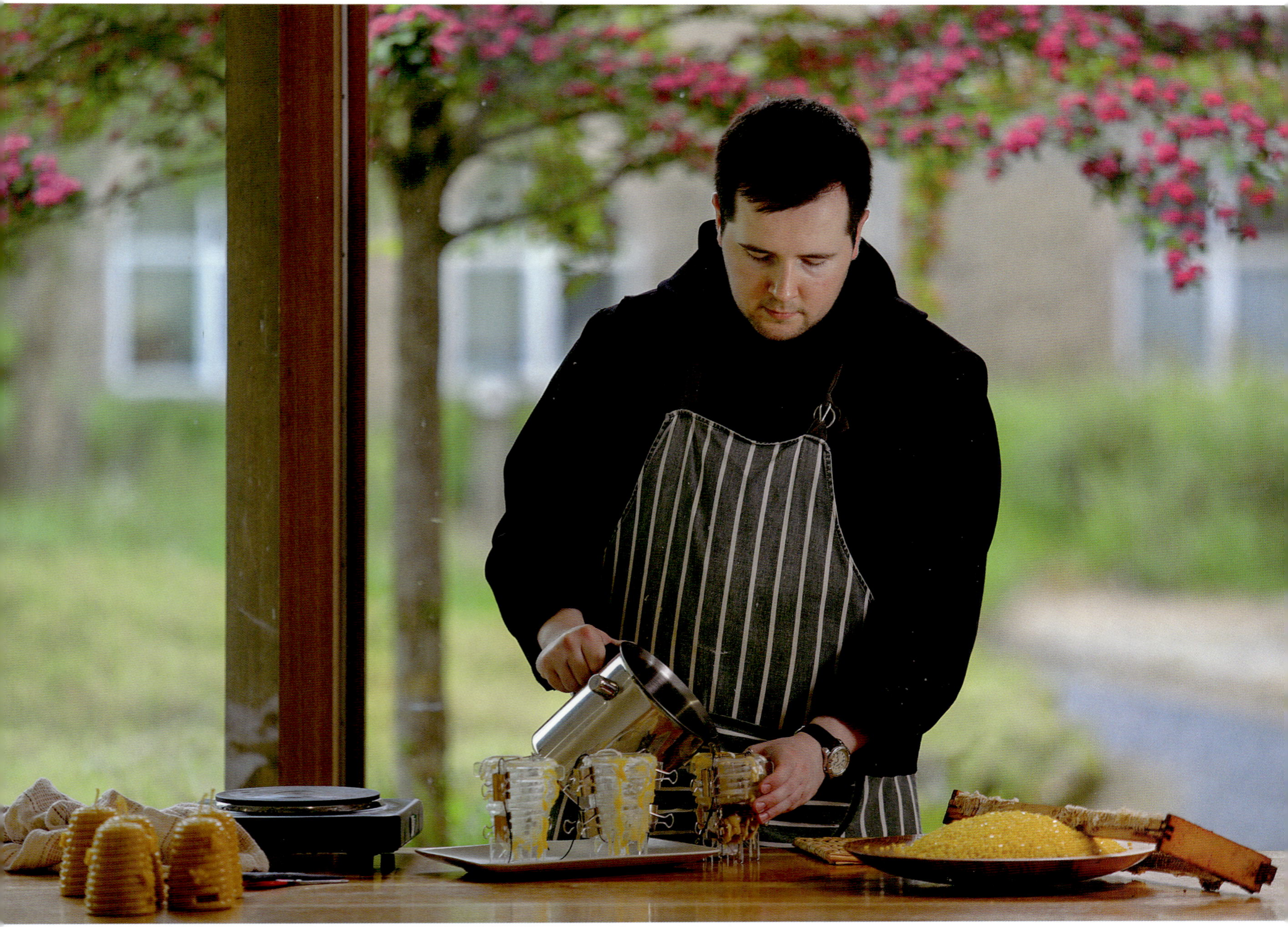

A Monk's Tale:

The Archivist

It is probably too easy, with the benefit of hindsight, to imagine that one had experiences or wonderings as a child and nostalgically to embroider these if they did occur. Crystal clear in my memory, however, is one wondering I had when I was nine years of age. While walking on the Curragh Plains, where I grew up, I wondered what real prayer is and resolved that whatever it is, I wanted to experience it. Equally clear is my stumbling on and reading, in 1964, Dom David Knowles' early book *The Monastic Order in England* (1940), which gave me my first glimpse of the Benedictine life and images of which, totally uninvited, constantly resurfaced.

In the Summer of 1968, I – now a student of history – was invited to Glenstal to the relatively new Ecumenical Conference. Within twenty-four hours of arrival, I knew that this was where I was going to spend the rest of my life. Always interested in the liturgy, I intuitively realised that here was a place where prayer, common and private, was the life-blood that held the place together and that the community was also part of a great tradition. Here, too, scholarship was respected and encouraged.

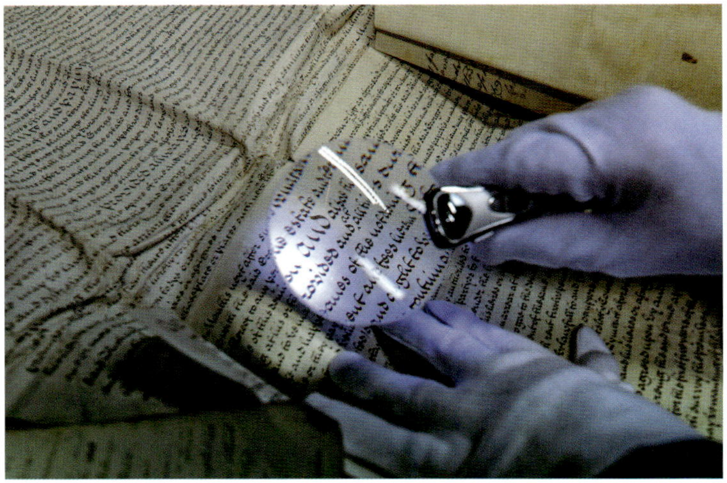

When a monk makes profession, he sings the *Suscipe*, a rather tear-jerking Latin chant, based on Psalm 118, v.116, which reads, 'Receive me, O Lord, according to your promise, and I shall live: and let me not be confounded in my hope'. The whole community joins him in this chant which expresses our shared project and goal. Like any way of life, the monastic path abounds in hazards and apparent impasses. Sometimes, the 'Receive me' chant can seem a huge mistake but after fifty years I am still singing it. And I am still trying to find out what prayer is.

Fr Henry

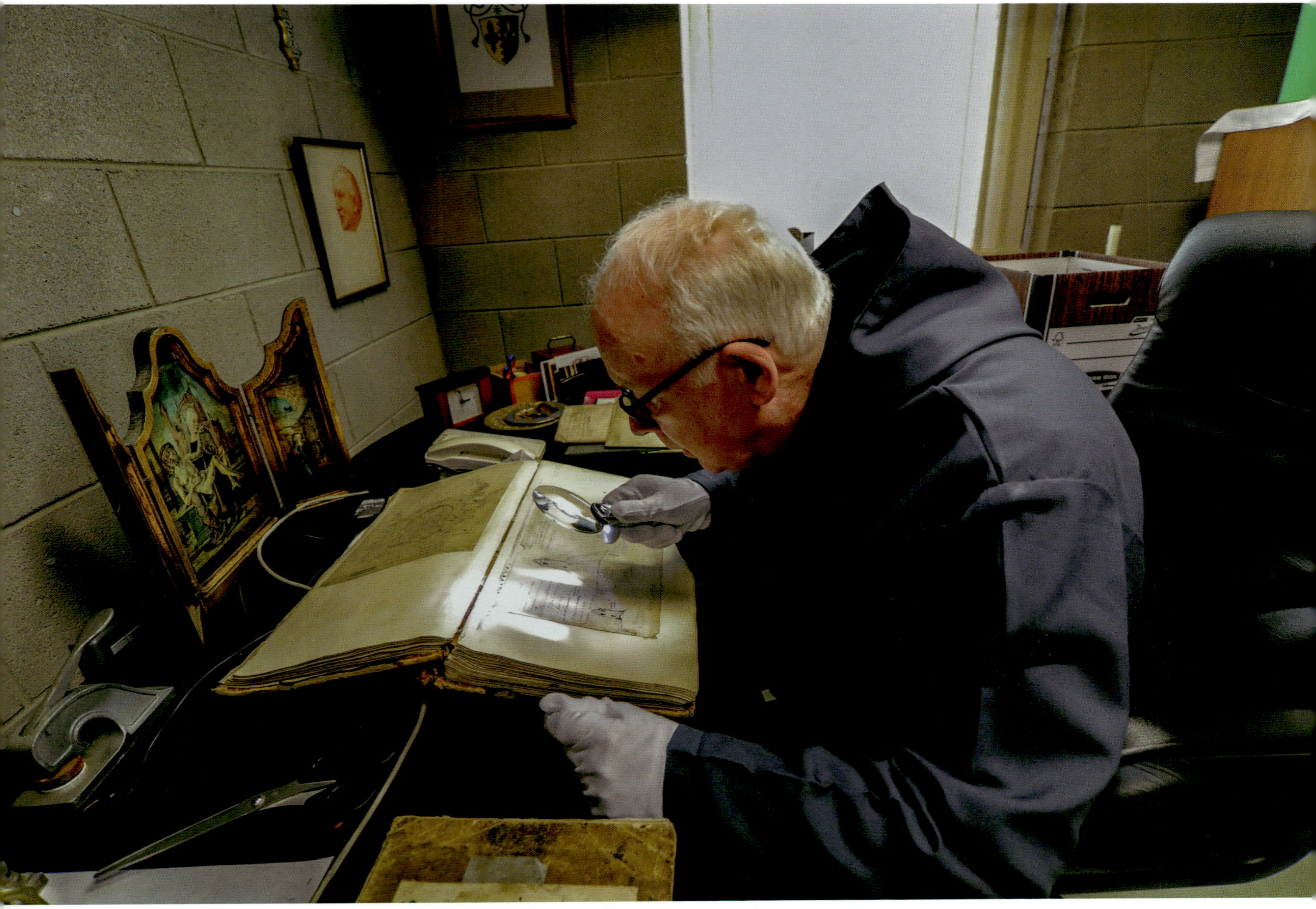

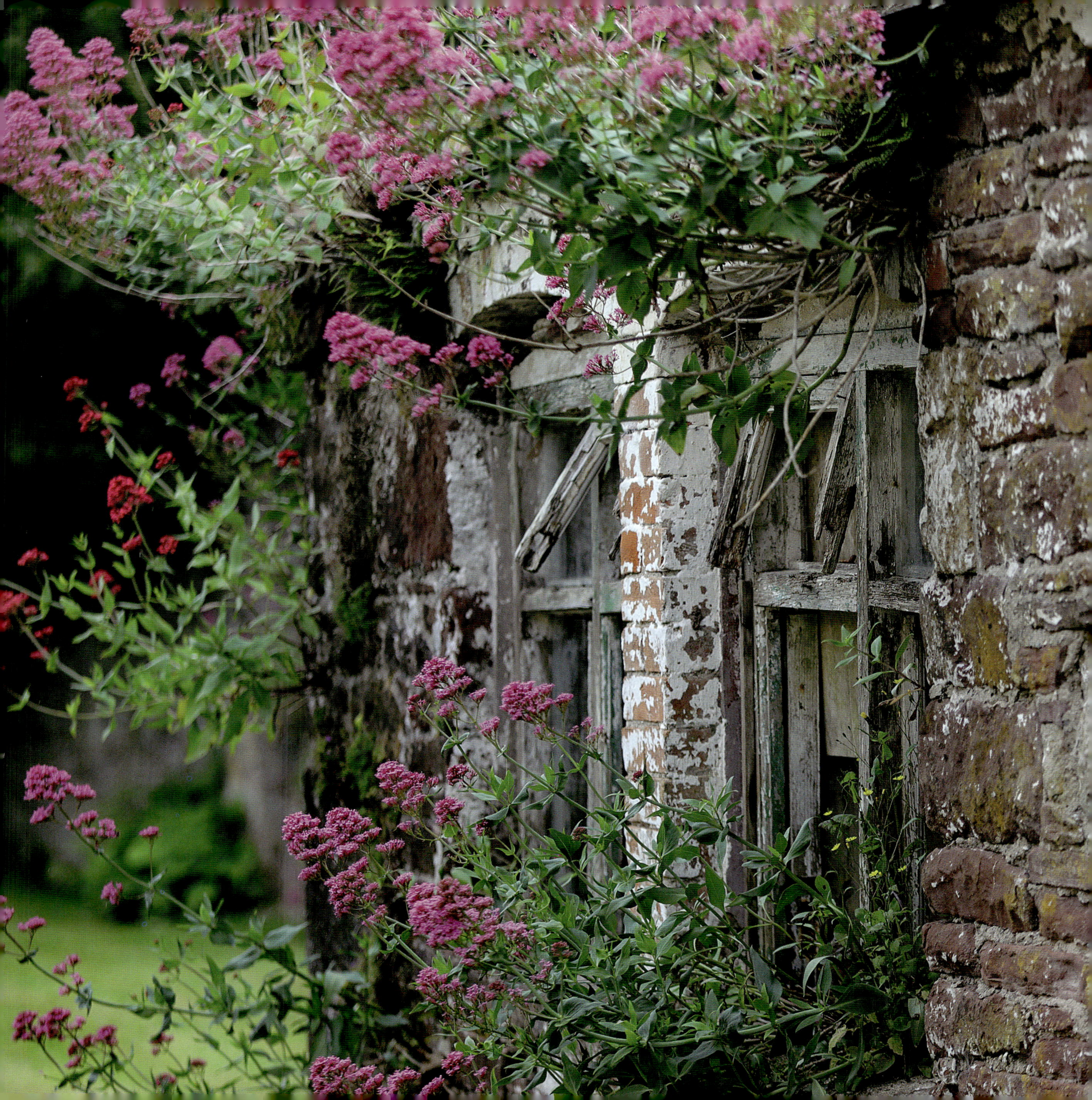

Summer

The word 'PAX' and a cross are emblazoned about the entrance to Glenstal as they are at the entrance to every monastery. Meaning 'peace', it represents our wish for anyone who comes here but particularly for those who arrive as guests and pilgrims and who, in St Benedict's words, 'are never lacking in a monastery.' Between groups, day-trippers and resident guests, the community receives around 8,000 visitors each year, not to mention those who come to attend the services or to walk the grounds. In recent years, through the generosity of a benefactor, we have improved the facilities for visitors, enabling us to better fulfil the Rule's instruction that 'every guest should be received as if they were Christ.'

None of this would be possible without the support and generosity of our staff. The housekeeping department ensures that both schoolboys and visitors enjoy a safe and secure environment. The receptionists see that visitors and callers receive a warm and efficient welcome while those in the bursar's office ensure we have the resources to pay for it. Although recently leased, the farm plays an important role in our environment and the well-tended paddocks and grazing cattle provide a bucolic backdrop to all that goes on here.

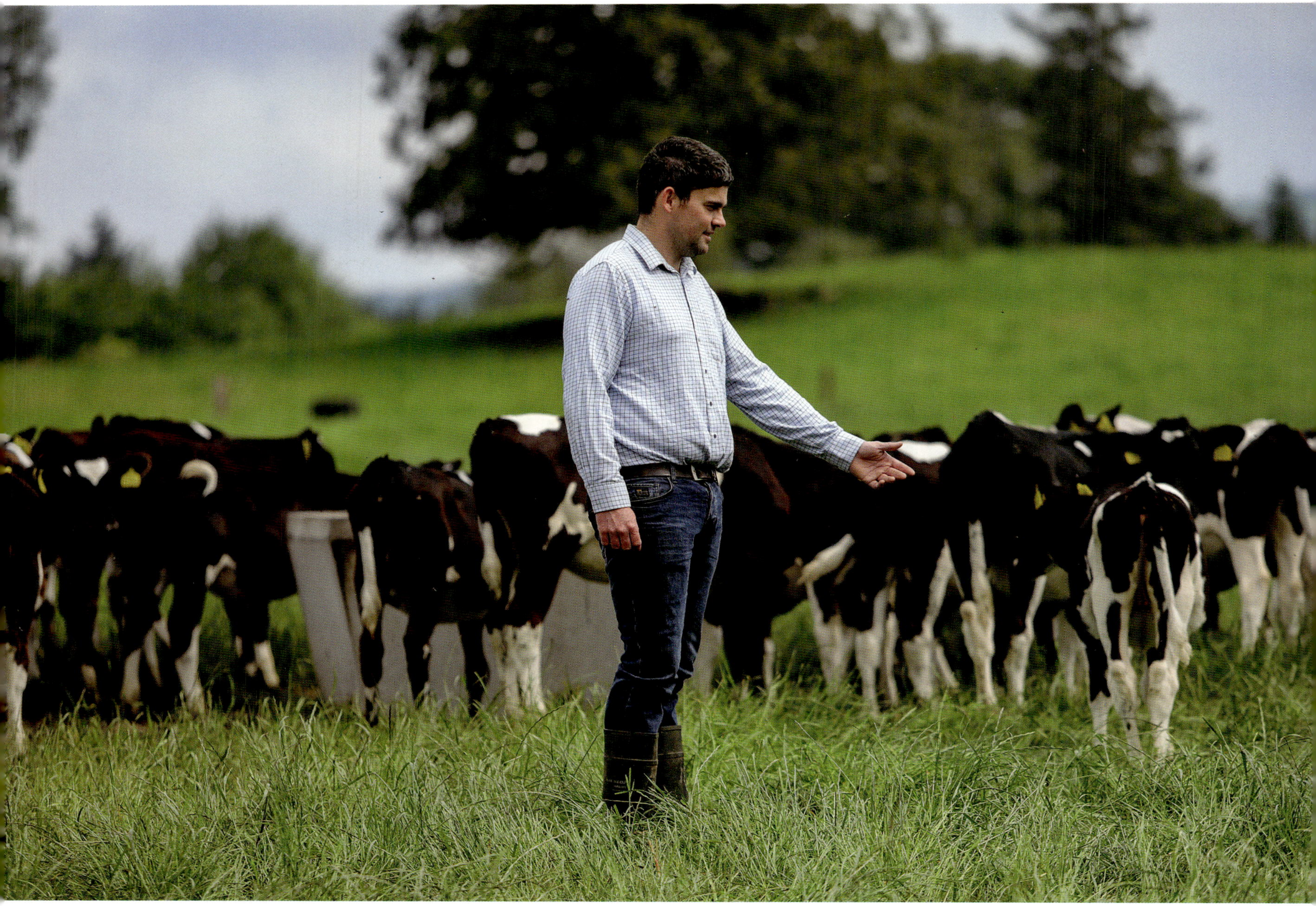

Vincent Crowe is the farmer at Glenstal Abbey farm where he tends a herd of 140 crossbred Jersey-Friesian cows. With the monastic community he is committed to maintaining the tradition of dairy farming, both as a source of income for the community and as a sustainable use of the land. This will entail developing the herd and updating the milking parlour.

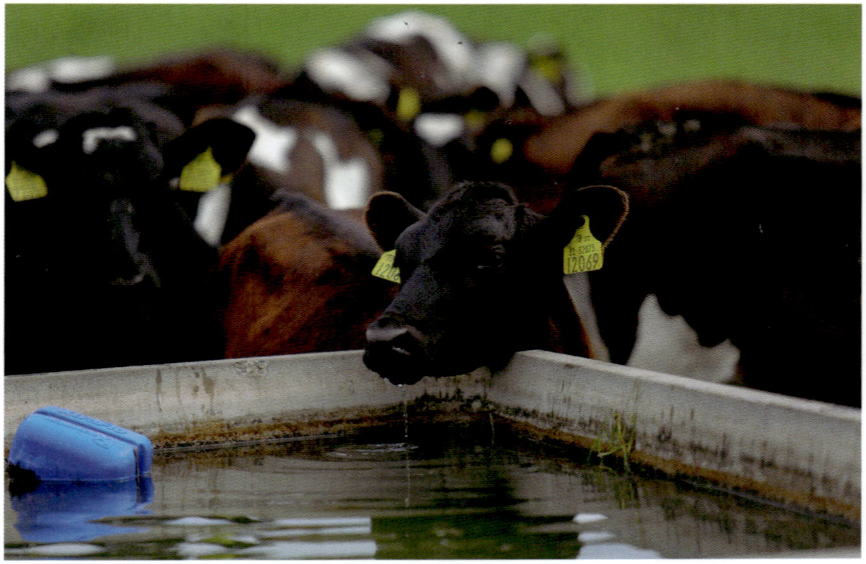

Johnny Davis, from Murroe, worked at Glenstal Abbey Farm for forty years, a job he has loved since he left school. Pictured here shortly before his retirement in July 2019, he and his wife Margaret lived in Glenstal where they raised their two sons, Gavin and Adrian. Although looking forward to retirement, he admits that he will miss the rhythm of life and work around the place.

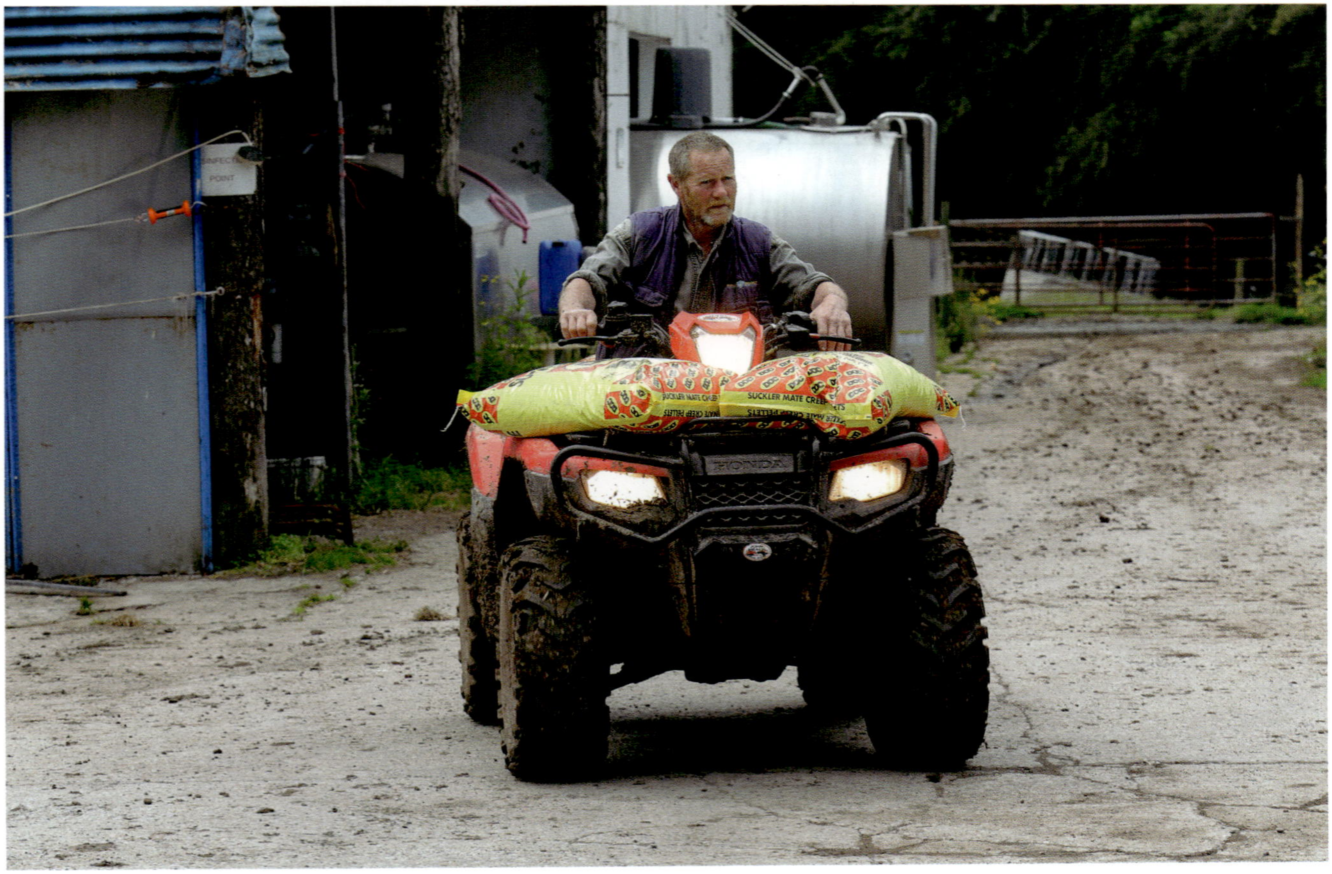

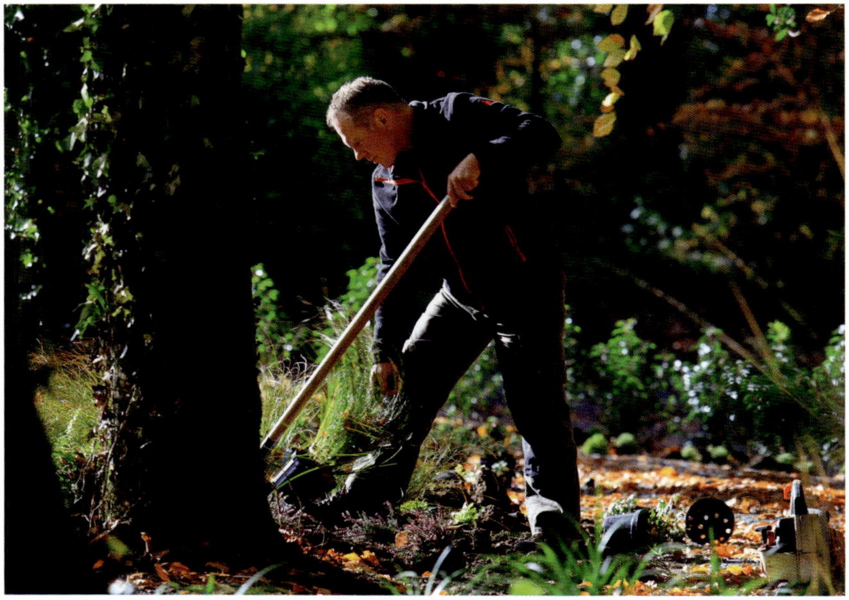

The housekeeping and maintenance departments keep the buildings and the grounds in trim and the catering staff accomplish the miraculous by providing a delicious diet with which neither the most fastidious teenager nor pickiest monk can find fault. Likewise, the nurses and infirmary team ensure that, regardless of age or stage, the sick are treated with reverence, respect and good humour. Since the community arrived here in 1927 we have been blessed with loyal and faithful employees who collaborate with us in trying to maintain Glenstal as a 'household of God.'

Left: Johnny Buckley at Glenstal Abbey gardens.
Below: Maintenance at the monastery from left to right, Gerard Gardiner, Paddy O'Connor, Maintenance Manager, Pat Daly, George Boyle, Brian Doherty, David Holmes and Eamonn Slattery.

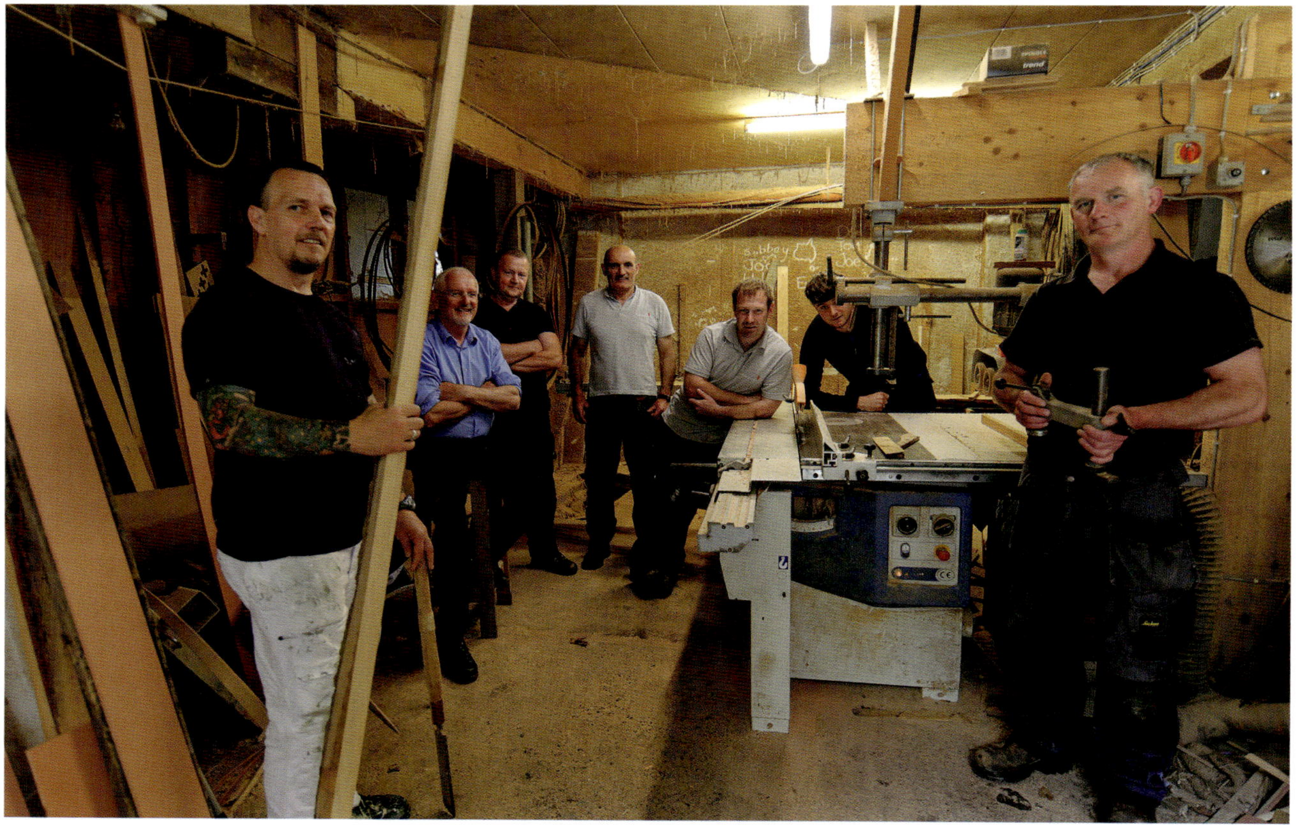

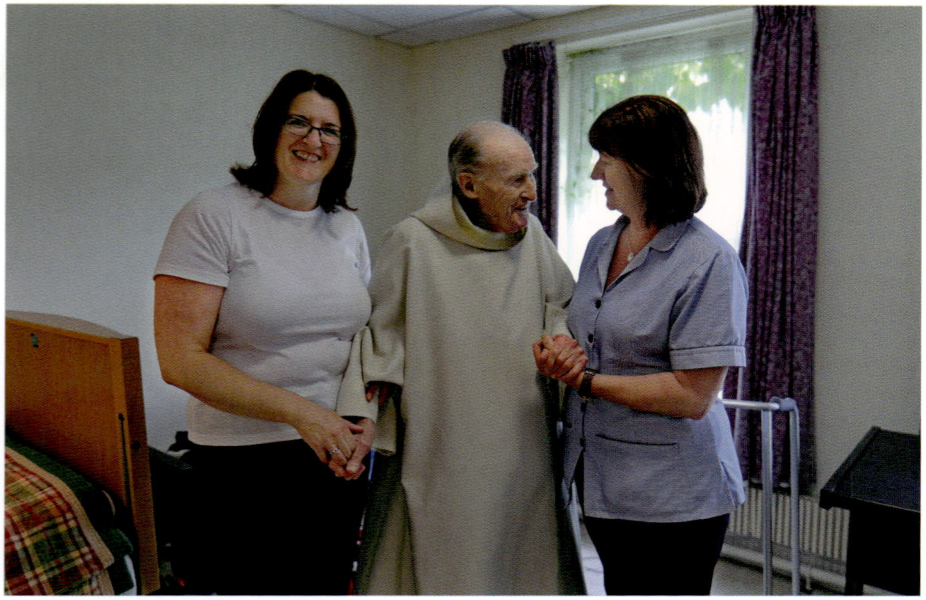

Left: Fr Anshelm with carers Tina Rainsford and Bernie Boyle, at Glenstal Abbey.
Below: front row, from left, Helen Maher, Deirdre Power, Mary Fitzgibbon, Jackie Hoban, back row from left, Mary O'Dwyer, Edel Guerin, Oonagh Bermingham, Mary Quigley and Carol Redfern.

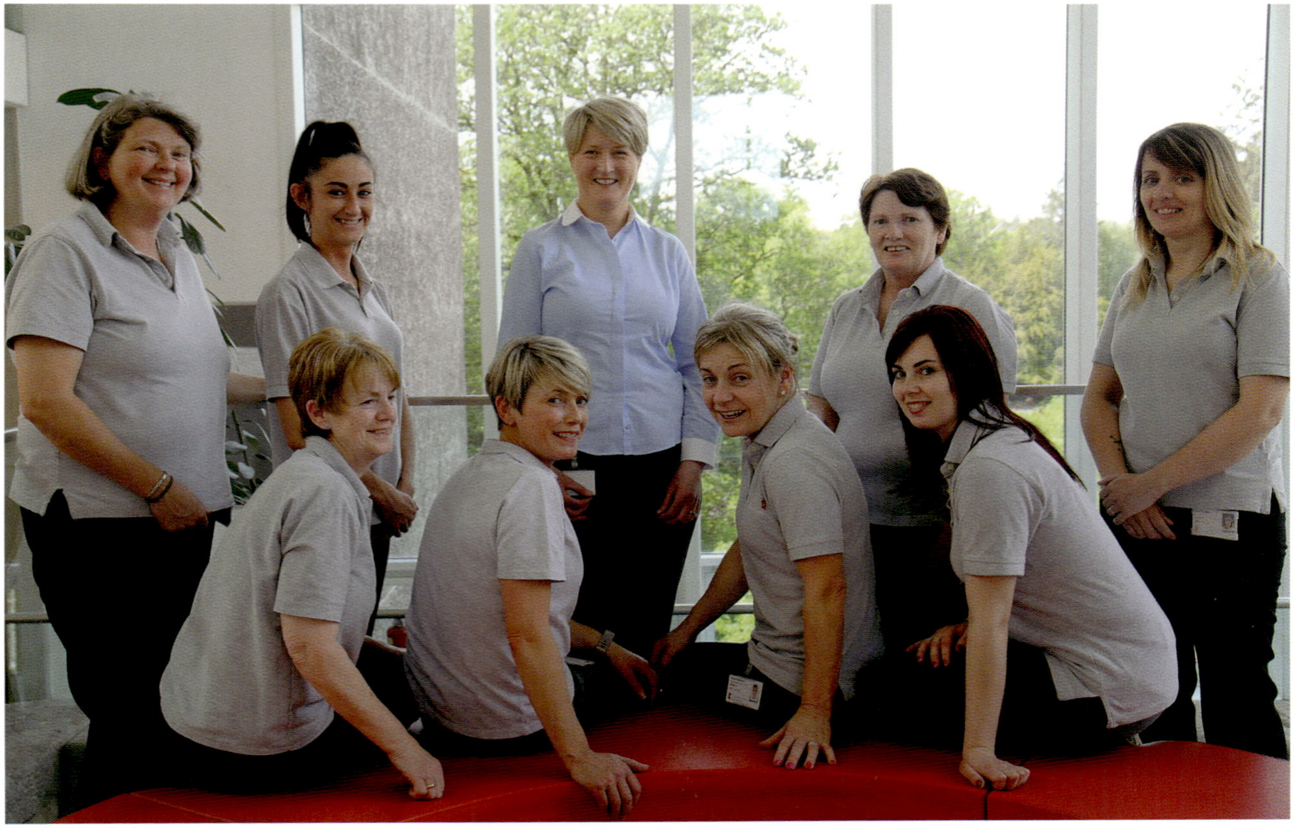

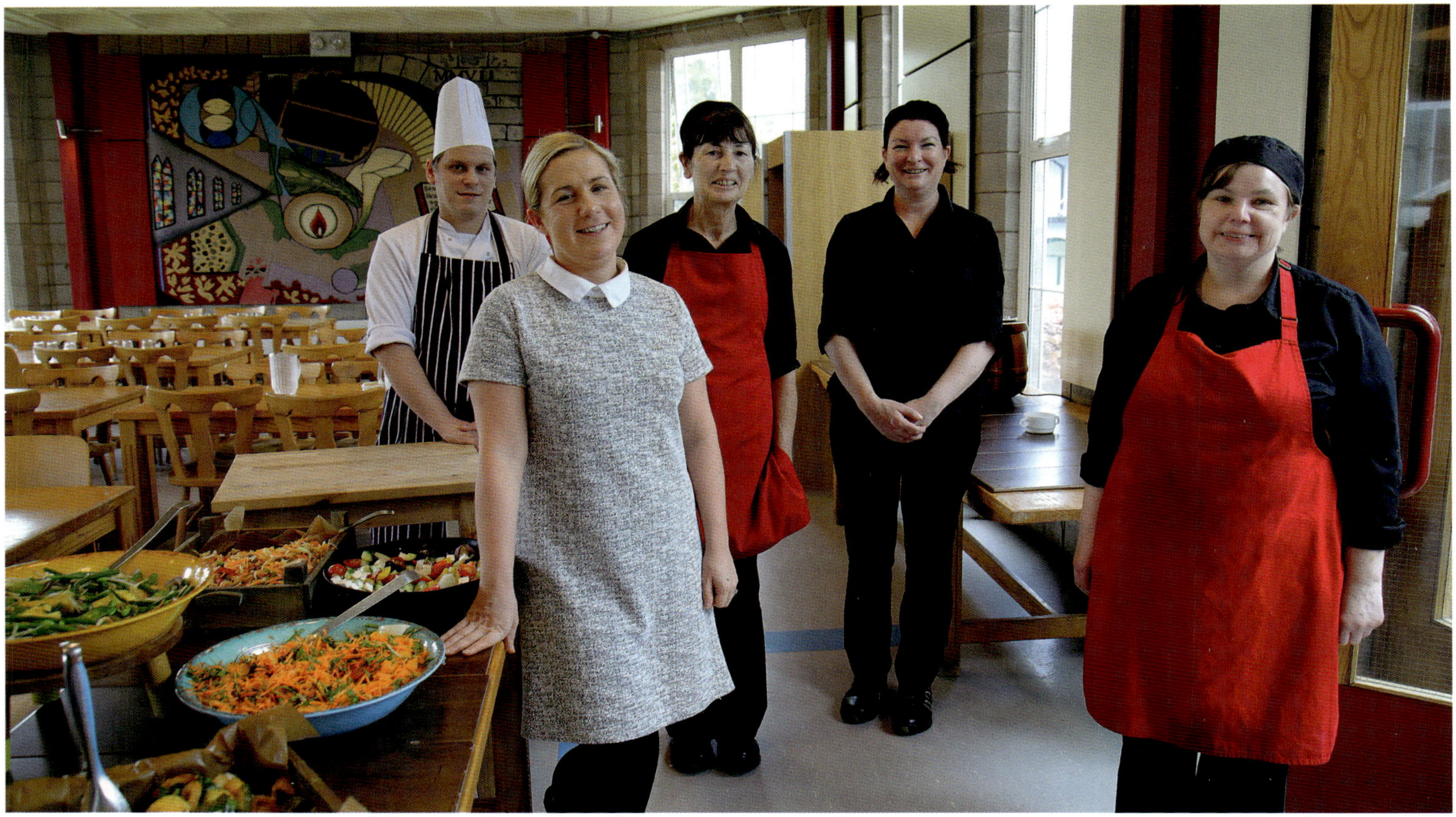

Above: Catering Staff at Glenstal Abbey School, Amy Byrne, Tomas Mydlek, Helen Rush, Wendy Cosgrove, Mags Wixted.
Right: Wendy Cosgrove, serving students Rory Woodcock and Clovis Hanbury-Tenison.

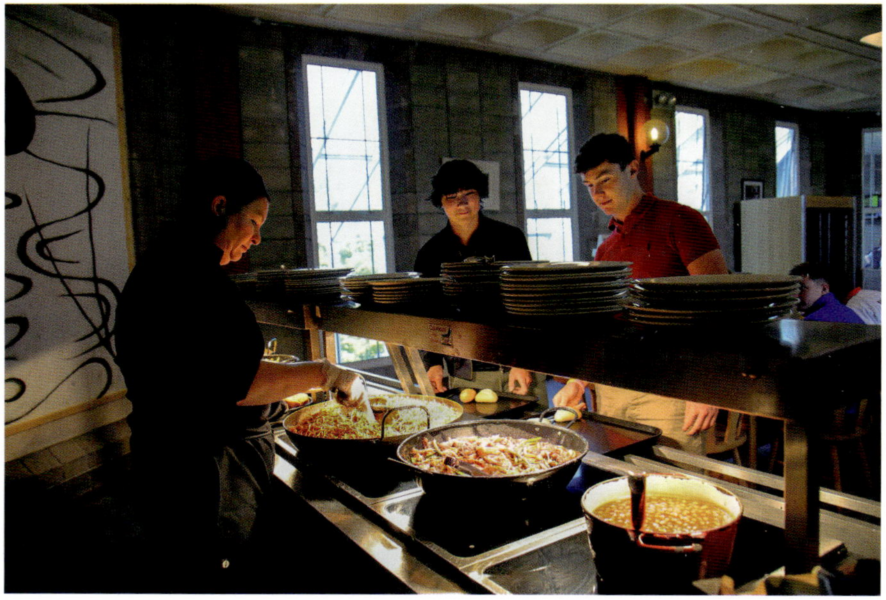

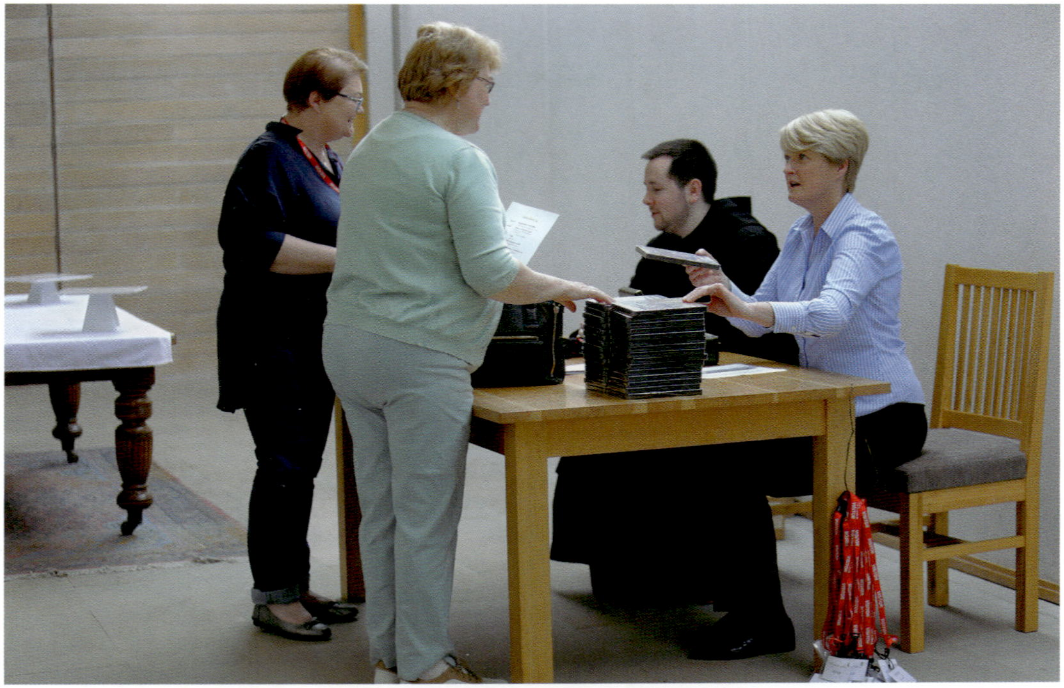

Left: Br Justin and Oonagh Bermingham greet Joan Finn, left and Ann Lawlor as they register for the annual Ladies Retreat.

Below: Fr Columba with a retreat group.

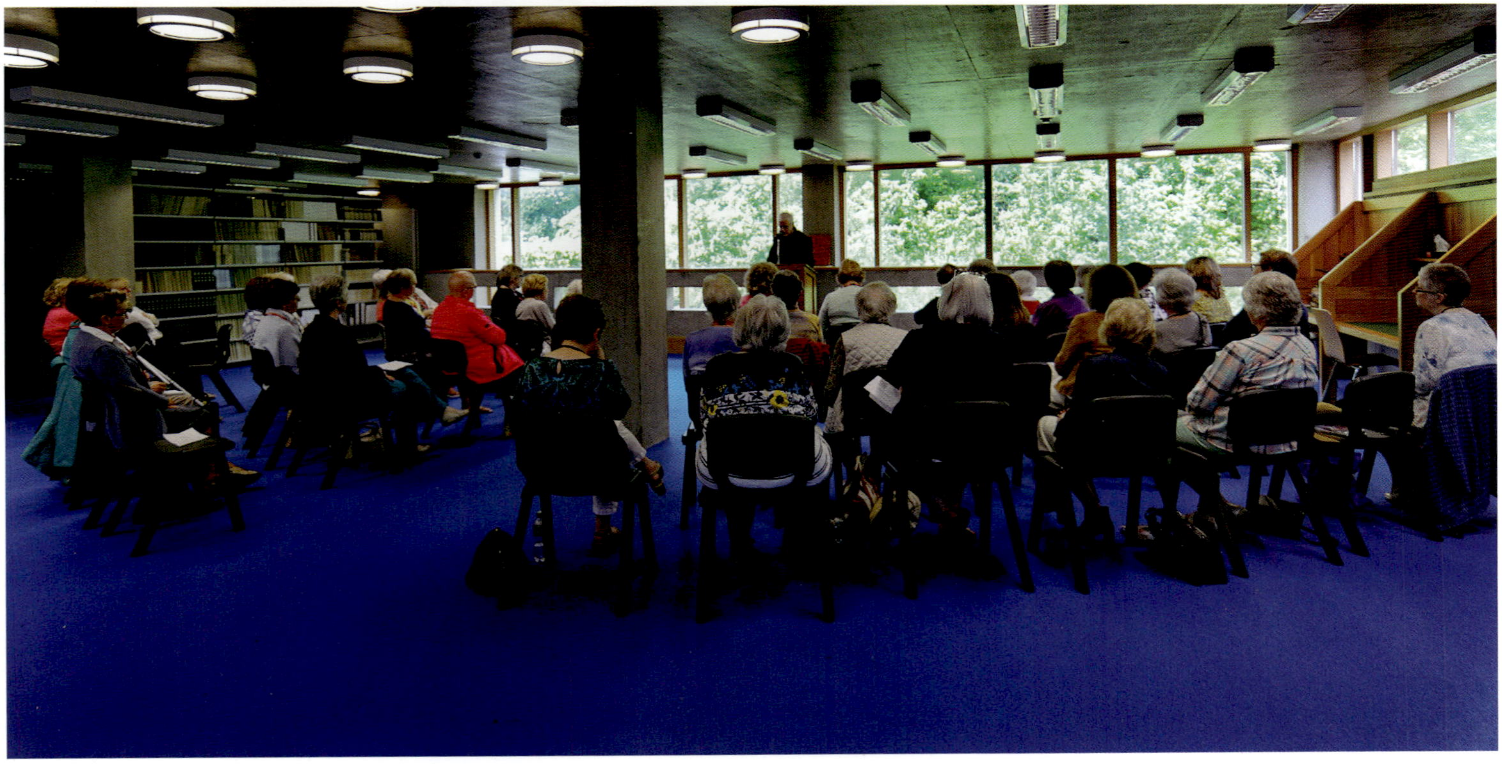

The Summer School Term

In the school, the rhythm changes as the third and sixth year boys focus on the preparing for the Junior and Leaving Certificate exams. On the sports front, the emphasis also changes as the various rugby competitions wind to a close, and tennis and track and field athletics take their place. For the seniors, the priority is finding a quiet place to study and striking a balance between books and recreation. The monastery library with its roomy study carrels is a favourite place in which to work, as is the school library where its star-vaulted roof and stone carvings provide ample material for distraction and daydreaming.

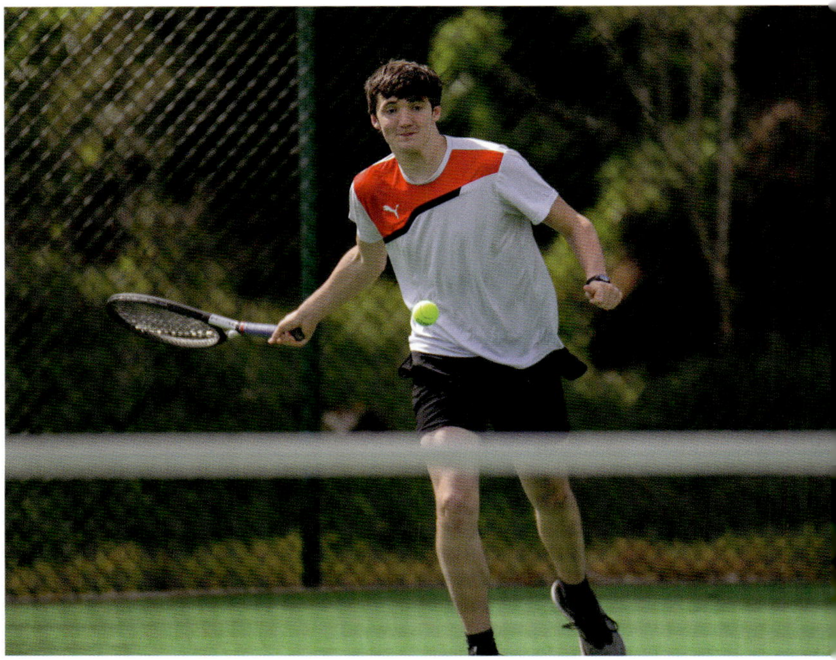

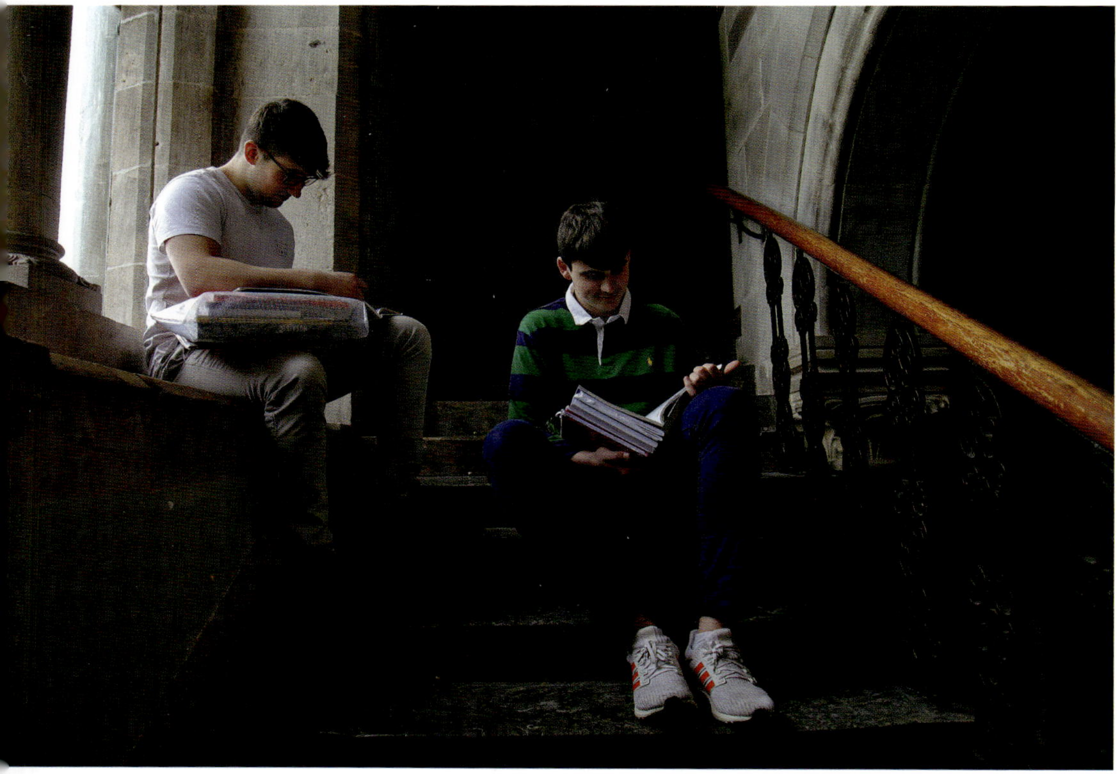

Above: Alfie Hales playing Tennis.
Left: Mike Twomey and Muiris Bulaeir preparing for the Leaving Certificate.

The highlight of the year is the annual Family Day at the end of May. This is a chance to showcase the year's achievements for parents, family and friends. In addition to various athletic events, there is a concert, an art exhibition and fundraising activities to support the annual trip to Kenya where fifth year students help renovate school facilities and provide some basic instruction in computer and English language skills. The day ends with the annual prize-giving ceremony. The period that follows is an important one for the sixth year students as they take their exams and transition into a new phase of relationship with the community and with the place.

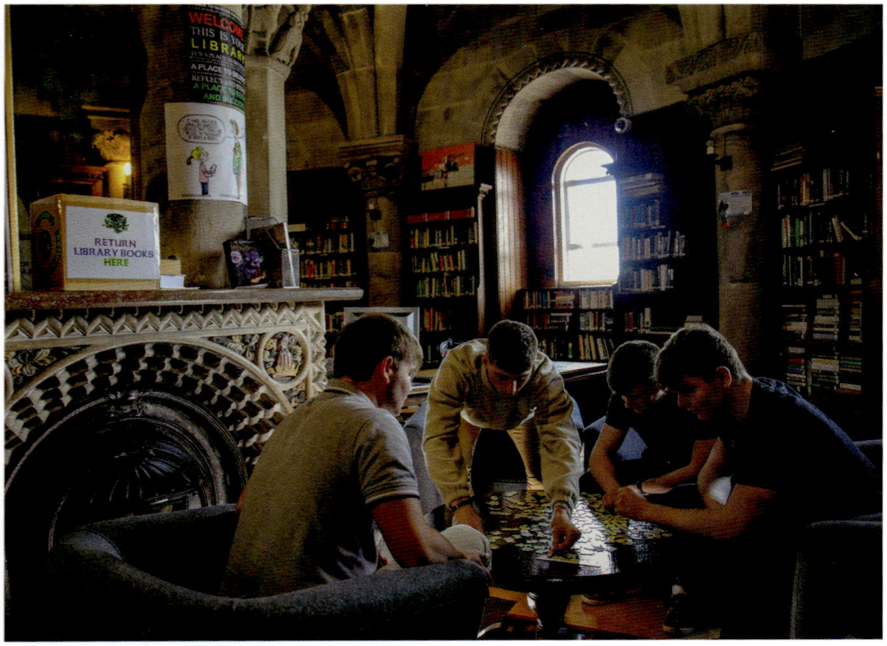

Right: Bill Fitzgerald, left, Jack Collins, J.D. O'Dea and Eoghan Fitzgerald, in the School Library.

Below: Deirdre O'Connell, Maths Teacher at Glenstal Abbey School.

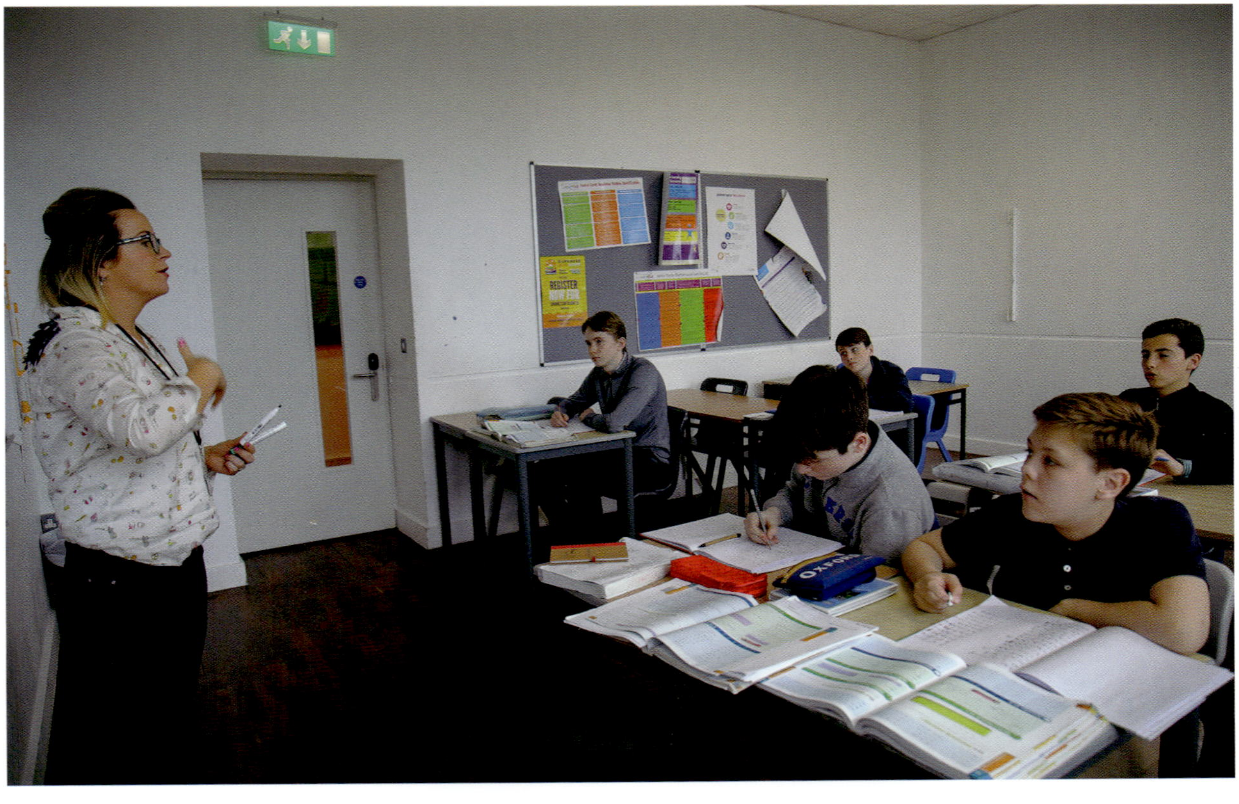

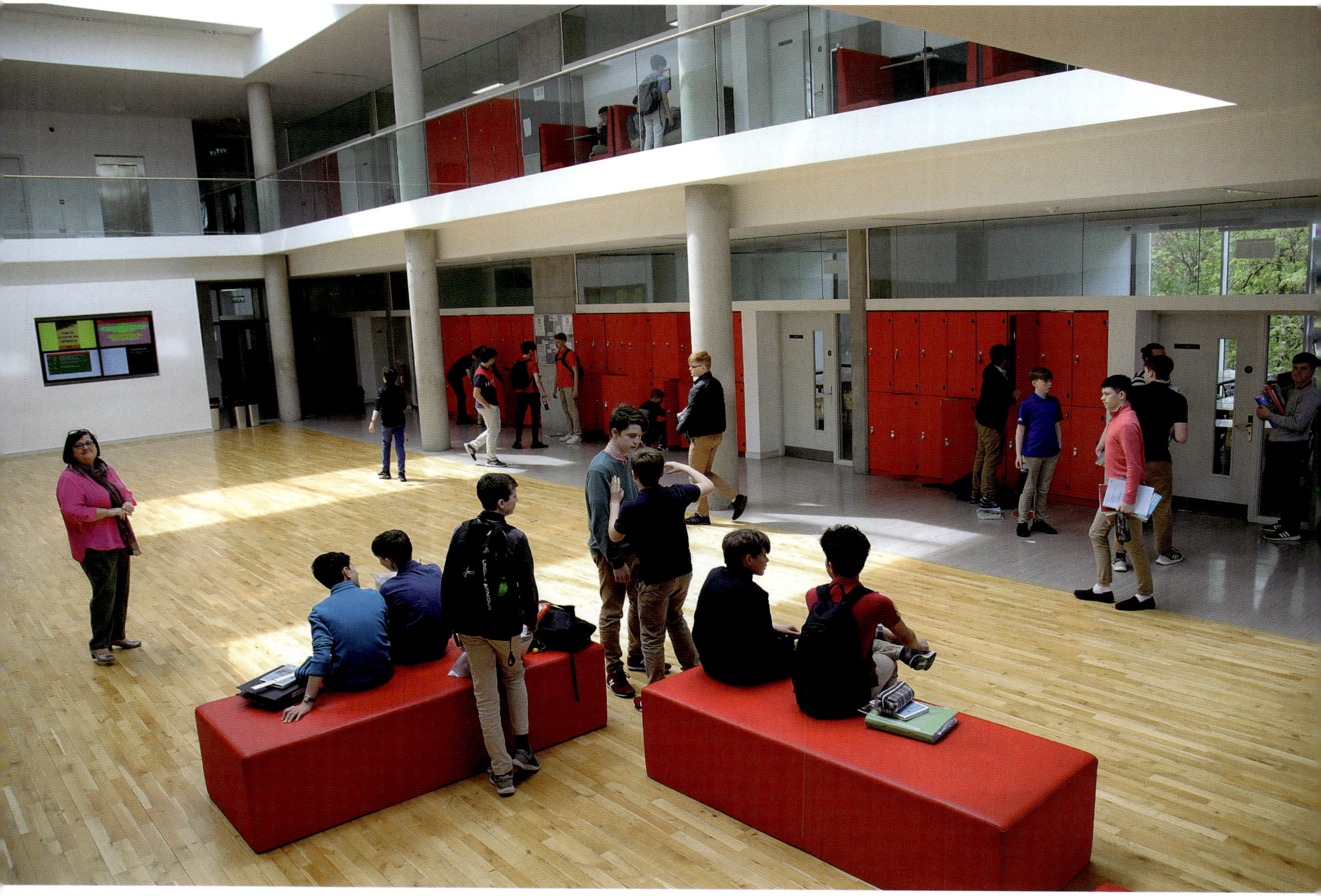

One of the highlights is joining the community for a festive meal in the monastery refectory. The emphasis on community and the atmosphere of boarding school mean that lifelong friendships are forged here and it is often the privilege of one of the brethren to assist at the wedding of former students, sometimes to help them through crises, and occasionally to commend them to God's mercy at the hour of death.

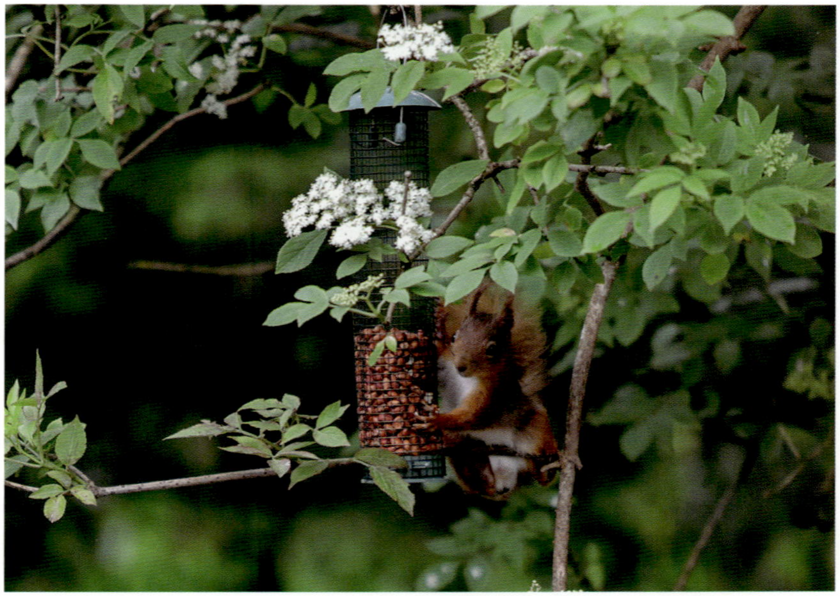

Glenstal is a game sanctuary, which means that monks are not the only form of exotic fauna. It is not uncommon to catch glimpses of deer, badgers and foxes in the gloaming. There is a healthy population of red squirrels, hares, rabbits and pine martens, though the latter have occasionally wreaked havoc in the hen run. Ducks, herons and coots make their homes on the lakes, and a pair of nesting swans with its clutch of cygnets has been a feature of the front avenue lake for years.

Each morning in late spring and early summer we go to Matins and Lauds to the sound of the dawn chorus and join our voices to theirs in the praise of God. Our winged friends are not without their challenges however. While we rejoice with the psalmist that 'the swallow has made a nest for her brood near your altar', someone has to clear up after her. And as for the bats...

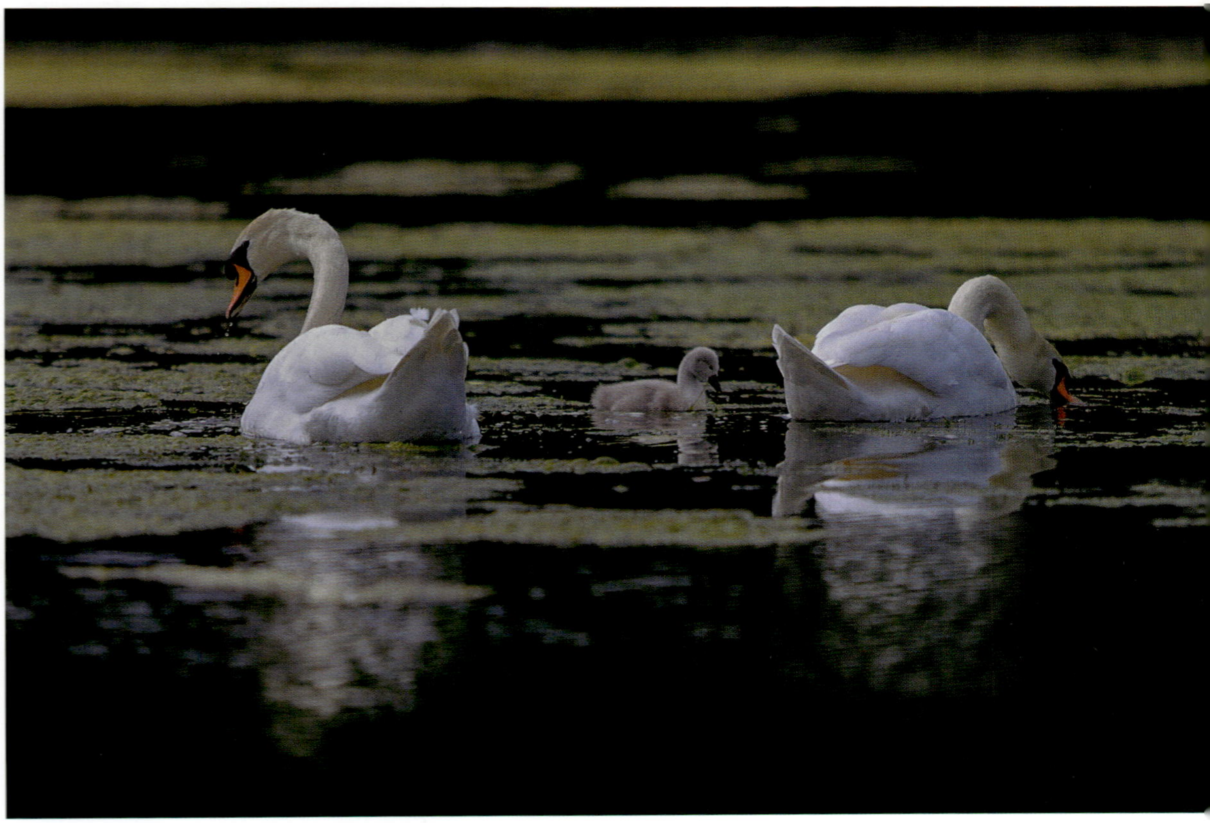

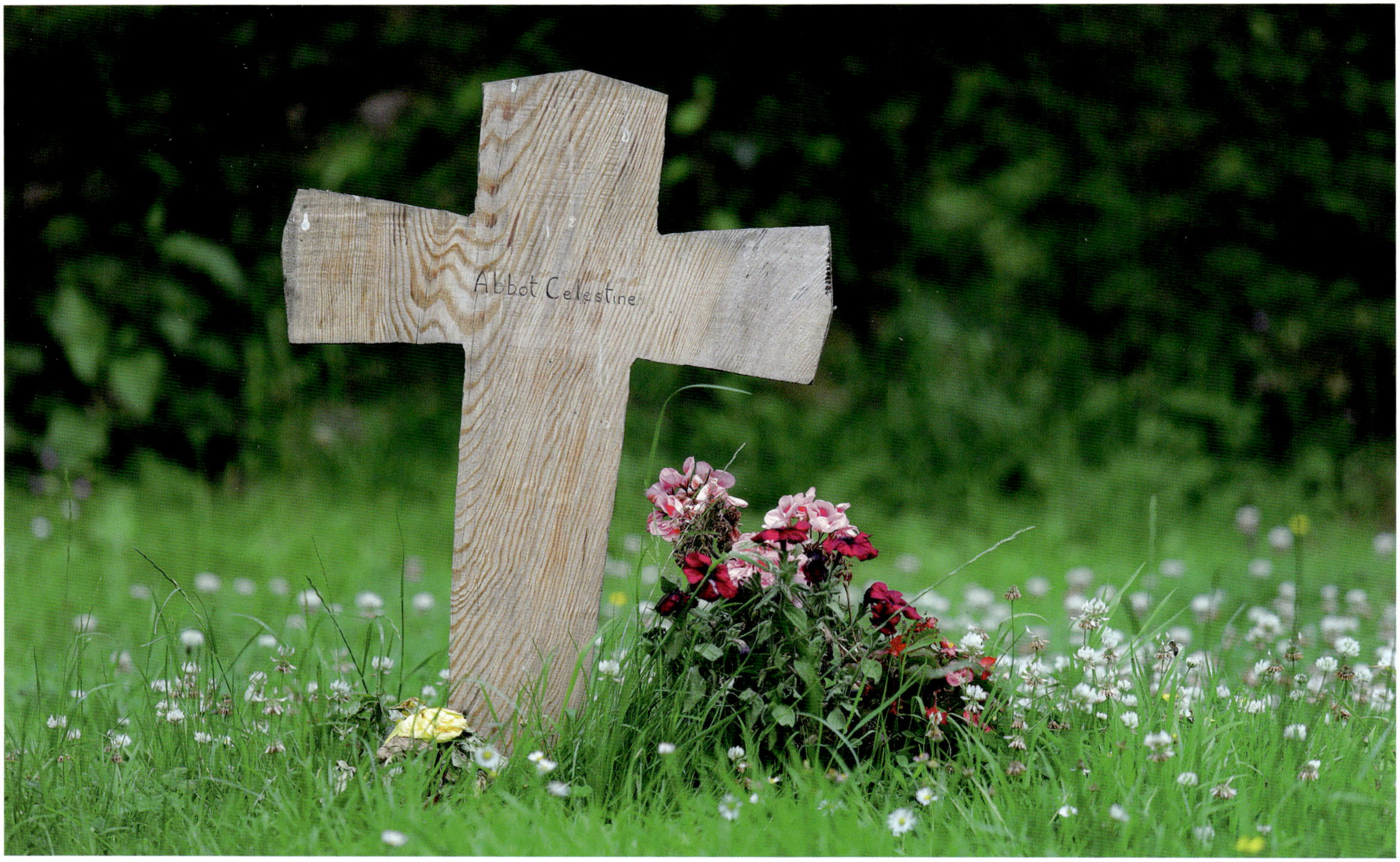

With the end of Eastertide the liturgy reverts to the uncomplicated rhythm of 'Ordinary Time.' After the intensity of Lent and Eastertide, there is something soothing about its uncomplicated cycle of psalms and readings and the plain green vestments at Mass. Certain celebrations stand out in this sea of green. St Benedict's day on July 11th is one such, as we commemorate the Father of Monks and Patron of Europe. For some it has a more personal resonance, being the anniversary of a significant milestone like monastic profession or ordination.

Likewise, the solemnity of the Assumption of the Blessed Virgin Mary on August 15th calls to mind the Holy Mother of God and the promise of heavenly life that is held out to all of us. Other events cannot be predicted and yet are intimately entwined in the life of the community. The death of Abbot Celestine was one such occasion. Blessed with a long and fulfilled life, he served the community in several leadership roles in the course of his 70 years in the monastery. For all this he was most notable for his devotion to the psalms, those hymns of praise, pain and petition that have been the staple of Jewish and Christian prayer for millennia. It is the custom here for pairs of monks to keep vigil with their deceased confrere on the night before his funeral, reciting the psalms over his body as he prepares to take his place in the heavenly liturgy. At the funeral Mass we sing the *Suscipe*, the prayer each monk makes at his profession, asking the Lord to sustain him in his life-giving commitment and not allow him to be confounded.

Right: Br Jarek, violin; Br Cyprian, piano.

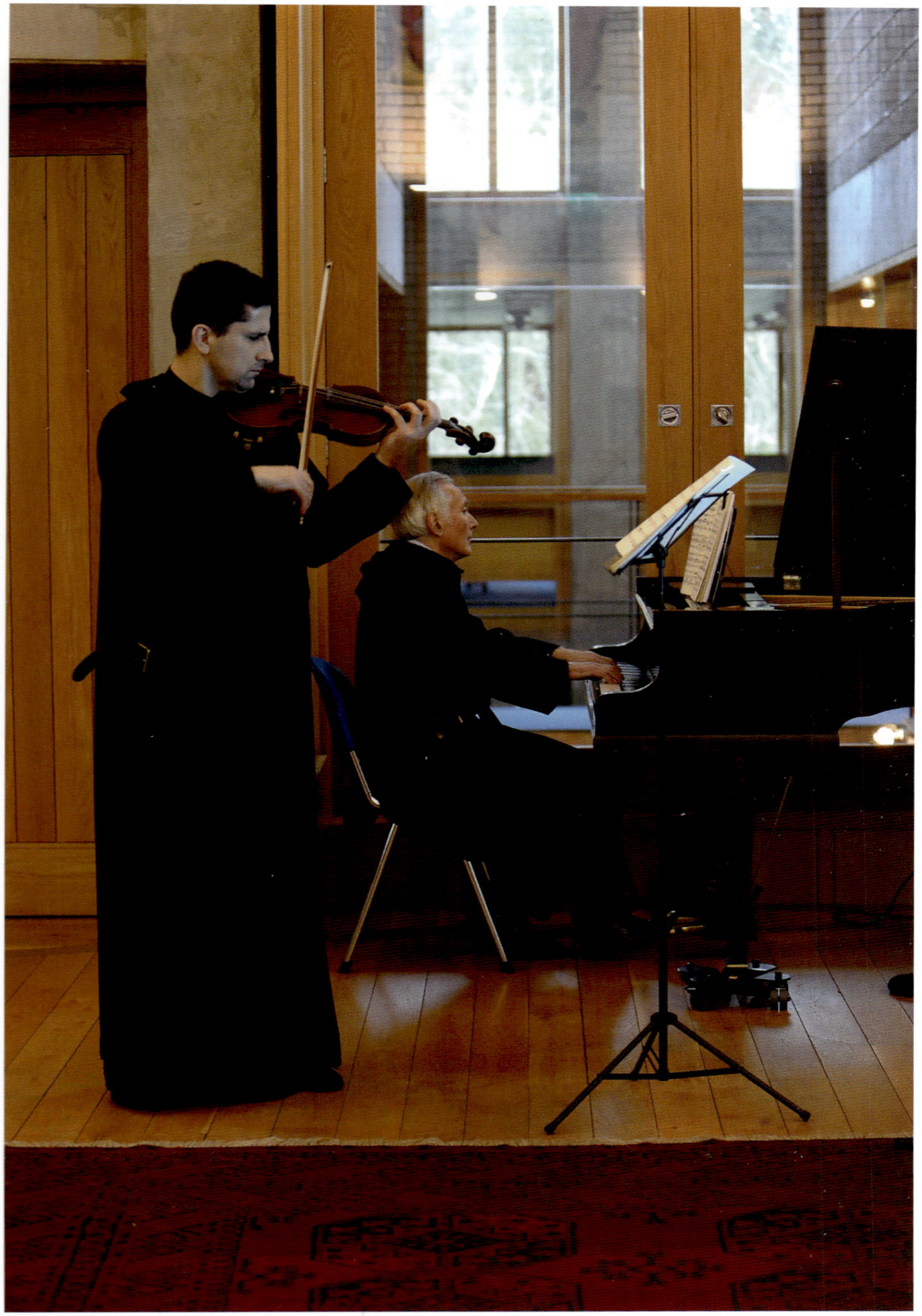

Within a fortnight sorrow turned to joy, as we celebrated the solemn monastic profession of Br Jarosław. A native of Poland, Br Jarek is an accomplished athlete, musician and scholar and one of a number of men who in recent years have found their way to Glenstal from far distant lands. Such additions enrich us, broadening our horizons and expanding our hearts, and the music and culture of his homeland was much in evidence in all our celebrations.

A Monk's Tale:

The Centenarian

On Saturday 6th October 2018, the first time in its history, the community of Glenstal Abbey celebrated the 100th birthday of Fr Placid. Although now resident in a nearby nursing home he returns to Glenstal for Mass and lunch each week. Reflecting in his homily on the long span of history through which Fr Placid has lived, Abbot Brendan said, 'You were born in the final days of World War I, in 1918. Benedict XV was Pope, Ireland was in the aftermath of the 1916 Rising and Europe was in deep shock at the sheer scale of the slaughter the First World War had brought. At that time Glenstal had not yet been founded as a monastery. Over the course of the last century you have seen nine different popes, four English monarchs, all nine Irish presidents and eighteen American presidents.'

He also recalled the dramatic circumstances of Fr Placid's return from Rome during World War II: 'As a student in Rome you experienced at first hand the Second World War, having to make your way home through occupied Italy into Vichy France, then over the Pyrenees and into Spain, thence to Portugal where you were able to get a flying boat to Foynes and eventually back to Glenstal. It sounds more like a chapter from the adventures of James Bond than a page from the life of a monk.'

Reflecting on the ups and downs of a long life, Abbot Brendan concluded: 'Those who walk with the Lord through life will know the joy of these words from the gospel, "Happy the eyes that see what you see, for I tell you that many prophets and kings wanted to see what you see and never saw it; to hear what you hear, and never heard it." Fr Placid, as you complete your one hundredth year, we wish you every blessing and good health. May God be with you as you continue your journey and may he bring us all to everlasting life.'

Fr Placid has served in many capacities in the monastery over the years, including several years as Conventual Prior in the years before the monastery became an abbey. As a scholar, his work is known worldwide in the fields of liturgical translation and in the study of the writings of Saint John Henry Newman. He maintains his scholarly interests to this day and, remarkably, for his centenary produced a new book on the idea of Mary as 'Custodian of the Incarnation' in Newman's writings

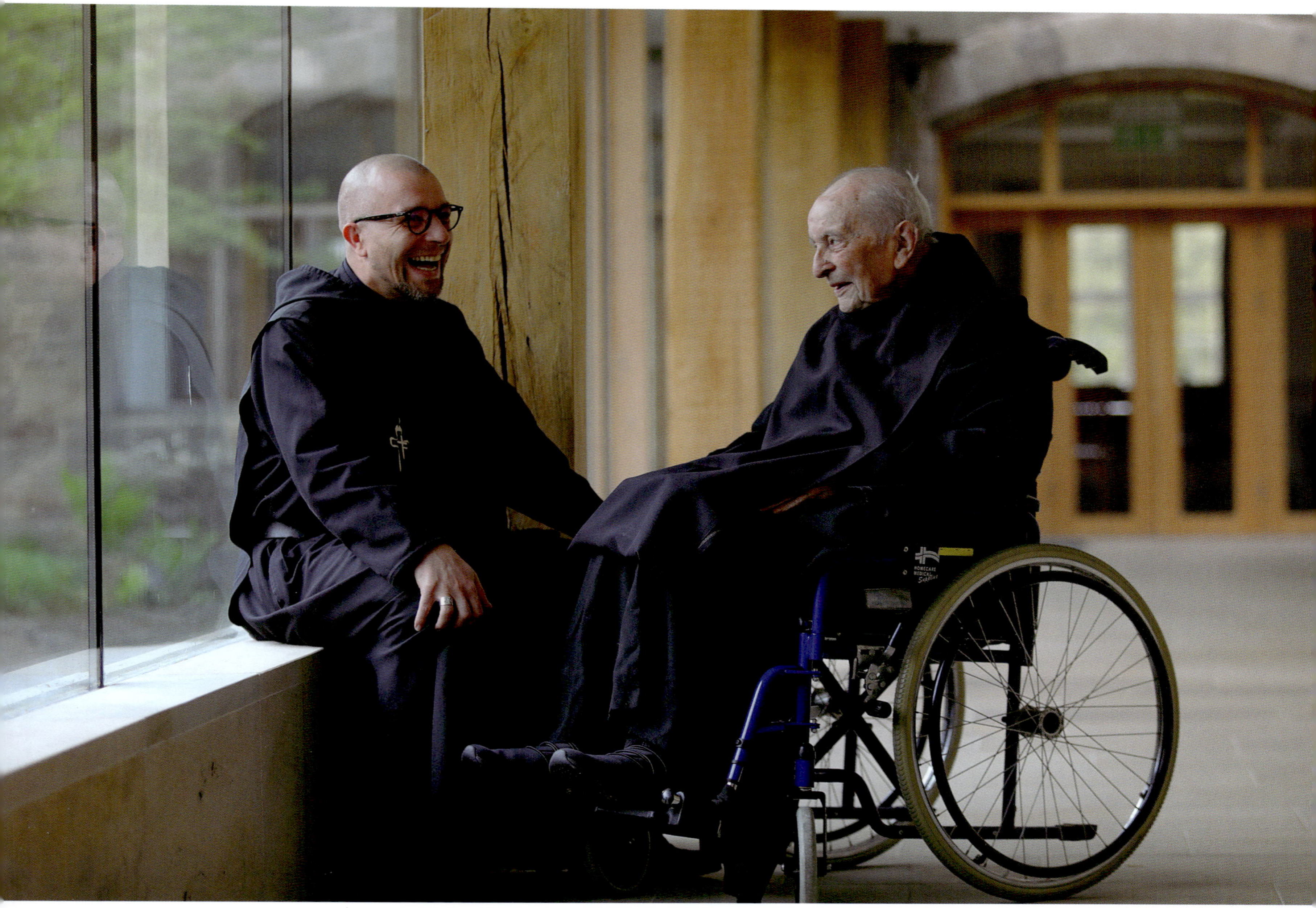

Fr Placid, 100, Ireland's oldest monk, with Fr Maksymilian, 39, one of Europe's youngest abbots.

A Monk's Tale:

Welcoming the Guest

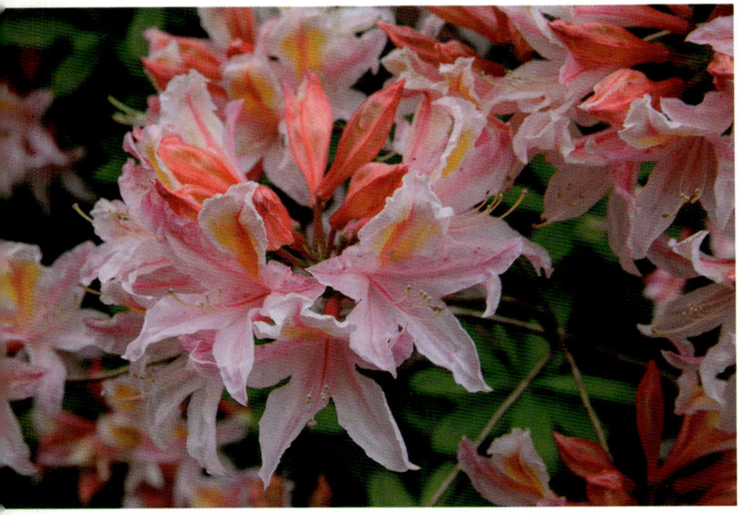

Glenstal, in the Benedictine tradition of hospitality has an open door to all who visit and all are welcome. People connect with Glenstal in all sorts of ways. Many come to participate in the liturgy, visit the church or simply walk the grounds. Others spend some days of reflection in the guesthouse or 'God Pods', and many others join in one of the day-retreats, courses or conferences during the year.

In recent years visiting day groups have become very popular. Also, increasing numbers of people are joining us for the liturgy and those public talks live-streamed on the web. For most, it seems to be a relaxing, reflective and restoring encounter. 'Pax' (Peace), inscribed over the portal of the monastery, the first word of welcome to all entering this place, is a word repeatedly used by many to describe their experience, having spent some time here.

Seeking God and allowing a space where God seeks us through a life of prayer and work is at the heart of monastic life. A particular listening is the key to this space; a listening with the ear of the heart, as St Benedict calls it. In welcoming a visitor, we invite you simply to tune in to this listening space and participate in this seeking and being sought. It is this space that is at the heart of hospitality, at the heart of welcome; a space where the visitor, the other, the outsider, the stranger can enter and simply be; a space where the other is listened to and heard. It is not a space that seeks by conformity to change from the outside, but rather allows growth from the inside. This truest hospitality welcomes, and allows the other discover and become their truest selves.

Br Pádraig

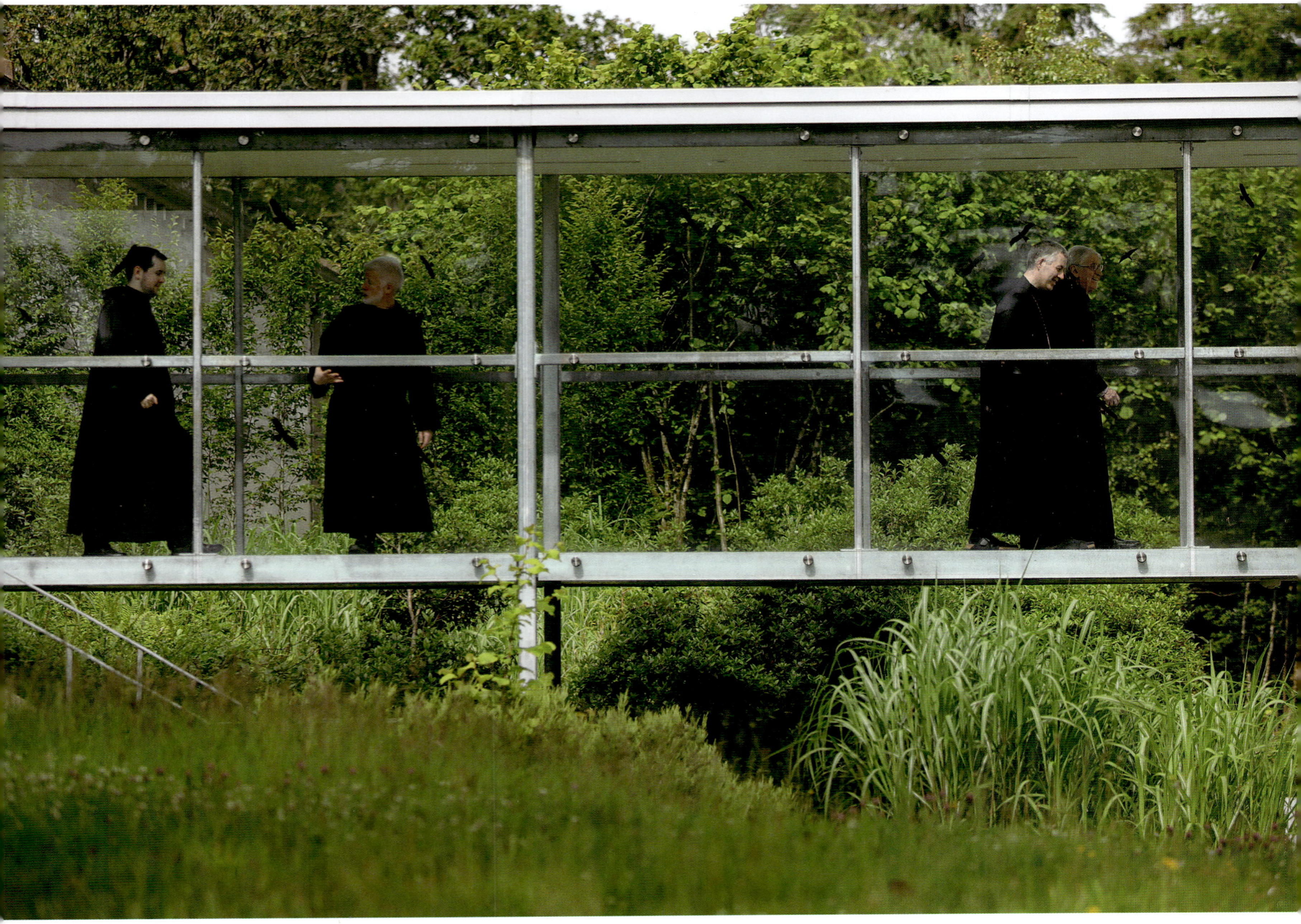

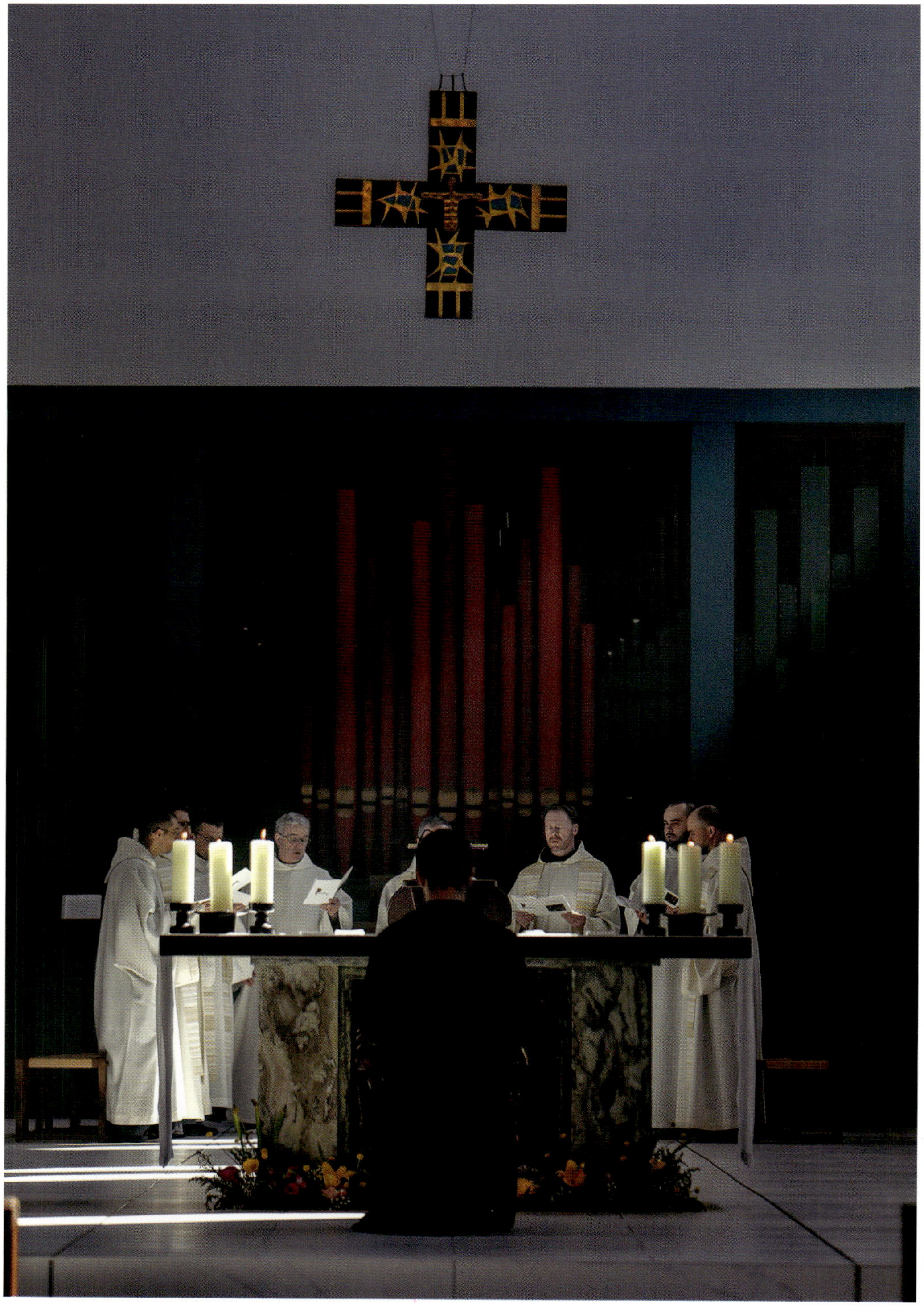

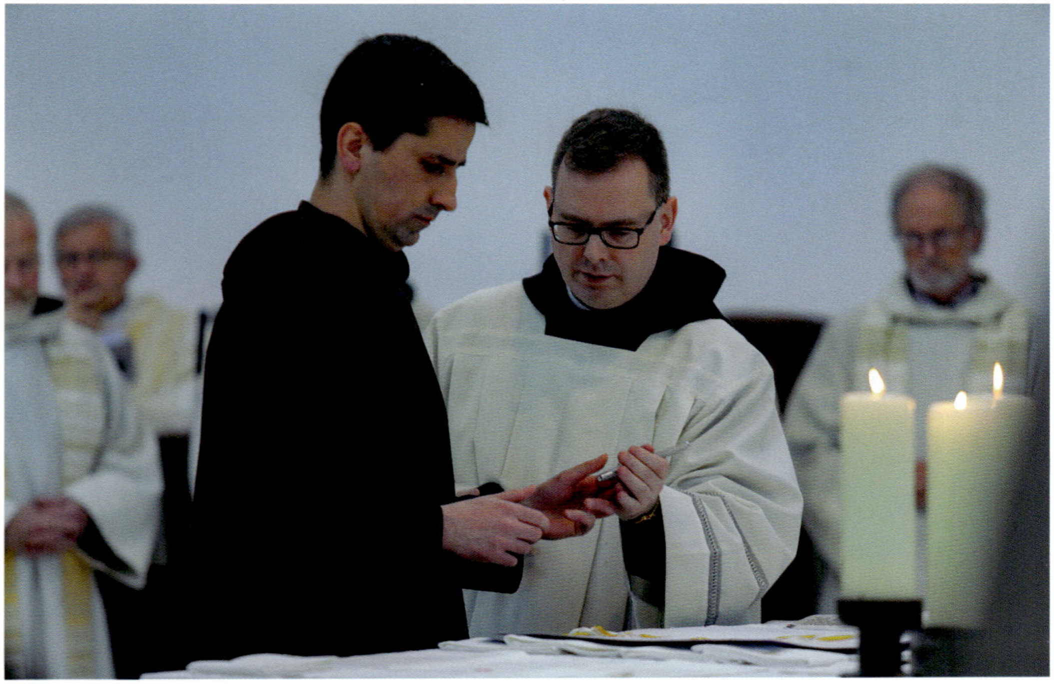

A Monk's Tale:

The Newly Professed

Throughout Ireland these days you will find very many Polish people who have come to make their living here. In fact, they have even become the biggest minority in the country. Why should Glenstal not have one of them too?

I was brought up in a traditional Polish Catholic family in southern Poland. My childhood, apart from significant involvement as an altar boy, was particularly marked by two activities: tennis and music. They filled the years of my youth. Though they seemed somewhat unusual in the Benedictine world in Poland, these interests turned out to be more than fitting in Glenstal. Therefore, it was a joy to me that during my first year in Glenstal I could work in the school as a tennis coach. As for the violin, I am truly grateful to the community here for the welcoming attitude that enabled me to smoothly incorporate my secular profession into daily monastic life.

In 2019 I made my solemn profession as a monk of Glenstal. Although I had spent some years in a monastery in Poland, only here, on Irish soil, did I become ready to be admitted definitively into the ranks of the monks. Thanks to the efforts of many of the monks and guests present at the profession ceremony, everyone could experience the thrilling beauty of the Benedictine liturgy. For me personally, it was an absolutely unique moment, when I heard the Abbot say in the homily: 'From now on you belong to God!'

I was really glad that my family could be with me on the day, along with some life-long friends from Poland, including a number of monks, and some newer friends made during my studies in Oxford.

Br Jarek

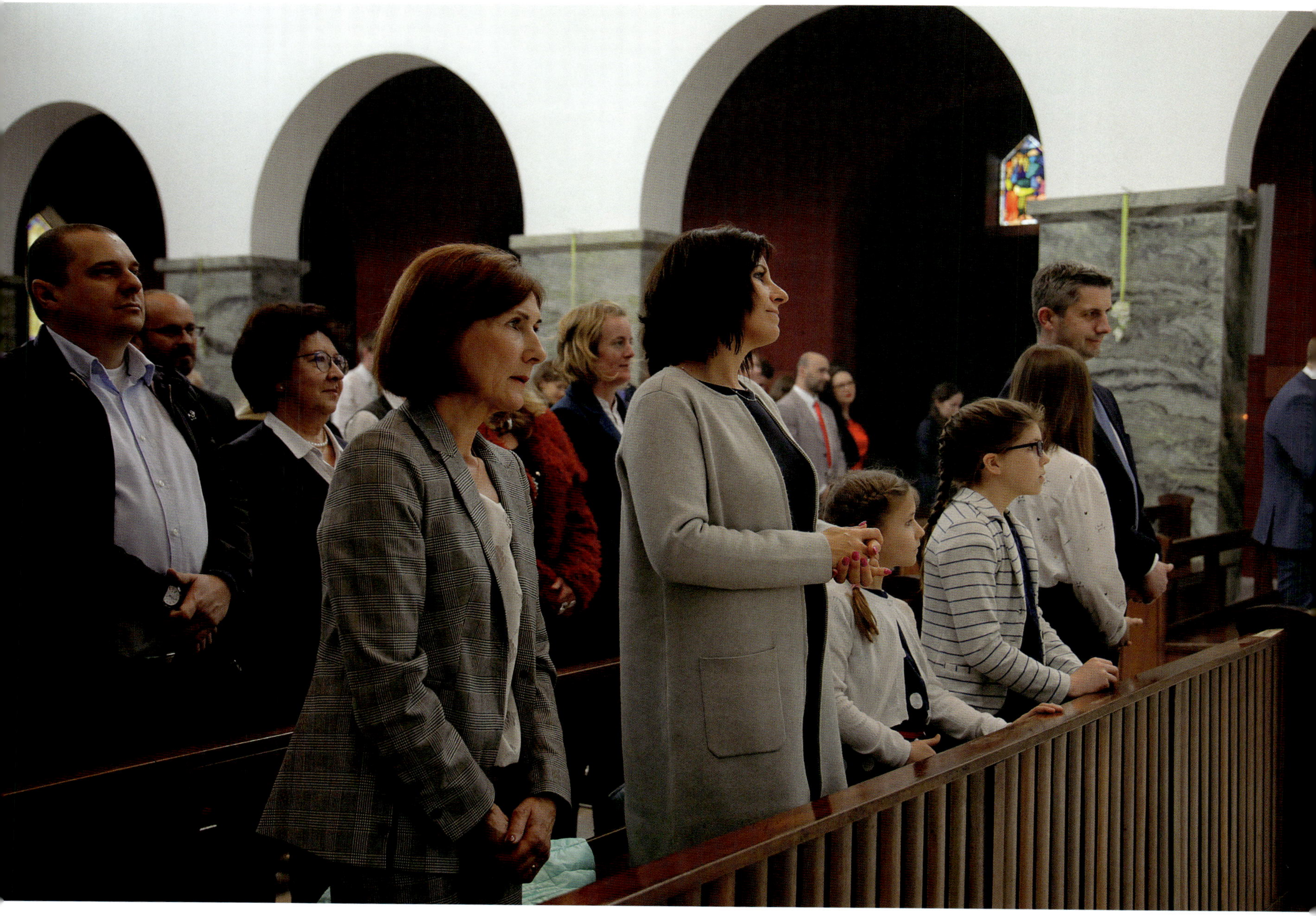

Br Jarosław's family witness his Solemn Monastic Profession.

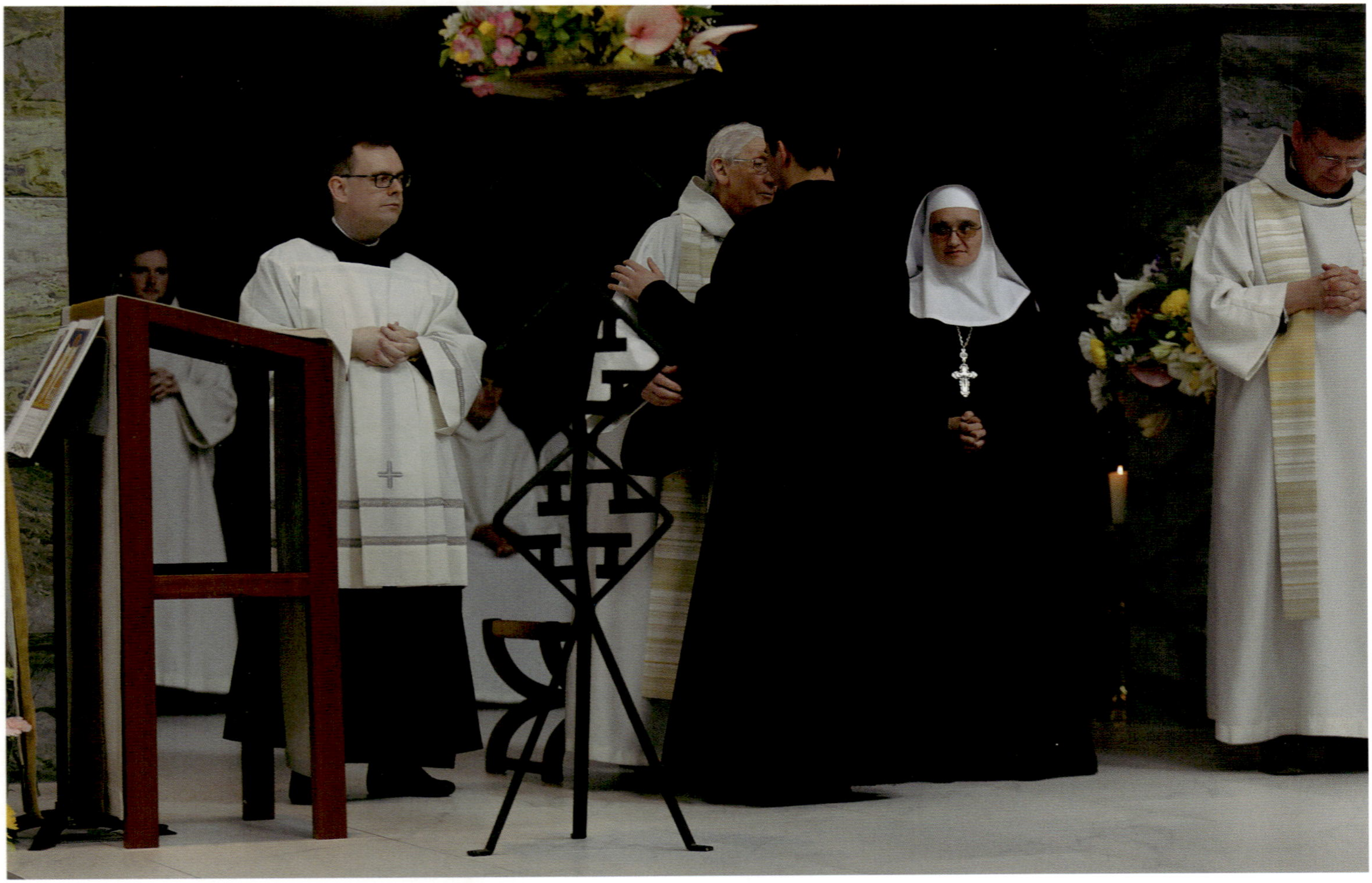

Brother Jarosław exchanges the kiss of peace with other Benedictine monks and nuns during his profession.

A Monk's Recipe:

Leek and nettle soup

Stinging nettles for this purpose are best picked when young and tender. They are high in iron and vitamin c and make a lovely peppery soup.

INGREDIENTS

45g	butter
110g	onion or leek
50g	green lentils
150g	potato, peeled and chopped
1ltr	chicken stock
150g	young nettles, washed and chopped
150ml	full-cream milk

Salt and pepper to season

Sweat off the potato and onion in the butter, and season. When they are soft, add the stock.

Cook off the lentils and add to the mix and bring to the boil. Add the nettle leaves and simmer for just a few minutes. Do not overcook

Add some of the milk and liquidize, adding milk to the consistency you like.

Bring it up to the boil again, and serve with a tasty Rosemary and Sea Salt Crouton.

Make sure to wear rubber gloves when picking and chopping nettles.

Br Pádraig

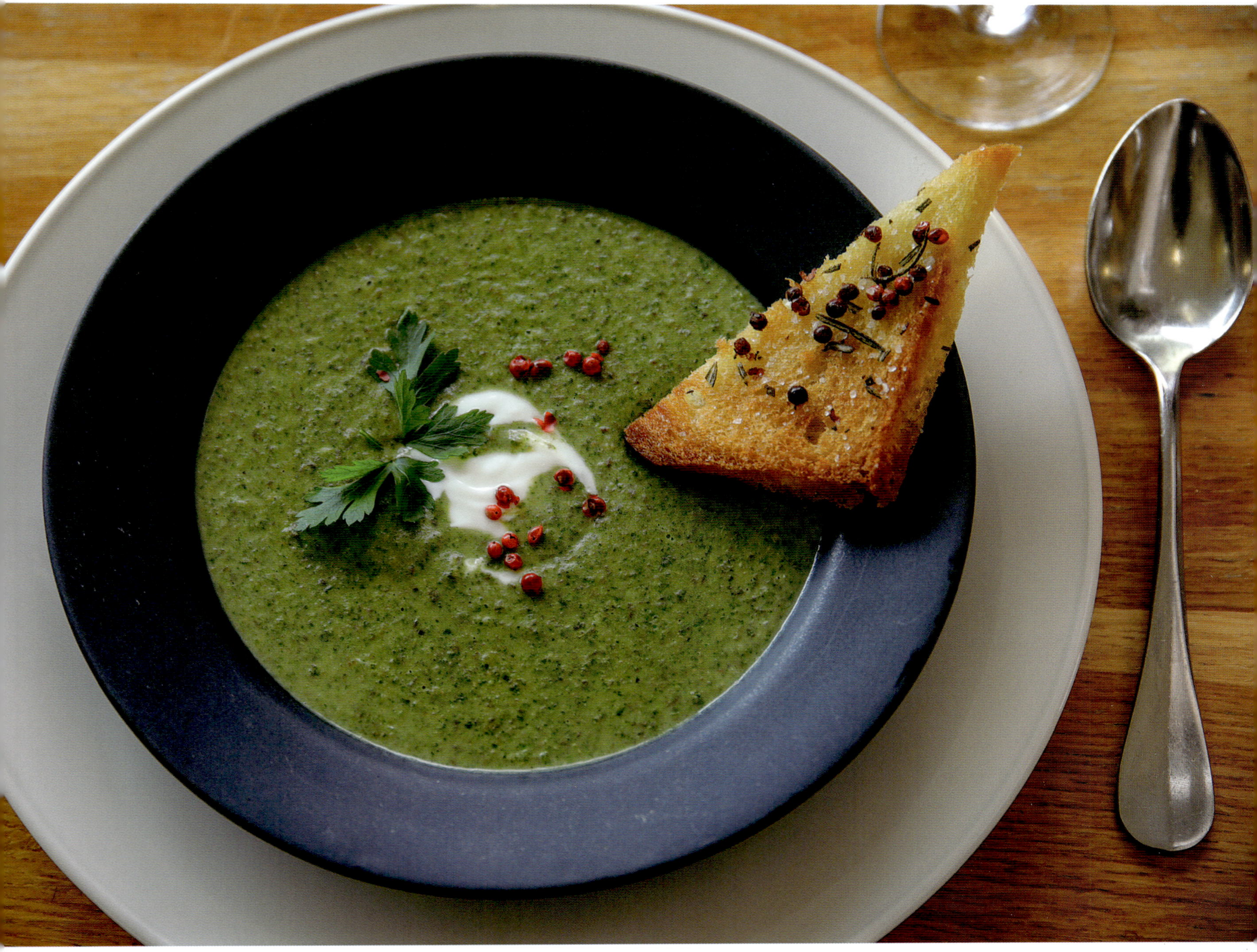

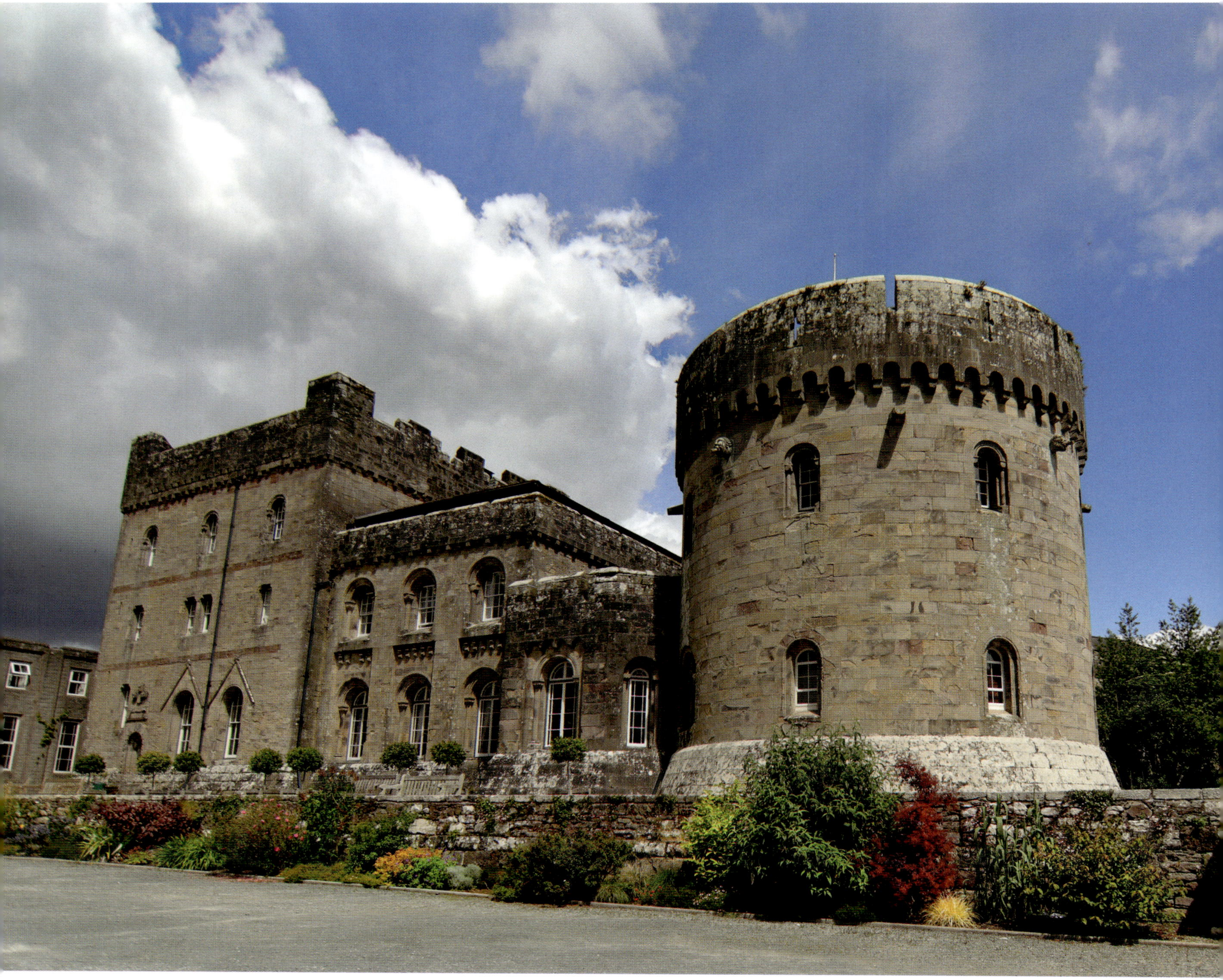

The preceding images and words have given an impression of the life, work and calling of the monastic community at Glenstal Abbey in the course of a single year. Yet, there is a sense in which the task of the monk, like that of every Christian, is timeless: to seek and strive after peace with eyes fixed on the Kingdom of God.

"

'To the monk heaven was next door; he formed no plans, he had no cares; the ravens of his father Benedict were ever at his side. He "went forth" in his youth "to his work and to his labour" until the evening of life; if he lived a day longer, he did a day's work more; whether he lived many days or few, he laboured on to the end of them. He had no wish to see further in advance of his journey than where he was to make his next stage. He ploughed and sowed, he prayed, he meditated, he studied, he wrote, he taught, and then he died and went to heaven.'

– St John Henry Newman, *The Mission of St Benedict*